THE HUMAN FUTURE REVISITED:

The World Predicament and Possible Solutions

Harrison Brown

W·W·NORTON & COMPANY·INC·

NEW YORK

Copyright © 1978 by Harrison Brown

Published simultaneously in Canada by George J. McLeod Limited, Toronto. Printed in the United States of America.

ALL RIGHTS RESERVED

FIRST EDITION

Library of Congress Cataloging in Publication Data

Brown, Harrison Scott, 1917–
    The human future revisited.

    Bibliography: p.
    Includes index.
    1. Economic history—1945–   2. Human ecology.
3. Forecasting. I. Title.
HC59.B764 1978   330.9'047   77-28951
ISBN 0–393–05663–5

1 2 3 4 5 6 7 8 9 0

To Theresa

Contents

Introduction

As a young man during World War II, I worked on the development of atomic bombs. There was a natural tendency for most of us who were engaged in such activity to brood about the ultimate consequences of this new weapon and to ask ourselves where humanity might be heading. In 1946 I wrote a book dealing with the dangers of nuclear war entitled *Must Destruction Be Our Destiny?* However, by the early 1950s I had come to appreciate that although nuclear war is indeed a terrible danger, other problems are in a very real sense even more dangerous. Such problems as rapid population growth, the growing affluence and complexity of industrial society, rapid technological change, and decreasing availability of resources can by themselves result in the collapse of our civilization, even in the absence of nuclear weapons. The massive deployment of ICBMs equipped with hydrogen warheads, coupled with the proliferation of nuclear capabilities in the world, serve only to make these basic problems more acute.

In 1954 I wrote *The Challenge of Man's Future*, in which I attempted to look into the future from the point of view of some of these other problems. Now, more than two decades later, I find the forecasts in that book to be both surprisingly and depressingly accurate. Although at the time of publication I was criticized by some as being overly pessimistic in outlook, the forecasts where they err were more often than not based upon overly optimistic assumptions. For example, although it was clear that U.S. crude oil production would probably peak about 1970, this did not seem to be a matter for really serious concern, since the United States had a great deal of coal and nuclear power was well on its way toward being a reality. Thus the very disturbing energy crisis in which we have been enmeshed since 1974 was largely unanticipated.

For similar reasons, it did not seem possible in 1954 that environmental problems on a truly global scale would reach serious proportions in the foreseeable future. Los Angeles had smog, but it was doing something about it. It seemed to me that environmental problems would be coped with once they were recognized. Now I realize that such optimism was completely unwarranted.

I also realize that I was overly optimistic about the prospects for the development of the poor countries. The social and political barriers to development have turned out to be considerably greater than I had imagined at the time.

Last, although I recognized that industrial civilization might perish worldwide, I more or less thought of this as happening, if ever, in a spectacular nuclear holocaust. I had not appreciated that industrial societies are really very fragile, complex systems which are subject to a variety of intentional as well as unintentional disruptions.

Much has happened in the world since World War II, and in my travels and studies during the intervening period I have learned a great deal that I didn't know when I wrote *The Challenge of Man's Future*. For some time I have believed that a reexamination of the human condition would be in order, approaching the basic issues from a different perspective than was taken earlier. This book represents that effort. In examining the issues, I have attempted to come to grips with these questions: To what extent do we humans still have some measure of control over the situation? To what extent is the situation out of our control?

Over the years I have become increasingly apprehensive about many developments, most of which are rooted in rapid technological change. In recent years my apprehensions have been amplified by the fact that these developments are rapidly converging—with consequences for mankind which are difficult to comprehend, yet potentially disastrous. The convergence point is not so very far in the future, probably within the lifetimes of most of us, certainly within the lifetimes of our children.

The recent serious perturbation in the international flow of crude oil was but a symptom of a complex, deep-seated, worldwide malaise which involves far more than the availability of energy. I suspect that it is like the trembling one feels near a volcano before the top blows off.

In this analysis I have attempted to emphasize that humankind is confronted by a network or web of interrelated problems, none of which has a solution which can be divorced from the solutions of others. The problems as well as the solutions are interdependent. We need much research if we are to understand them, let alone solve them.

I have also attempted to emphasize that we are faced with the task of managing a gigantic, complex, global system which we really don't understand, for it lies out of the ken of our conventional managerial experience.

In spite of these difficulties I am by no means without hope—if I were, I would not have written this book. I am convinced that there are many steps we can take to buy precious time for ourselves. We can, if we have the will, make substantial progress in the next quarter century toward the elimination of hunger and poverty in the world. We can greatly decrease the likelihood of a nuclear holocaust. Above all we can obtain a better understanding of ourselves in relation to each other, our institutions, and the world which is our common home.

In short, I believe that although the dangers which confront us are immense, we nevertheless have it in our power to create a new level of civilization—an abundant, just, and peaceful world in which people can not only develop to their fullest terrestrial potential—they can reach out to the stars as well.

H.B.

Pasadena, California
August 1977

Acknowledgments

I am deeply indebted to the Rockefeller Foundation for providing the grant which made it possible for me to take the time to undertake the research and much of the writing which has gone into this book. I am also grateful to the California Institute of Technology where most of the research and writing was done.

The Japan Society (New York) and the International House of Japan made it possible for me to spend one month in Japan in 1975, studying some of the problems of Japanese society. The Yomiuri Shimbun made it possible for me to continue those studies in 1976.

In 1975 the Rockefeller and Ford Foundations together provided funds which made possible a several-month study concerning the vulnerabilities of industrial societies which was conducted jointly with Guy Pauker of the Rand Corporation. Some of the materials and conclusions from that report have been incorporated into the chapter on Vulnerabilities. I am indebted to Dr. Pauker for many hours of lively conversation and debate, both in the United States and with colleagues in Europe.

Mrs. Darcy Williams took care of producing a legible manuscript and of managing other important matters concerning this effort. I am indebted to her for her patience and her dedicated efforts.

Ms. Elizabeth Krieg and Ms. Pat Pahl were most helpful in the collection of data and materials, some of which were quite obscure.

Last, I am grateful to my wife, Theresa, who has been patient and helpful in more ways than she suspects.

THE HUMAN FUTURE
REVISITED

CHAPTER I

The Fissioning
of Human Society

Technology is the only field of human activity in which
there has been progression. The advance from Lower Pa-
laeolithic to mechanized technology has been immense.
There has been no corresponding advance in human socia-
lity, though advances in this field have been called for by
the changes in social conditions that have been imposed
upon mankind by its technological progress.
—Arnold Toynbee, *Mankind and Mother Earth*

(1)

Our planet was born several thousands of millions of years ago and in our
thinking about man's future we must always keep this vastness of time in
mind. From the very beginning there has been a ceaseless interplay of chemical reactions leading to the emergence of molecules of increasing complexity.
As the physical conditions on earth changed and chemical reactions progressed, complex molecules emerged which were actually capable of reproducing themselves. In other words, these molecules were able to catalyze the
formation of new molecules, identical to themselves, from the atoms and
molecules of their environment. In a very real sense those early replicating
molecules were the first living "things" on earth. And molecules like them
provide the basis for life on earth today.

In time, replicating molecules became associated with other molecules and
eventually there emerged very complex agglomerations of molecules which in
turn could reproduce themselves. We call them "cells." Still later, complex
replicating combinations of cells emerged. All of these replicating or living
"things"—molecules, single cells, and combinations of cells—coexisted and

competed with each other for the raw materials they needed for their replication. Some species died while others thrived. New species were continuously emerging, giving rise to new competitions. Thus did *chemical* evolution give way to *biological* evolution.

The story of the biological evolution of the earth is one of breathtaking complexity and beauty. Quite early we see the emergence of organisms which utilize the sun's energy directly. In view of the fact that all life requires energy, and since the sun's rays provide the largest and most dependable source of energy on earth, these organisms—plants—became the dominant life form. Virtually all other forms of life became dependent upon plants for their survival.

Seemingly endless varieties of plant life emerged in the sea and on land. Although nonplant (animal) life has always been less abundant than the plant life upon which it depends, it too has evolved in wondrous and almost endless ways. The fossil record tells us about the emergence of animals with a diversity of supportive and protective structures, the evolution of vertebrate animals in the sea, the development of the lung, and the movement of vertebrate life to the land. The record tells us about the emergence of the body thermostat, live birth, and mammals; about those mammals which we call primates, which lived in trees, walked erect, and socialized; about the emergence at least 2 million years ago of that special kind of primate which we call man.

Although early man lived much as did the other animals about him, he was different. Like other animals he did what he could to keep from being killed. But his brain was different from those of most other animals. Humanity was endowed with what we call the power of conceptual thought, which enabled it, among other things to conceive of tools, to make them and use them. Conceptual thought enabled humans to ask questions and to answer some of them, to solve problems and to communicate with others. Learning became cumulative and was passed from one generation to the next, each generation having a fund of knowledge somewhat greater than its predecessor's. Something completely new, of high survival value, had been added to the evolutionary scene.

Thus primitive man with his tools spread over the surface of the earth, hunting and fishing and gathering edible plants for his food. The controlled use of fire, one of the more powerful of man's inventions, extended the range of foods which could be eaten and the range of climates which were habitable. Clothing helped him survive cold winters. A variety of tools made of stone and wood increased the efficiency of his hunting and fishing.

Eventually this hunter and food gatherer inhabited all of the continents. By that time, he had become the dominant animal on the earth scene. His actual numbers were small—the earth in its natural state could not have supported more than about 10 million persons leading a food-gathering existence, or only about one person for every 16 square kilometers of land area. But the power of his brain and of his tools, which supplemented and extended his natural physical capabilities, made up for his paucity of numbers. Thus did biological evolution give way to cultural evolution.

To be sure, man lived in a rugged world which was filled with many dangers. Every human being led a precarious existence and life expectancy at birth must have been quite short—perhaps no more than 25 years. But human beings collectively had emerged as a biologically stable species which could not easily be driven to extinction.

Human beings are gregarious and prefer to live in groups. Hunters and food gatherers collected in tribes which wandered over the countryside, always seeking areas where game and other forms of food were plentiful. But the very low density of available food in nature placed an upper limit on the size of a nomadic tribe or self-contained family group. In general, the maximum radius of operation of hunters from a tribal center was about 25 kilometers. This represents the approximate distance that a hunting party could travel. kill game, and bring it home before it spoiled. Under these circumstances, in areas of average natural fertility, the hunters of a tribe could not support a population of much more than about 200 persons. Thus, when the earth was "saturated" with human beings living within the framework of a food-gathering culture, the population of some 10 million persons was divided among about 50,000 tribes, each of which had a "territory" amounting to about 3200 square kilometers. Of course, the actual size of a tribe's territory depended markedly upon the biological productivity of the region.

A part of the biological stability of primitive society stemmed from the fact that once it had spread over the world, only the most gigantic disasters could eradicate at any one time more than a small fraction of the 50,000 tribes which existed worldwide. In the event that a few hundred or even a few thousand tribes were eradicated by war, disease, or famine, the remaining tribes were little affected and would quickly fill the empty spaces through a combination of reproduction and migration (see Figure 1.1). By that time virtually the only way the human species could have become extinct would have been as the result of a cosmic catastrophe or through the emergence of still another species which was better able than man to cope with the same environment. Thus far the latter has not happened and is unlikely to happen for as long as cultural evolution relegates biological evolution to a less important position in the terrestrial scheme of things.

Eventually a new cultural mutation with tremendous survival value ap-

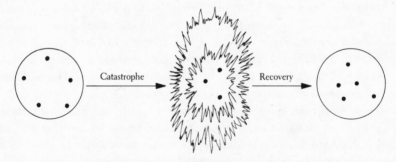

FIG. 1.1. Food-Gathering Society

peared in human society. First, man found that he could protect animals which were useful and destroy those which were not, and, later, that some useful animals could be bred in captivity. Still later he found that he could protect useful vegetation and encourage its growth, and then he learned to collect and plant seeds. These new technologies—animal domestication and agriculture—made it possible for several hundred people to inhabit a region which in its natural state could not previously have supported more than one person. Groups of humans which made use of these new technologies multiplied; those which did not were driven to extinction.

The changes brought about by agriculture were enormous and came rapidly. By ensuring permanent food supply, the cultivation of plants made permanent settlement possible. Since in the new culture, as in the old, people liked to live in groups, villages emerged, surrounded by the fields in which the farmers worked. Because there is a limit to the distance a farmer is willing to walk to his field in the morning and walk home again in the evening, the number of persons who can live in a village and be supported by the products of the surrounding fields is limited. In areas of average productivity, villages have populations of 200–300 persons. Such village sizes are common in the greater part of China and India today.

Thus regions which in preagricultural times might each have accommodated 1000 individuals divided among perhaps 10 nomadic tribes, now accommodated about 500,000 individuals divided among some 2000 villages. This new scheme of things was even more resilient than the older one from a biological point of view. If a few score villages were decimated as the result of war, pestilence, or famine, it was only a matter of time before the places left vacant by the catastrophe would be filled once again through reproduction and migration (see Figure 1.2).

Agricultural technology developed to the point where, on the average, farmers were able to produce somewhat more food than was needed by their families. This surplus, which was never very large, was nevertheless extremely important, for it meant that some people could engage in full-time activities other than farming. Some became potters, others made weapons and tools, others became soldiers and priests. This phenomenon accelerated the pace of technological change and eventually led to the emergence of cities—a development which gave culture a new form.

The great cities of the ancient empires emerged in locations, usually on waterways, which enabled them to draw upon large areas for their food and raw materials. A typical city of some 300,000 persons might have drawn upon a region inhabited by about 3 million peasants divided among 10,000 or more villages. The city was the center of the government and culture of the region. In exchange for food and raw materials, it provided such manufactured goods as the peasants could afford to buy, military protection, and public works projects, such as irrigation canals.

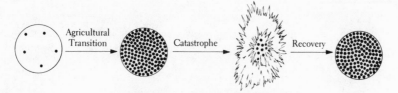

FIG. 1.2. Transition to Peasant-Village Culture

Basically, however, the cities in the ancient empires were far more dependent upon the villages than the villages were dependent upon the cities. When a city was destroyed by war, earthquake, or social upheaval, the peasants in the neighboring villages would continue their normal activities, little disturbed by the catastrophe. Eventually a new city might emerge in the region, perhaps also destined eventually to be destroyed (see Figure 1.3). In the stream of history we see the debris of countless cities, each of which arose from a substratum of peasant villages, prospered for a while, and eventually perished.

(2)

A major key to man's cultural evolution was his gradually acquired ability to control energy. Indeed, the concepts of "civilization" and "controlled use of energy" are inseparable.

When manlike creatures first emerged upon the earth, their primary need for energy was in the form of food to nourish their bodies, and amounted to some 3000 calories* daily. The controlled use of fire, which greatly extended the variety of foods which could be eaten and the range of human habitation, increased per capita energy consumption to about 8000 calories per day, corresponding to the heat that would be released by burning a little over 1 kilogram of coal per day, or somewhat over 400 kilograms of coal each year. Thus, the maximum consumption of energy by humans in preagricultural times probably amounted to no more than the equivalent of some 4 million tons of coal annually.

Although the invention of agriculture and animal domestication resulted in a tremendous upsurge in human population, it initially had little effect upon per capita energy demands. As beasts of burden partially replaced men in tasks requiring the concentration of energy, such as plowing, perhaps an additional 4000 calories were added to the average individual's energy consumption. This brought the total energy requirement to about 12,000 calories, or the

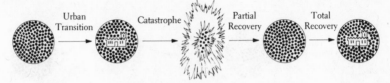

FIG. 1.3. Urban Civilization

equivalent of burning some 600 kilograms of coal per person each year. By the beginning of the Christian era, the population had grown to some 250 million persons, corresponding to a worldwide energy demand equivalent to burning some 150 million tons of coal annually.

Prior to Roman times, the primary motive power for tools and machinery was human muscle power. Although the ox had been used for many centuries for plowing and the horse had been used extensively for rapid transportation of people and materials, the concentration of energy for accomplishing specific objectives was generally obtained by the use of large gangs of people. Slavery was an accepted social notion in antiquity, and gangs of slaves were used to provide motive power for ships, for constructing roads and aqueducts, moving massive machines, and constructing great public works. Animals were seldom used for these purposes. Why?

In those days a harnessed horse could pull four times as much as a man. But the businessmen of the time, knowing that the animals each consume four times as much food as a man, could see no particular advantage to the use of animals, and they could see many disadvantages. Indeed, the flour

---

* The food calorie, or "large calorie," equals 1000 gram calories.

mills of ancient Rome were driven by two men or one donkey, and there appears to have been little economic incentive to prefer the latter.

We now know that the reason a horse could pull only four times as much weight as a man was the poor harness design which resulted from ignorance of horse anatomy. The harnesses of the time prevented the horse from exerting its full available strength, which would have enabled it to pull fifteen times as much as a man. It was not until the Middle Ages that the breast-strap or postilion harness was acquired from the Mongol tribes that invaded Europe. The horse collar was also introduced, and by the twelfth century was in general use throughout Europe. Following these developments, animals quickly replaced man as a source of power for the concentration of energy. By that time per capita energy consumption was probably equivalent to burning about 1300 kilograms of coal per person per year. As the population during the Middle Ages was about 400 million persons, total human energy demand amounted to the equivalent of burning about 500 million tons of coal annually.

Although sailing vessels were used in antiquity and the waters of rivers were used to transport ships and materials downstream, wind and water were not used for motive power for tools and machinery until Roman times. The oldest known reference to a water mill was made by one Antipater of Thessalonica, who wrote in the first century B.C.:

> Cease from grinding, ye women who toil at the mill; sleep late, even if the crowing cocks announce the dawn. For Demeter has ordered the nymphs to perform the work of your hands, and they, leaping down on the top of the wheel, turn its axle which, with its revolving spokes, turns the heavy concave Nisyran millstones.

These early mills were used primarily for grinding grain and had an output of about 0.5 horsepower—which was about the same as mills operated by two slaves or a donkey. Such small mills gradually spread, reaching Ireland in the West and China in the East by the third and fourth centuries A.D.

A larger and considerably more efficient mill was constructed in the first century B.C. by a Roman engineer. At Venafro on the Tuliverno, near Naples, the remains of such a mill have been found which had an output of about 3 horsepower and permitted the grinding of between 300 and 350 pounds of grain per hour. When we compare this with the output of but 15 pounds of grain per hour of a mill operated by two men or a donkey, we see that a truly major breakthrough had been achieved. The output of this early Roman mill was higher by far than that of any other power resource of antiquity.

In its time this early mill was revolutionary and expanded industrial possibilities more than nuclear energy has expanded industrial possibilities today. Yet for reasons that appear extremely complex, the Roman (or Vitruvian) water mill spread very slowly. Many of the factors that contributed to this slow spread, as in the case of nuclear energy today, appear to be economic, social, and psychological in nature. Heavy investments were required in order to ensure a steady flow of water and to provide the machinery that could make use of a more concentrated output of energy. In an age when individual capital was invested primarily in slaves and land, there was little impulse toward industrialization which required appreciable capital investments that could depreciate with time.

The grinding of grain in Rome was centralized, and during the early Empire unemployment in the city was apparently a serious problem. The emperor Vespasian (A.D. 69–79) is said to have refused the building of a water-driven hoist "lest the poor have no work." Clearly, had the centralized grain grinders been converted to water mills, the situation would have been aggravated—a problem of a type that has occurred repeatedly in history. There is no evidence of a rapid increase in the number of water mills until the fourth century A.D., some 400 years after their first appearance in Italy. There seems to have been an acute shortage of labor during that century, and this may have contributed to the spread.

The period in Europe following the disintegration of the Roman Empire was hardly favorable to technological progress. Indeed, the practical knowledge of machinery possessed by the Romans was not surpassed until the eighteenth century. Yet in spite of this, the number of water mills increased steadily between the tenth and twelfth centuries and appears to have doubled every 50 to 100 years. The mills came to be applied to mining and metallurgy as well as to grinding grain.

The windmill was apparently unknown to both the Greeks and the Romans. It was of eastern origin and spread slowly across Europe in the thirteenth century. This source of concentrated power, like the water mill, was limited by nature, a factor that undoubtedly contributed to its gradual spread. Also, laborers objected to its installation. In the sixteenth century, for example, craftsmen protested against windmills, claiming that they would throw many people out of work. (A mechanical saw, driven by a windmill, was destroyed near London by a riotous mob in 1768.) Nevertheless, by the mid-eighteenth century the waters and winds together were providing the greater part of the mechanical power available in Europe.

Controlled energy is essential for the production of mechanical power. It is also essential for the production of sufficiently high temperatures to make pottery or to obtain metals from their ores.

Copper was the first metal to come into widespread use on a substantial scale. In actuality copper is not very abundant in the earth's crust, but the metal can be obtained fairly easily from its ore. The reduction temperature is fairly low, so that smelting can be accomplished in a simple furnace. Once the technology of extracting copper was developed, the use of the metal became widespread in the ancient civilization and the demand for the ore grew rapidly.

In this situation the high-grade deposits of ore close to the ancient urban centers were soon used up. Egypt, for example, quickly depleted her own copper reserves and had to develop an elaborate network of trade routes that enabled her to import copper from as far away as the British Isles and Scandinavia. Even so, high-grade ores of copper were uncommon enough to limit use of the metal. Copper did make possible a number of new technologies, but farmers, who were by far the greater proportion of society, were almost unaffected. Their implements continued to be made of stone, clay, wood, and leather.

Gold is considerably easier to extract from its ore than is copper; often the "ore" is metallic gold itself. As one might expect, therefore, the use of gold appears to predate the use of copper by a considerable span of time. Gold, however, is one of the rarest metals in nature, so that its ores are extremely scarce. Its rarity precluded its widespread use, except in small quantities for ornament and as a medium of exchange.

Iron is considerably more abundant in the earth's crust than is copper, but it is a much more difficult metal to win from the ore. The reduction temperature is high, and furnaces capable of attaining it were not developed until about 1100 B.C. The new high-temperature technology appeared first in the Middle East and quickly spread westward. The general availability of the ore made it possible for metal to be used on an unprecedented scale. New tools of iron helped transform Europe from a land of dense forests to a fertile cropland.

England entered the business of iron production richly endowed with iron ore. Forests were also abundant, and the trees were used to produce charcoal, which in turn was used to reduce the ore to the metal. These resources enabled England to become a major producer of iron for the world.

By the sixteenth century the island, which had once been covered with trees, was confronted by a shortage of timber. Deforestation had taken place rapidly, in part to increase the area of agricultural land and to provide wood for building, fuel for heating, and charcoal for the iron industry. Faced by the shortage of wood, England made increased use of coal, and by the seventeenth century coal was being substituted for wood in a number of localities as a fuel.

Numerous efforts were made to use coal as a substitute for charcoal in the manufacture of iron, but although coal will reduce iron ore to the metal, the impurities in it render the properties of the metal quite unsatisfactory. By 1709 Abraham Darby, after much effort, learned to drive off the volatile materials in coal by preheating, and succeeded in using the product, called "coke," to smelt iron ore. Although the product was reasonably satisfactory, in part because the coal he used had a low proportion of sulfur, coke-produced pig iron did not rival charcoal iron in quality until about 1750. From that time, however, England's vast coal resources were available for iron manufacture and the iron industry grew very rapidly. As the practice of smelting with coke spread, the quality of the iron improved and the costs dropped, thus making the metal more generally available and encouraging its more widespread use.

The linking of coal to iron has been second only to the development of agriculture in its impact upon the course of human history. Almost immediately this new development greatly increased the demand for coal. Miners had to dig ever-deeper shafts, and underground water became a major limiting factor in coal mining. In 1705 Thomas Newcomen and John Calley designed an engine which was moved by steam and which could furnish the power to pump water from the mines. By the mid-eighteenth century more than a hundred Newcomen engines were in use. In 1765 James Watt constructed a steam engine that required only one-third the coal consumed by a Newcomen engine per unit of power output, and the following year a steam engine was used for the first time for purposes other than pumping water—to blow air through a blast furnace. By 1785 the steam engine had also been harnessed to power looms and spinning machines. These developments quickly led to the consolidation of small industries into large factories. It was only a matter of time before the steam engine was applied to both land and sea transport, and eventually to the farm. The Industrial Revolution had begun.

Following the advent of the steam engine, per capita demands for energy increased rapidly. In part this increase resulted from the replacement of human labor by machine labor. In part it resulted from the fact that people wanted luxuries, and the new sources of energy, properly harnessed, made those luxuries available. But in large measure the increase stemmed from the fact that the ready availability of large quantities of energy created a new environment for the human species within which a new culture emerged. Machine culture rapidly replaced agriculture.

Prior to the Industrial Revolution coal had not been used very widely, although there is some evidence that it was used in Europe as early as the twelfth century A.D. But by the late nineteenth century coal was providing the greater part of the 75,000 calories per day required by the average person who lived in industrial society. This corresponded to burning nearly four tons of coal per person each year.

After the invention of the steam engine, technological developments followed each other rapidly. By the beginning of the nineteenth century men had conceived of the screw-propeller steamboat, the threshing machine, and the sewing machine. The same century saw the appearance of the water turbine, the internal combustion engine, and the steam turbine. In the early twentieth century the gas turbine and the jet appeared. The electrical generator revolutionized communications and the transmission of power.

The most important characteristics of the Industrial Revolution have been rapid change and rapid increases of rate of change. Since the beginnings of the epoch, mankind has seen the emergence of almost innumerable technological innovations that have competed with existing ways of doing things and have further released man from physical labor. It is now generally recognized that technological innovation has been a prime contributing factor to economic growth, perhaps equaling the combined effect of the classical factors of land, labor, and capital.

Successful innovations have driven many older technologies to extinction and have resulted in higher productivity, greater consumption of energy, increased demand for raw materials, accelerated flow of materials through the economy, and increased quantities of metals and other substances in use per capita. The history of industrial development abounds with examples. The steam-powered iron ship, for example, appeared in the late eighteenth century and competed with the wind-powered wooden ship. As the number of the former increased, that of the latter decreased (see Figure 1.4). By 1890 the tonnages of the two types of ships were equal. Not long afterward, the sailing ship as a practical merchant vessel was virtually extinct.

This evolutionary competitive process in which a new technological species drove an older species to extinction brought many benefits. Perhaps most important, travel times between continents were lessened considerably. Transport costs (including inventory costs) were likewise lessened. Much heavier loads could be accommodated. But all of this was at the expense of greatly increased consumption of energy per unit of material transported. Monetary costs went down; energy costs went up.

A second example of technological competition was the replacement of horses and mules by steam and gasoline power as prime movers on the farm. Prior to the Civil War in the United States, horses and mules were the primary means for concentrating energy. In the nation as a whole, which was primarily agrarian, there was approximately one horse or mule for every four

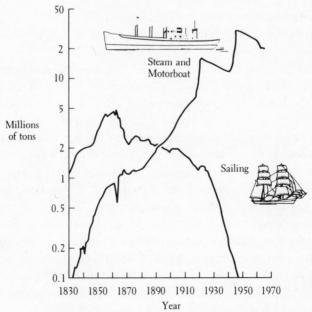

FIG 1.4. Tonnage of U.S. Merchant Vessels

persons, a situation which prevailed for many decades. But steam power was introduced to the farm shortly after the Civil War and by the turn of the century was providing major competition to horses. Had the internal combustion engine not been introduced to the farm in 1906, the steam engine undoubtedly would have driven the horse to extinction as a working farm animal. Instead, by 1930 the internal combustion engine had driven the steam engine to extinction on the farm, and by 1970 the farm work animal was also virtually extinct[1] (see Figure 1.5).

This major technological transition led to considerably increased farm production per man-hour worked and to decreased costs in monetary terms. But the costs in terms of energy, both to power the new equipment and to manufacture it, were greatly increased.

As technological innovations followed each other with breathtaking rapidity, and as society adjusted itself to the innovations, energy expenditures rose rapidly as well. Often innovations did not compete directly with existing technologies but made it possible to do things that had not been possible previously. Not infrequently, innovations were introduced as luxuries—the telephone and the automobile, for example. But as society evolved around these

[1] In 1972, farm work animals accounted for less than 0.5 percent of the available horsepower of prime movers on farms in the United States.

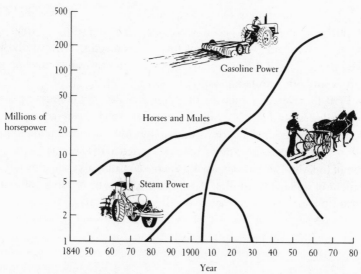

FIG. 1.5. Horsepower of Prime Movers on Farms in the United States (Excludes Automotive)

innovations, they were transformed from luxuries to necessities. And virtually all such innovations were accompanied by increased energy consumption—some large, some small, but collectively they grew exponentially.

Indeed, sources of energy themselves provide important examples of technological competitions—although in this case tempered by considerations of resource availability. In the early history of the United States wood met the

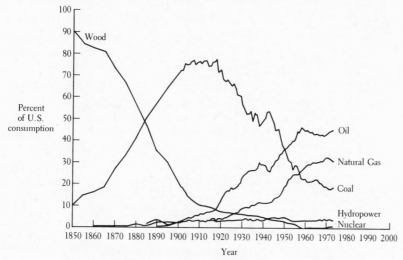

FIG. 1.6. Competition Between Fuels in the United States

overwhelming proportion of the nation's energy needs. By the middle of the nineteenth century coal had become an appreciable competitor to wood, and in the early twentieth century petroleum was competing successfully with coal. By the middle of the twentieth century natural gas was competing successfully with both petroleum and coal (see Figure 1.6).

By 1970 the average person in the United States was consuming about 250,000 calories per day, some 80 times as much as had been required by individual primitive men. This corresponds to the annual consumption of some 11 tons of coal per person—some six times as much as the average for the population of the world as a whole. World energy consumption had grown to the equivalent of some 7000 million tons of coal each year, or some 1800 times the total human need when man was still a food gatherer.

(3)

Since World War II the gap in wealth between inhabitants of industrialized and unindustrialized countries has widened at an accelerated pace. Indeed, a striking pattern has evolved amounting to no less than a fissioning of human society into two quite separate and distinct cultures—the culture of the rich

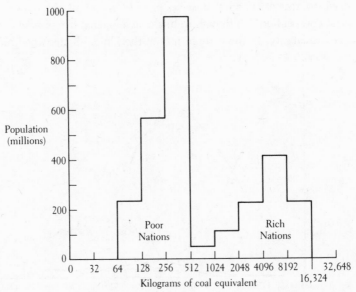

FIG. 1.7. Per Capita Energy Consumption

and the culture of the poor, with very few people living in between these two extremes.

Average per capita energy consumption is a useful indicator of wealth. Figure 1.7 shows the numbers of persons in the world who live at various average levels of energy consumption as expressed in kilograms of coal equivalents per person per year (1970). At the lower end of the scale, 235 million persons live under circumstances where their average energy consumption is the equivalent of between 64 and 128 kilograms of coal each year. At the upper end of the scale, 225 million persons consume on the average 130 times as much energy per person each year as is consumed by the poorest.

A nearly identical pattern of evolution can be seen when we examine per capita steel consumption or per capita gross national product (in constant dollars). Both show two peaks in their distribution and provide a convenient division of nations into the "rich" and "poor" categories. The average characteristics of each category, including the relatively small group living between the two extremes of wealth, are shown in Table 1.1.

TABLE 1.1

Average Population, Energy Consumption, and GNP in 1970

	RICH NATIONS	INTERMEDIATES	POOR NATIONS
Population (millions)	954	234	2,440
Energy consumption (millions of metric tons of coal)	5,680	384	717
Per capita energy consumption (kilograms/person)	5,950	1,640	293
Per capita GNP (U.S. dollars 1973)	2,720	846	169

We see from these figures that the rich countries, which have 27 percent of the population of the world, account for 84 percent of the world's total energy consumption. Further, the divergence between the rich and the poor is increasing, largely because of rapid population growth in the latter. In 1960 the average person in a rich country consumed 18.5 times as much energy as a person in a poor country. By 1970 this ratio had grown to 20.5. At 1970 growth rates the ratio will reach 40 by the year 2020.

A graphic comparison of the populations and levels of consumption of fossil fuels by the rich and poor countries is shown in Figure 1.8 in which the

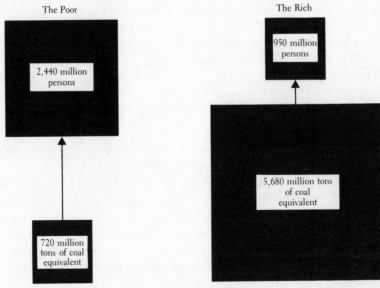

The Poor

2,440 million persons

720 million tons of coal equivalent

The Rich

950 million persons

5,680 million tons of coal equivalent

FIG. 1.8. Energy Consumption and Population in the Rich and Poor Nations

areas of the squares are proportional to the numbers of people and quantities of fuel consumed. Table 1.2 shows some selected growth characteristics.

Were the rates of growth of energy consumption and population which prevailed in 1970 to continue, by the year 2020 per capita consumption of

TABLE 1.2

Selected Average Growth Characteristics of Rich and Poor Nations

	RICH NATIONS	POOR NATIONS
1970 population (millions)	954	2,440
Annual population growth rate	0.8%	2.5%
1970 per capita energy consumption (tons of coal per year)	6.0	0.29
Annual growth rate of energy consumption	5.2%	5.6%
2020 population (millions)	1,400	8,500
2020 per capita energy consumption (tons of coal per year)	54	1.4

energy in coal equivalents would rise to 54 tons in the rich countries and to 1.4 tons in the poor. By that time the population of the world would be 10.5 billion, some 1.4 billion of whom would be rich and 8.5 billion of whom would be poor. Consumption of energy in the poor countries alone would rise to a level considerably higher than total consumption in the world today, while total world consumption of energy would approach the equivalent of 100 billion tons of coal annually. The ultimate consequences, were such developments actually to take place, are awesome to contemplate.

Thus we now find ourselves in a divided world: the wealthy part is characterized by growing affluence and the poor part is characterized by growing population (see Figure 1.9). Growing affluence and its counterpart, growing

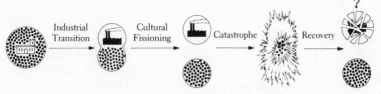

FIG. 1.9. Industrial Civilization

population, are transforming human society dramatically. Each phenomenon in its own way is determining the ultimate destiny of humanity.

Clearly, something is bound to give long before A.D. 2020 is reached. Current growth rates simply cannot persist much longer. Of consuming interest is the *manner* in which growth rates will change. Will rates of population growth and per capita consumption change as the result of premeditated, willful, constructive actions on the part of the world's people? Will they change as the result of such factors as malnutrition and disease, environmental degradation, and decreasing resource availability? Will they change as a result of continuing conflict between rich and rich, between poor and poor, and between rich and poor? Or will growth rates change as the result of a major catastrophic world upheaval?

CHAPTER II

The Richest
of the Rich

I was 7 when I saw the first automobile come into Boston.
They said man would never get to the North or South Pole,
but when I was 14 they got to the North Pole and when I
was 16 they got to the South Pole. I was 23 when they first
had the human voice on radio. All the things I'd been told
would never happen, happened.

—R. Buckminster Fuller,
Interview in *PHP*, Tokyo,
February 1977

(1)

When European settlers first came to North America they found seemingly
endless expanses of virgin fertile land. The colonies which later became the
United States found it relatively easy to produce an abundance of the basic
necessities of life. Population grew rapidly, in part because of the abundance
of food and in part because of immigration. For some time industrialization
took place very slowly, largely because of England's mercantile policy. The
colonies were expected to send raw materials to England and to be a market
for finished goods. Laws prevented them from industrializing in any substantial way.

Following the American Revolution, some 50 years after the Industrial
Revolution had started to transform English life, the process of industrialization began in the United States in earnest and it accelerated quickly.
By the early nineteenth century textiles had become a big business. Metals industries were established in the midwest, where major deposits of iron and

coal were located. Americans turned to inventing and by 1860 had invented most of the farm machinery in use today.

The population of the United States grew at a prodigious rate. In 1790 the population was somewhat less than 4 million. By 1860 it had grown nearly eightfold to 31 million. By the turn of this century it had grown to 76 million. Increased industrialization brought with it increased urbanization, with the result that by 1860 over 16 percent of the population was living in towns and cities of over 8000 people. By the turn of the century over 40 percent of the population were town and city dwellers. As urbanization increased, a new phenomenon appeared: fertility began to decrease and families became smaller, so the rate of population growth diminished somewhat. By 1900 the average number of children borne by one woman had dropped from eight to four.

The United States was able to accumulate capital by producing excess agricultural products and selling them to European nations. Thus, although its rate of industrial growth did not exceed its rate of population growth until about 1890, considerable capital had been accumulated by that time. Following 1890, as the rate of industrialization increased and the rate of population growth decreased, there was a rapid increase in the general availability of goods. The Age of Affluence had begun.

The rapid evolution of the United States into the most affluent nation on earth was made possible by a number of situations and developments. On the physical side there was ample arable land for production of agricultural products. Wood, coal, and petroleum were plentiful as fuels. The hydropower potential was considerable. Deposits of iron and copper ores were substantial. The political, economic, and social systems encouraged entrepreneurism, innovation, and risk taking. New kinds of institutions such as the land-grant colleges accelerated the accumulation and application of technical knowledge in both agriculture and industry. The Civil War and two world wars gave enormous impetus to industrial production. New techniques of industrial organization and production greatly increased productivity both in industry and in agriculture. By the end of World War II the United States had changed from a rural agricultural nation to an industrial giant in which individuals had more material possessions and richer diets than the inhabitants of any previous or contemporary society.

A major contributor to these developments was the tremendous explosion in agricultural production. A part of this explosion stemmed from farm use of the internal combustion engine and the fact that one liter of gasoline burned in a 1-horsepower engine yields the energy equivalent of seven man-days of hard physical labor. In the United States that is the equivalent of buying labor at a cost of 2.5¢ per man-day.

Another part of the explosion stemmed from the intensive application of science and technology to the improvement of crop yields. Still another part involved the considerable improvement of efficiency in transforming cereals into animal products.

High and increasing levels of agricultural production per hectare resulted from liberal applications of fertilizers and pesticides. As one result of these and other developments, for example, the yield of corn in the United States was more than doubled between the early 1950s and the 1970s.

But the tremendous increases in crop yields in the United States also depended on very large inputs of energy from fossil fuels. Over 50 percent of this energy is now consumed directly in the form of fuel for tractors and other machinery and of electricity. The balance is consumed indirectly: about 20 percent for producing the fertilizers, another 20 percent for manufacturing the farm machinery, and about 10 percent for miscellaneous inputs such as irrigation.

Thus, the tremendous inputs of science and technology (including large inputs of energy from fossil fuels), together with the unusually large ratio of fertile arable land to people in North America, led to an unprecedented capacity for the production of surplus food. On the average, Americans were able to feed themselves a very rich yet relatively inexpensive bill of fare and still export agricultural products to others at prices which most rich countries were willing and able to pay. Indeed, U.S. agricultural production became so large that requests for cash purchases could easily be met and in addition substantial shipments of foodstuffs could be made to poor countries. Further, in order to avoid excessive production surpluses, the U.S. government for many years paid its farmers considerable sums of money to keep substantial areas of good farmland idle.

The concentration of large quantities of energy resulted in increases in industrial productivity which were almost as impressive as those achieved on the farm. Since the turn of the century the industrial production per man-hour worked has increased more than fourfold. In substantial measure this increase has resulted from the efforts of industry to reduce labor costs. Substitution of energy from fossil fuels for human energy was one approach. Others included the assembly-line approach to production, the careful organization of work operations (making use of time-motion studies), psychological testing, simplification of design, and the use of electronic control over many aspects of industrial operations.

In 1850 agriculture contributed three times as much as did industry to our national income. A century later, in 1950, manufacturing was contributing four times as much as agriculture. By 1975 the contribution of industry exceeded that of agriculture by a factor of seven.

In reality, agriculture itself had become an industry, indistinguishable in most respects from other industries. It had become dependent upon a vast array of high-technology inputs ranging from fertilizers and pesticides to complicated machinery, fossil fuels, and computers. Indeed, the tremendous increases in agricultural productivity per man-hour worked became far less impressive when the labor costs of the diverse inputs were taken into consideration. And the fossil fuel inputs to agriculture grew to the point where they approached the energy content of the crops themselves.

(2)

It has become increasingly clear that technological change has played an enormous role in the economic and social development of the United States. The rapid growth of the U.S. economy cannot be explained satisfactorily solely on the basis of the accepted classical ingredients of economic growth: capital, labor, and land. The missing ingredient is a combination of interrelated elements which have variously been called "innovation," "technical change," "scientific and engineering advance," "research and development," "advances of knowledge," "education," "improved communications," "improved techniques of management," and "training of labor." Although economists disagree among themselves as to the relative importance of these elements, studies indicate that over the years they have collectively contributed at least 50 percent of the annual growth of the United States economy, and probably even more. Certainly they played a major role in carrying the United States far ahead of the rest of the world economically during the first half of the twentieth century.

Until the latter part of the nineteenth century most technological innovations came into existence through individual inspiration and efforts. The history of the United States abounds with examples of individual inventor-entrepreneurs such as Whitney, McCormick, Bell, Ford, and Edison. But following the creation of the land-grant colleges in 1862, a steady shift took place in the methodology of bringing innovations into existence. Research at agricultural experiment stations increasingly became a group effort. As the theoretical basis for the methodical application of the known laws of nature improved, random trial-and-error approaches to the solution of problems diminished in importance. Gradually it was realized that the returns on investments in systematic applied research could be very high. In time, numerous industries created departments for research and development. Even so, by 1921 total investments in research and development nationwide amounted to but $150 millon, corresponding to about 0.2 percent of the GNP. By World War II this had risen to $570 million, corresponding to 0.6 percent of the GNP.

During World War II, U.S. science and engineering were mobilized into a vast array of major projects aimed at helping the military effort. Some of the projects, notably those which produced the proximity fuse, radar, and the atomic bomb, were spectacular successes. The research management experiences gained at that time were applied effectively after the war to a wide variety of programs, most of which were either military- or space-oriented. By 1953 total research and development expenditures had risen tenfold above the 1940 level. By 1973 such expenditures exceeded $30 billion annually, corresponding to about 2.5 percent of the GNP. Scientists and engineers combined represented more than 2 percent of the labor force.

A vast array of new products and services emerged. The transistor, which had been developed during the war, made possible the modern computer, the pocket radio, and a vast array of electronic gadgetry which had not been possible in the days of the vacuum tube. As computer memories increased, major revolutions in information handling and storage took place. There were corresponding revolutions in photoreproduction. Satellite technology opened up new possibilities in long-distance communication; computers which were far removed from each other geographically could be linked together.

In the chemical field a variety of new products appeared, ranging from agricultural pesticides to synthetic fibers, to optical fibers. Tens of thousands of new drugs were developed by the pharmaceutical industry. Agricultural scientists developed large arrays of new plant varieties, and food technologists devised increasingly sophisticated techniques for processing, packaging, and marketing foods. In the transportation area, air transport systems were made increasingly effective and contributed to the near-extinction of domestic intercity passenger travel by train. Internationally, long-distance passenger service by ship became virtually extinct. Shipment of freight by air opened up numerous possibilities, particularly for the shipment of goods which had high value per unit weight.

Important as the postwar U.S. research and development program was, the dominant part of it was military-aerospace oriented. In 1955 military programs consumed about 47 percent of the U.S. R&D dollar. By 1960 the military share had climbed to 52 percent, following which the proportion began a slow relative decline, reaching 28 percent in 1973. In the meantime, after

1958 space R&D programs grew rapidly. The space share peaked in 1965 at 20 percent, following which it also slowly declined.

The great concentration of the U.S. R&D effort upon military and space-oriented problems had a profound effect upon the universities and upon the training of engineers. Quite naturally, major emphasis was placed upon areas where jobs were available, as distinct from areas of critical societal problems which were less well financed, such as construction, pollution, mineral resources, energy, transportation, agriculture, crime, waste management, and health delivery systems.

As the total budgets for R&D increased in the United States, budgets for "basic research" increased as well. "Basic research" usually means research which is undertaken for its own sake and which might provide important insights into the workings of nature without reference to any specific useful application. Quite apart from its intrinsic intellectual value, such research is essential if we are to continue to solve practical problems. In the long run the solution of practical problems is dependent upon the quantity, quality, and availability of knowledge concerning the physical, biological, and social behavior of matter—including human beings and other living organisms. In 1955, expenditures for basic research amounted to somewhat less than 10 percent of the total R&D budget. The proportion grew with time and since 1970 has remained at a level close to 15 percent.

The United States emerged from World War II as the research colossus of the world. In the years immediately after the war the basic research output in the United States was greater than that of the rest of the world combined. But as the other more technologically advanced nations recovered from the effects of the war and began once again to engage in basic research activities, the proportional contribution from the U.S. declined, reaching about 40 percent in 1967. Although more recent statistics are not available, it is doubtful that U.S. contributions to basic research in 1975 amounted to much more than a third of the world total.

Thus the U.S. research and development effort ranged over the decades from the work of relatively isolated individual inventors and research workers to those of huge research complexes involving tens of thousands of people. The accomplishments of that effort have been impressive, but they would have amounted to little in the absence of meaningful coupling with organizations which were willing and able to transform research findings into production and marketing. For a long time this involved entrepreneurs, often the inventors, who were willing to take risks and to locate others who would share risks. As time has passed, the importance of individual entrepreneurs has lessened and the importance of large organizations has increased.

A substantial part of the contribution of research, including invention, to U.S. economic development has been made by persons and organizations willing and able to take risks and closely allied to the inventors or developers. It is by no means certain that this situation will continue. For a complexity of reasons, the atmosphere in the United States is now becoming less favorable for the risk taker.

(3)

Until the turn of this century the United States was one of the world's most dramatic examples of explosive population growth. In 1790 (the time of our first census) the population was somewhat less than 4 million. By 1900 it had grown nearly 20-fold to reach 76 million. In large measure this growth resulted from a very high level of fertility.

As we have seen, for the greater part of the nineteenth century America was predominantly an agricultural nation in which life was a constant struggle against nature. Large numbers of children were an economic asset since most of the work was accomplished by physical labor. The average woman in 1790 could expect to give birth to seven children by the time her family was completed. Of course, many women died while they were still in their childbearing years and others were sterile, so a considerable number of women gave birth to a dozen or more children during the course of their lifetimes.

Nevertheless, for reasons not well understood, the fertility rate dropped steadily during the nineteenth century. By 1860 it had fallen to five children per woman and by 1900 it had fallen to 3.3. This phenomenon seems to have reflected a desire on the part of couples to have fewer children and also seems to have been more pronounced in the cities where children were less of an economic asset than they had been on the farm. In any event, the drop in birth rate was achieved without benefit of modern contraceptive techniques and can be attributed to a combination of postponed marriage, coitus interruptus, abstinence, and abortion.

The drop in fertility rate was in large measure compensated for, however, by a high level of immigration, particularly from Europe. Also, in the eighteenth century large numbers of Africans were brought as slaves to work on the farms, predominantly in the southern states. There were no significant restrictions on immigration until after the Civil War when slavery was abolished and Chinese immigrants were excluded. Even so, during the last half of the nineteenth century the rate of immigration appears to have amounted to between 20 and 25 percent of the birth rate.

The final ingredient which determines the rate of population growth is the death rate. During the nineteenth century the death rate was high by modern standards, although the abundance of food gave rise to a healthier than average population when compared with the rest of the world at that time. By 1900 the death rate had fallen to 17 deaths per 1000 population each year, about twice that of today. With a birth rate of 32 per thousand and an immigration rate of 8 per thousand, this meant an annual rate of population growth of 2.3 percent, about the same as that in many developing countries today. High though that rate of growth seems, it nevertheless represented a drop from a 3.3 percent rate of annual growth early in the nineteenth century.

The total fertility rate continued to fall early in this century and reached a minimum of about 2.1 children per woman during the Great Depression of the 1930s. With the onset of World War II the fertility rate started to increase, and peaked at about 3.6 in the middle 1950s. Throughout the 1960s and 1970s the fertility rate declined. The decline seems to have stemmed partly from a real desire on the part of younger people to have fewer children and partly from the availability of more effective contraceptives and the legalization of abortion.

At the same time, patterns of immigration changed considerably. During the first decade of this century about 40 percent of the population growth was attributable to immigration. After World War I there were strong pressures to restrict the influx of people, and following the Immigration Act of 1924 the rate of immigration fell markedly. During the 1930s more people left the United States than entered, but during the 1960s immigration accounted for about 16 percent of our total population growth. In 1970 the immigration rate was about 2 compared with a birth rate of 18 per thousand persons.

During the period 1900–1970 death rates as well as birth rates fell by nearly 50 percent and have now reached the point where most people live well beyond their periods of maximum fertility. Further decreases in mortality rates will primarily affect older persons who have already passed through their childbearing years and thus will not have major impact upon our rate of population growth. What happens to our rate of population growth in the future will be determined largely by what happens to fertility, by immigration policies, and by illegal immigration.

Fertility rates depend upon the behavior patterns of people, which are neither well understood nor easily predicted. Nevertheless, the trends indicate that we are heading for an average family size of two children. Indeed, this situation was reached in 1972 and may well prevail in the years ahead. But even were we able to retain this low fertility rate on a permanent basis, births would continue to exceed deaths for the rest of this century and well into the next.

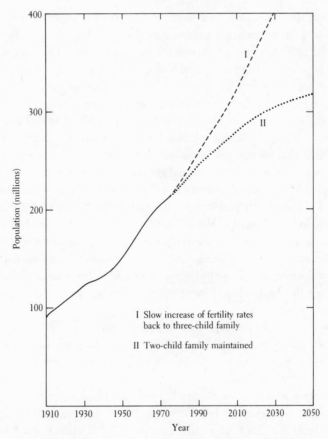

Fig. 2.1. Estimated Population Growth of the United States

Assuming present levels of immigration, and modest continued lessening of mortality, the population will reach 300 million by about 2025. However, in view of the changeable nature of fertility, the two-child family might not be a truly stable element of our society for some time, in which case the population in 2025 could conceivably be as high as 400 million. Figure 2.1 shows two projections of future U.S. population growth.

In the years ahead, changing age distribution is likely to be a far more important population characteristic than is population growth. In 1900, persons 65 years of age and older accounted for but 4 percent of the population. By 1970 the proportion had increased to about 10 percent. Because of the downward trend of the birth rate, our population will continue to grow older in average age. If the two-child family pattern and current mortality rates prevail, the population of persons 65 years of age and older will eventually level off at about 16 percent while the proportion of persons 18 and younger will decrease from the present 34 percent to 24 percent. As these changes in age distribution take place, there will, of course, be changes in the labor force. But except for dislocations, such as that produced by the "baby boom" of the 1950s, those changes will come slowly. Given a continuing pattern of two children per family, the proportion of persons 18–64 years of age will change, but very slowly, from the present 56 percent to 60 percent.

The most serious aspect of the aging of the population will continue to be the problems involved with the care of the aged. In 1900 there were only about 3 million persons in the United States 65 years of age and older. By 1970 there were 20 million such persons. By the turn of the next century the number may well approach 30 million. This very large increase will give rise to extremely serious problems of providing adequate financial support, health care, and roles which are valued in our society. Should there be major breakthroughs in the prevention or treatment of cardiovascular disease or carcinomas, the population of the elderly will increase still further and the strains upon the system will be correspondingly greater.

(4)

In the years ahead, the movement as well as the growth of population will continue to be an important determinant of the nature of American society. America has been a nation of migrators since the time the new nation was created by immigrants from Europe, together with their offspring and black slaves. This situation is likely to prevail during the next few decades.

The first major migration consisted of the movement of the early settlers, primarily from the British Isles, Spain, and Germany, to the New World. It is estimated that perhaps a quarter of a million people left the British Isles for America in the seventeenth century to establish colonies on a continent inhabited at the time by about a million Indians. In the eighteenth century, the total migration from Europe may have been as much as 1.5 million. During the same century, between 250,000 and 300,000 Africans were brought to the colonies to serve as slaves. By the time of the first census in 1790, the European population in the colonies had grown to more than 3 million. There were about 700,000 black slaves, concentrated primarily in the South, and another 60,000 free "nonwhites." The Indian populations in the colonies themselves had been decimated, and had ceased to be a factor of any consequence. The total Indian population east of the Mississippi at the time is estimated to have been well under 100,000.

At the time of the first census the average complexion of the population as a whole was considerably darker than at present, for one out of every five persons was classified as "nonwhite." In the South, however, the proportion of blacks was much higher, for a third of all families owned slaves and the average slave-owning family could count eight blacks among its possessions. The slave trade was cut off in 1808, but the number of slaves in the United States continued to grow through reproduction, at a rate which was about the same as the growth rate of the white population, not counting the increasing flow of immigrants from Europe. By 1860, the last census prior to the abolition of slavery, the slave population had grown to about 4 million.

The second great migration was the massive movement of people to the West. At the beginning of the nineteenth century the United States was a relatively small country, primarily confined to the strip of land between the Atlantic Ocean and the Appalachian Mountains. In search of more farmland, settlers crossed the mountains into Tennessee and Kentucky. As new territories were added the movement to the West accelerated, and by the beginning of this century literally millions of persons had moved westward. At the time it was the largest and most rapid movement of population in history.

The third great migration was from the farm to the city. The new agricultural technology lessened the need for farm labor. The new industrial technology increased the demand for labor in the cities. Thus, the farm laborer was both pushed and pulled toward the cities, with the result that urban centers grew rapidly in both size and number. By the end of World War II nearly two-thirds of the U.S. population was urbanized and 12 urban areas had grown to a size of a million or more persons. By 1970 the urban population included nearly three-quarters of the population and there were 26 urban areas each with a million or more population.

Accelerated immigration from other countries—the fourth great migration—also played an important role in city growth. During the period 1820–1974, nearly 50 million people came to the United States, approximately three-quarters of them from Europe. A substantial proportion of these immigrants settled in the larger cities and became a source of relatively inexpensive labor for the newly developing industries. The flow of immigrants varied from decade to decade, depending in part on the economic and political situations in their home countries and in part on their visions of the economic opportunities awaiting them in the United States. In the single decade 1905–1914 over 10 million immigrants made the journey—one-fifth of all persons to immigrate to the United States up to the present time.

In 1790 there were about four whites for every black in the U.S. population. As a result of increasing immigration this ratio increased steadily, reaching 8.8 in the 1930s. Since then, the ratio has been decreasing as the result of the differing birth rates between blacks and whites, or more correctly between poor and rich. By 1974 there were 6.7 whites for every black. Similarly, as a result of the changing immigration the percentage of foreign-born in the U.S. population has changed substantially. Until World War I about 16 percent of the U.S. population was foreign-born and little more than half the population was native white of native parentage. With the advent of laws controlling the numbers of immigrants, the percentage of foreign born fell steadily, reaching 4.7 percent in 1970.

Early in this century more than 90 percent of all blacks were still living in the southern states to which their ancestors had been brought as slaves. Most were attached to the soil—indeed, according to the census of 1910, only one-quarter of all blacks were living in towns and cities. During World War I the need for labor to run industries in the North, coupled with the changing economy in the South, led to the first large migration of blacks from South to North. This process was accelerated with the passage of legislation in the 1920s designed to curtail sharply the flow of immigrants from overseas. The black exodus from the South slowed somewhat during the Depression years of the 1930s but was greatly accelerated during World War II. By 1950 only two-thirds of all blacks were living in the South; by 1973 the proportion had dropped to about one-half.

Even more dramatic was the flow of blacks into the cities. By 1960 two-thirds of all blacks were residents in metropolitan areas. By 1973 the urbanized proportion had increased to 75 percent. The economic, social, and political consequences of this vast migration were enormous. In a period of time which was breathtaking in its brevity many large northern industrial cities, as well as most of the southern ones, found themselves with a population of blacks which approached or exceeded that of whites.

(5)

The invention of the internal combustion engine in the late nineteenth century greatly accelerated the substitution of machines for horses and men on the farm and thus accelerated the movement from farm to city. It also made possible the development of the mass-produced private automobile, for which Americans developed an instant, deep, personal, and emotional attachment. By 1900, some 8000 private motor vehicles had already been registered. By 1913, the number of this new-found and exciting luxury had grown to more than a million. By 1923, when the number of vehicles exceeded 10 million, the automobile was well on its way to being transformed from a luxury to a necessity. At the outbreak of World War II the number exceeded 30 million. The 100-million mark was passed in 1973, which corresponded to one car for every two persons. To accommodate these vehicles, nearly 4 million miles of streets and highways were built and 110 billion gallons of gasoline were consumed annually. The rapid growth of per capita automobile ownership (see Figure 2.2) suggests that the number of motor vehicles is not likely to stop growing until there is one for every person of driving age.

As with earlier technological innovations, the automobile—and its close relatives the bus and truck—competed with established technologies, in this case the railroads and electrified municipal transport systems. The private au-

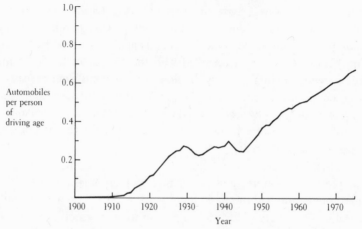

FIG. 2.2. Automobiles per Person of Driving Age in the U.S., 1900–1975

tomobile and the bus together quickly captured the lion's share of intercity passenger traffic from the railroads. After World War II, the airplane combined with the automobile to drive the passenger-carrying railroad to near-extinction. At the same time, the truck ate heavily into the railroad's share of the freight business.

Of all the changes brought about by the internal combustion engine, however, perhaps the most spectacular was within the cities themselves, where a quite different transportation technology existed.

Of the 50 largest cities in the United States, 39 are ocean or river ports where water transport has played a major role in the import of food and raw materials, the export of manufactured products, and the movement of people. In these cities, industries were established close to the ship terminals and workers lived near the industries, since walking was the primary mode of transportation. Goods, and to a certain extent people, were moved about by horse-drawn conveyances and streets and roads were designed with this in mind. For the most part, however, trips to and from work and shopping were accomplished on foot.

With the arrival of electrical power, the streetcar, the elevated train, and the subway appeared on the scene. Workers could live farther away from their factories and offices. Then the motor vehicle completely destroyed the balance which had been achieved. Because of the low density of automobiles and trucks in the early stages of the transition, the advantages of shifting from the horse to the engine were immediate and the population of the new vehicles increased extremely rapidly. The motor-powered truck quickly displaced the horse-powered wagon as well as the river barge. The taxi and private car displaced the horse-drawn carriage and the ferryboat. The new vehicles utilized the existing streets which had been built on the scale of the horse-drawn wagon, and it was only a matter of time before traffic became chaotic.

Nevertheless, upper-income families made use of the new mobility to move to the suburbs. As families left the central city, lower-income groups moved into the houses that had been vacated. In time the structures deteriorated and became the familiar tenements of modern city slums. A clear pattern of city decay emerged in which the central core of the port area disintegrates and is not rebuilt, and a new city emerges at the periphery of the old one. As it decays, yet another ring of new city emerges farther out. As the process continues, the overall efficiency decreases and the city becomes less competitive economically.

Over the years, for reasons of economic necessity immigrants to the United States would seek out those areas of cities where they could live least expensively. Often these were the areas vacated by the well-to-do, which had become slums. As the immigrants' economic fortunes improved they, or their children, moved away from the central city to less difficult environments, eventually to become indistinguishable from those who had preceded them.

The great decline in the flow of immigrants from overseas coincided with the accelerated in-migration of blacks from the South, who also sought out areas where they could live least expensively. They too gravitated to the slums. But once there, their problems differed considerably from those of their European predecessors. First, their visibility made it difficult for them to be accepted socially and economically into the white mainstream of American life. Second, their extremely primitive rural background prevented their adjusting easily to urban life. These problems led to an acceleration of urban decay and to social unrest of a magnitude previously not experienced in American life.

The movement of blacks into the central cities led to the accelerated flight of whites to the suburbs, disturbed by increasing levels of crime and violence and the deterioration of schooling. The mobility which had been bestowed upon them by the automobile made it possible for them to settle at great distances from their jobs. The sharp increase in the numbers of automobile commuters led to the construction of seemingly endless successions of divided highways, expressways, freeways, bridges, and tunnels. It also inevitably led to traffic congestion which, in spite of all remedial measures, continued to worsen with time.

As these tremendous demographic and social changes were taking place, agricultural and industrial production per man-hour worked continued to rise, and per capita income grew to the point where ordinary laboring people could afford to buy goods which previously could only be afforded by the rich. Between 1900 and 1950 the per capita GNP in constant dollars rose 2.5-fold and a large part of this increase went to purchase homes and automobiles, to install plumbing, electricity, and telephones, and to shift to richer diets. Between 1950 and 1973 the per capita GNP, again in constant dollars, increased by another two-thirds. By that time more than 80 percent of all households owned one or more automobiles; almost all homes had electrical refrigerators and television sets; washing machines, clothes dryers, freezers, and air conditioners were the rule rather than the exception. The age of mass consumption had arrived and it became clear that with continued increases in per capita income virtually all households would eventually own the full spectrum of machines and appliances.

In the meantime, as changing technology resulted in increased agricultural and industrial productivity, the composition of the labor force began to change rapidly, moving away from areas of production toward the services. Between 1950 and 1975 manufacturing and agricultural output per man-hour worked doubled and quadrupled, respectively. In the same period the proportion of blue-collar and farm workers in the working population decreased from 52 to 36 percent, with a corresponding increase in the proportion of white-collar and service workers. By 1975 nearly two-thirds of all workers were in the service area, ranging from professionals in health care and education to technicians, sales workers, bank tellers, bookkeepers, postal clerks, bus drivers, policeman, fireman, and household workers.

(6)

The age of mass consumption was made possible by vast increases in the consumption of a variety of raw materials such as ores of iron, copper, and aluminum, but most notably in the consumption of energy in the form of oil, natural gas, and coal. Energy in increasing quantities was required to power agricultural and industrial machinery, reduce iron ore to metal, run trucks and automobiles, light cities, and heat homes and offices.

For countless millennia solar radiation, operating through the mechanism of photosynthesis, was man's primary energy source. This continued to be true for some time after the onset of the Industrial Revolution, as charcoal (made from wood) remained the preferred, but increasingly more expensive, agent for reducing iron ore to metal. Households in the United States were prodigious consumers of fuelwood for cooking and heating. As late as 1850 wood supplied 90 percent of the fuel used in the United States, with coal accounting for the balance. Nevertheless, coal quickly became the primary industrial fuel, so useful was it for steel manufacture and the generation of steam power.

By 1885 the railroads had become the most important users of coal in the United States, closely followed by coke ovens. By 1910 fuelwood accounted for little more than 10 percent of energy consumption in the United States, with coal accounting for nearly 80 percent. Oil, natural gas, and hydropower accounted for the balance.

Oil first came into substantial use in the United States about 1860. At that time its cost (measured in 1970 dollars) was about $20 per barrel. Its initial use, in the form of kerosene, was in lamps to provide light, and later in stoves to furnish heat. But a series of technological developments rapidly changed the pattern of use. The development of the incandescent electric bulb decreased the demand for kerosene. But early in this century fuel oil came into widespread use to power steamships. This was followed in turn by the rapid upsurge of the internal combustion engine after World War I, and by the use of oil for residential and commercial heating.

By 1948 the price of U.S. oil had fallen from the original $20 per barrel to about $3.50 per barrel (all in 1970 dollars). By that time coal was being purchased by the electric utilities at an average price of about $12 per ton. At these prices oil was about one-third more expensive than coal if one were to judge the two fuels solely on the basis of their respective energy contents. In spite of this differential, however, petroleum use increased dramatically. In part this was due to the emergence of the internal combustion engine and, associated with it, the immense popularity of the automobile. But in addition, oil actually displaced coal in a number of markets. The railroads turned to diesel power; households turned to heating oil; power companies turned to fuel oil.

The problem of competition between fuels is an extremely complex one, involving many factors like transportation costs, ease of handling, efficiency of use, and cleanliness, in addition to original cost. Oil is a liquid and can be transported by pipeline and tanker considerably less expensively than coal can be transported by train or by slurry pipeline. Oil lends itself to automatic handling more readily than coal. Petroleum can usually be burned more cleanly than coal with respect to emissions of particulate matter and oxides of sulfur.

The availability of natural gas in large quantities also contributed substantially to the changing energy picture. Gas is associated with petroleum and is a premium fuel in the sense that it provides heat with high efficiency and with unequaled convenience and cleanliness. For many years, due to a lack of transmission facilities, the price of natural gas could not reflect this premium value. But as the vast network of gas pipelines evolved in the United States, the price came closer to reflecting the real value.

In 1948 the price of natural gas at the well was about one-eighth the cost of coal per unit of energy content, and practically free when compared with petroleum. But the cost of transporting and distributing gas is substantial; thus, for many years the main cost of gas to the customer was the transportation cost. Between 1950 and 1970 natural gas accounted for more than half the growth in total energy supply in the United States and the price of the fuel at the well increased rapidly. As gas has become more popular, there have been increasingly frequent difficulties stemming from a progressively more acute shortage of fuel at the well. During the severe winter of 1976–1977 the lack of adequate availability of natural gas reached crisis proportions.

In the latter part of the nineteenth century total energy demand in the United States increased at a modest rate of 2 to 3 percent per year. The rate of growth increased after 1900, then decreased following World War I, and became negative during the Great Depression. Since World War II growth has been considerably more rapid, and in the decade 1960–1970 averaged nearly 4.8 percent annually. By 1970 energy consumption in the U.S. exceeded the equivalent of 11 tons of coal per person each year (see Figure 2.3). As total needs grew, competition between fuels led to the emergence of oil as the primary fuel in the United States. About 1950 oil and coal were of equal importance. During the following quarter-century oil made even greater inroads, and by 1973 it was providing 46 percent of the nation's energy. Natural gas was the second most important fuel, providing 31 percent; coal accounted for 18 percent, and hydropower 4 percent.

For several decades the United States exported considerable quantities of petroleum products. However, the gap between imports and exports gradually narrowed and after World War II the United States entered a dramatic new era in which it imported more petroleum than it exported. By 1960 the U.S. was importing 18 percent of its petroleum requirements. By 1970 this had

FIG. 2.3. United States Energy Consumption Per Capita, 1900–1970

risen to 23 percent, and by 1973 to 35 percent. Since 1970 virtually all of the expansion in U.S. energy consumption has come from petroleum imports.

A major reason for this development was price. Vast reservoirs of oil were found in the Middle East and Venezuela which could be extracted at low cost. Indeed, by the early 1970s the incremental cost of Middle Eastern oil at dockside in the Persian Gulf was 10¢ per barrel, including a 20 percent return on all investments. Needless to say, the oil companies operating in the Middle East did not sell the crude oil for 10¢ per barrel. For a lengthy period the Persian Gulf price was $1.25 per barrel, giving a profit or "rent" of $1.15 after deducting the 10¢ cost. Even so, this was a bargain, for transportation charges were kept low by improved tanker technology. Under these circumstances imports rose rapidly—a development of considerable concern to domestic producers.

In the early years of the development of Middle Eastern oil, the companies with concessions in the region kept most of the "rent" or extra profit. But gradually the governments of the Middle Eastern countries have increased their shares. Since the creation of the Organization of Petroleum Exporting Countries (OPEC) in 1960, they have managed to keep most of it and put themselves in the position of being able to dictate what the price will be.

Although the growing dependence of the United States upon imported oil was a matter of concern to many students of the situation as early as 1950, the sequence of events in Western Europe and Japan was even more serious. Coal was available in both areas, but neither was endowed with appreciable petroleum deposits. So inexpensive was oil from the Middle East that the economies of Western Europe and Japan became dependent upon imported petroleum for their survival.

Thus the stage was set for collective action by the Organization of Petroleum Exporting Countries, which by 1973 consisted of Saudi Arabia, Iran, Venezuela, Nigeria, Libya, Kuwait, Iraq, the United Arab Emirates, Algeria, Indonesia, Qatar, Ecuador, and Gabon (an associate member). Prior to the Arab-Israeli war of October 1973 the price of OPEC oil was about $2 per barrel. By the end of 1973 the price had been raised to $3.44, and to more than $10 by the end of 1974. In addition, the Arab oil-producing nations cut off oil supplies to the United States during the Arab-Israeli war and the embargo lasted until March 1974.

The collective OPEC actions coupled with the embargo caused a number of serious dislocations throughout the world. The industrialized nations had to pay greatly increased sums for fuel to keep their societies functioning, and this in turn led to substantial balance-of-payments problems.

For the moment, the trap which has snared the importing countries is extremely strong. It isn't that other petroleum deposits won't be found—they probably will be. It isn't that other forms of energy can't be effectively put to use—they certainly can be. It isn't that per capita energy consumption can't be decreased without lowering living comfort—this certainly can be done. The difficulty is *time*, which is a commodity that cannot easily be purchased. Time is needed to intensify exploration. Time is needed to undertake the necessary research and development. Time is needed to build new plants, relocate industries, change ways of life.

The rich importing countries have little choice but to push in these new directions as rapidly as they can. But for the next decade at least they are destined to remain in the trap which they unthinkingly helped build themselves. From that trap they can look forward to further price increases and intensified political pressures—and backward to actions they wish they had taken 10, 20, or 30 years ago.

(7)

As the U.S. economy grew, consumption of resources other than energy grew as well. The provision of the goods which are deemed by most people to be essential in modern industrial society necessitates adequate supplies of raw materials. Each year we extract huge quantities of ores, minerals, and rock from the earth's crust, concentrate them into materials which can be injected into the industrial complex, then transform the materials further into finished products. In the course of this process much of the material ends up as scrap, which sometimes is recycled and sometimes wasted. The finished products in turn are purchased and used, eventually to become obsolete. Some of the materials in the obsolete objects are recycled; others are discarded, eventually to become widely dispersed. During this process, vast quantities of energy are required for mining and quarrying, beneficiation, the reduction of ores, manufacture, recovery of scrap, and the disposal of waste.

The process of industrialization in the United States has now carried us to the point where we produce close to 700 kilograms of raw steel each year for every person. Associated with that steel, we produce as well about 25 kilograms of other metals, such as aluminum, copper, zinc, lead, and tin; and nearly 10 tons of nonmetallics such as stone, sand, gravel, cement, clay, phosphate rock, common salt, lime, gypsum, and sulfur. These quantities are increasing on a per capita basis; of course, on a total basis they are increasing even more rapidly.

After World War I, the United States became the greatest producer and consumer of steel in the world. Per capita consumption rose from 140 kilograms in 1900 to 300 kilograms in 1910, to 400 kilograms during World War I, and to 600 kilograms during World War II. It is now about 700 kilograms per person (see Figure 2.4). Estimates suggest that we have in use in the United States some 10 metric tons of steel per person. Of this, the greater part exists in the form of heavy structural shapes, reinforcements, pilings, nails, staples, and wire fence. About 8 percent of the steel, or 750 kilograms per person, is in the form of private automobiles, trucks, and buses. The per capita amount of steel in use appears to be increasing slowly at a rate of about 1 percent annually.

Each year on a per capita basis about 350 kilograms of steel either becomes obsolete or is lost as the result of corrosion or other processes. Of this, about 150 kilograms (over 40 percent) is recovered and returned to the steel plants as scrap. The balance of about 220 kilograms will probably never be recovered. The mean lifetime of all steel in use appears to be some 25–30 years, although the lifetimes of the products in use vary greatly. Some products, such as cans, might be in use for only a few weeks or months. Steel in motor vehicles might be in use on the average about 10 years, in ships for about 25 years. Steel structural shapes such as girders and concrete reinforcements might be in use for a half-century or more.

Cycles of other materials used in modern industrial society are similar to

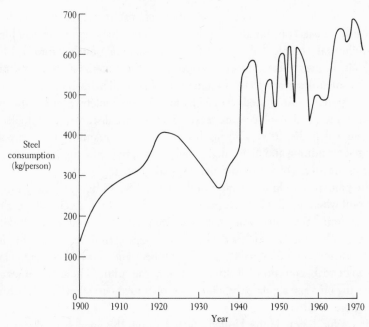

FIG. 2.4. United States Per Capita Steel Consumption

that of steel, but the relative proportions of the substances which flow in the various tributaries and branches vary. To take one extreme, gold is sufficiently valuable that losses in production of the metal and losses in use are very small. Efficiency of scrap recovery is high, witness the fact that even gold inlays from extracted teeth are almost always recycled. The mean lifetimes of most other metals in use appear to be shorter than that of steel. It is estimated that for every person in the United States we now have in use about 150 kilograms each of copper and lead, 100 kilograms each of zinc and aluminum, and 20 kilograms of tin.

Large as the quantities of metals in use are, and the volumes of metalliferous ores which must be dug up and processed to support a human being in our society, the quantities of nonmetals consumed each year loom even larger. Since World War II the annual per capita consumption of stone, sand, and gravel has risen by a factor of nearly 2.5 to about eight tons per person, and that of cement has risen by a factor of four, to one ton per person. In the same period, per capita consumption of phosphate rock rose by a factor of four and that of ordinary salt rose by a factor of two. In order to meet our needs for raw materials and the products derived from them, we transport nearly 15,000 ton-kilometers of freight each year per person.

In the early years of industrialization it seemed that the U.S. endowment of high-grade mineral resources was inexhaustible. But as time passed it became necessary to process ores of decreasing grade. At the turn of this century, for example, we were processing copper ore in the United States which averaged 4.0 percent copper. By 1925 the grade had dropped to 1.5 percent, and by 1950 to less than 1.0 percent. By 1970 the average grade was 0.6 percent.

In principle such a trend can continue virtually forever. But as the grade decreases, more technology must be utilized and greater quantities of rock must be handled. This means that greater quantities of energy must be consumed. Thus the United States could—in principle—be independent of copper imports for the indefinitely long future.

At the same time, when it turns out to be more expedient to import copper than to produce it at home, this is done. The United States has been a net importer of copper since 1939, and at the present time we satisfy about 6 percent of our needs with imports from Canada, Peru, and Chile.

The same principle of offsetting decreasing grades with increased technology or importation has applied to virtually all of our mineral resources. As the high-grade iron ore of the Lake Superior region dwindled, processes were developed for large-scale treatment of low-grade material to produce high-grade agglomerates. Also, in recent years about one-third of the iron ore consumed in the United States has been imported, largely from Canada, South America, and Africa. In addition, we import considerable quantities of steel from Japan and Europe.

The proportion of U.S. mineral consumption which is now satisfied by imports varies greatly. We have become almost completely dependent upon imports for our aluminum, cobalt, chromium, and manganese. We are largely dependent upon imports for our zinc, nickel, mercury, tin, and platinum. If absolutely necessary we could develop an independence from imports by encouraging substitutions and by processing domestic materials of lower grade. This would, however, take a great deal of time to bring about, require the investment of considerable capital, and necessitate appreciably higher prices. Indeed, the minerals trap in which the U.S. finds itself is analogous in many respects to the energy trap.

(8)

As the United States became increasingly industrialized, factories poured ever-larger quantities of waste into lakes and rivers, as well as smoke and noxious vapors into the atmosphere. As cities spread out in all directions, farms and woodlands were covered with asphalt and concrete. Emissions from automobile engines polluted the air over cities. The cities themselves generated increasing quantities of liquid and solid wastes which had to be disposed of in some manner. Changed farming practices led to increased soil erosion and to pollution from fertilizers and pesticides.

As recently as 50 years ago the United States was plagued by a variety of water-borne diseases such as typhoid, cholera, and dysentery. Better treatment of sewage and drinking water largely eliminated those diseases, but new sources of contamination created new hazards. The widespread use of fertilizers resulted in contamination of surface and ground waters with nitrates, to dangerous levels. Chemical contaminants, such as pesticides, detergents, trace metals, and hydrocarbons, became major sources of water pollution which have to be watched for on a continuing basis. Some of the chemical contaminants were suspected of being cancer-causing agents. Pollution of lakes, rivers, and coastal areas reduced levels of dissolved oxygen and in many cases killed fish and other living organisms.

Air pollution has been a problem of urban centers practically from the beginning of large-scale industrialization. Because coal was at first the major fuel, large quantities of soot were ejected into the air. Less conspicuous, but also present, were fumes of sulfur and nitrogen oxides, sulfuric acid, and hydrocarbon peroxides which irritated the respiratory system. In time the problem of soot was fairly well brought under control, particularly as the nation shifted more and more from coal to oil and natural gas. But as per capita energy consumption increased, ever-larger quantities of irritating chemicals found their way into the atmosphere. The internal combustion engine accelerated this process; today, the automobile and the electrical generating plant contribute the greater part of the pollution present in city air.

Cities over which the air moves a great deal are less subject to prolonged periods of exposure to noxious airborne gases. But some cities, Los Angeles for example, experience long periods during which the air is stagnant and the fumes increase in concentration. The contaminants cause watering of the eyes, coughing, impaired breathing, and even death. Usually, a large proportion of those who die have had preexisting heart or lung diseases.

From time to time the air becomes stagnant over cities which are usually relatively free of heavy pollution, sometimes with devastating effect. In 1952 a prolonged temperature inversion caused the air over London to stagnate for a period of five days. During this time some 4000 more persons died than would normally have been expected to die in a five-day period. New York City has likewise experienced periods of atmospheric stagnation which have caused a higher than normal number of deaths. Studies indicate that nonsmokers living in cities which experience frequent periods of heavy air pollution develop respiratory problems two or three times more frequently than those who live in cleaner communities. Residents of communities with persistently high pollution levels have higher death rates than residents of other communities. Children who are exposed to heavy pollution appear to suffer a greater risk of developing lung diseases such as emphysema or chronic bronchitis as adults. The death rate from lung cancer for urban residents is twice that for rural residents, even after making allowances for smoking.

Other air pollutants have caused severe health problems. Carbon monoxide from automobiles interferes with the ability of blood cells to carry oxygen, and can seriously interfere with coronary and central nervous system functions. Inhalation of airborne asbestos fibers has produced bronchogenic cancer and mesothelioma. The inhalation of beryllium often results in a progressive lung disease. Airborne mercury can affect the central nervous system. Because of lead emissions from automobiles, children who live in cities have appreciably higher concentrations of lead in their bodies than do rural children; they may also be particularly susceptible to lead damage of the central nervous system.

As Americans became wealthier, they not only bought more things, they also threw more away. Each year the average city dweller generates more than one ton of solid wastes which must be disposed of in some manner. The quantities on a per capita basis appear to be doubling about every 50 years. If we add wastes from agriculture, livestock, mines, and factories, the total comes to more than 10 tons per person per year.

A large part of the solid wastes generated by households consists of combustible materials, such as garbage and paper, which can be incinerated. But a substantial proportion consists of noncombustible objects, such as cans, bottles, and other objects. In addition, some 8.5 million automobiles are junked each year, together with large numbers of obsolete refrigerators, washing machines, and other appliances.

Over 50 percent of the junked automobiles are recycled, but those which are not create eyesores. Very little is being recovered at present from other urban wastes. Many cities simply bury their wastes in landfill—a process which is ugly and often unsanitary. Others incinerate the wastes and then bury the noncombustible residue.

Disposal of solid wastes is becoming an increasingly difficult problem, in part because available land for disposal is in short supply and in part because the present techniques themselves create new pollution problems. It is now becoming generally recognized that present methods of disposal are extremely wasteful and that, sooner or later, most of our discarded materials must be recycled in such a way as to provide energy and fertilizers along with other useful raw materials.

Industrial society now confronts Americans with a broad range of hazards which are new to the human experience. There is now little question but that pollution of the environment creates serious biological health hazards—not to mention the psychological ones which result from noise, overcrowding, and ugliness. We have conquered a variety of diseases which have plagued mankind for millennia, such as smallpox, cholera, and typhoid. At the same time, the conditions of life which we have created are apparently accelerating the spread of two diseases which are presently the leading causes of death in our society—cardiovascular disease and cancer.

It is now widely believed that a substantial proportion of cancer deaths are caused by a variety of man-made aspects of our environment, such as tobacco smoke, air and water pollution, exposure to certain chemicals and radiation, and the food we eat. Pesticides and food additives are everywhere. Some combinations of pollutants are now known to be more damaging than the sum of their separate effects. It is suggested that such environmental effects can help explain the fact that cancer deaths have been increasing more rapidly than can be accounted for simply on the basis of the aging of the population.

In addition, as people have become more affluent their diets have changed. We consume far more meat, dairy products, sugar, and processed foods than we did a few decades ago; and we eat fewer fresh fruits, vegetables, and wholegrain cereals. There is growing evidence that this changed diet—rich in fats, sugar, and cholesterol, and low in complex carbohydrates—may be a major contributing factor to the rapid increase in deaths from heart disease and related ailments.

(9)

U.S. involvement in World War I was a symptom of the fact that the nation had become a world power. Even so, U.S. expenditures for World War I were nominal by today's standards. The initial cost of the war to the U.S., apart from the lives lost, was about $26 billion—barely enough to keep today's Department of Defense operating for three months. The total cost of U.S. involvement, counting interest on loans and veterans' benefits, has been about $50 billion, which would support today's defense establishment for six months.

In the interval between World Wars I and II our military expenditures were little more than token, but the Second World War propelled us to a level of military expenditure unprecedented in our history. Our total expenditures for that war to date have been 10 times those for World War I, an amount that would keep our present defense establishment operating for five years.

Following World War II, with Japan and Germany defeated and the rest of Europe prostrate, the United States diverted much money and effort to the task of reconstruction. Those collaborative efforts were successful. At the same time the relationships between the U.S. and the U.S.S.R. deteriorated to the point where the leaders of both nations believed that war between them was a very real possibility. Thus, each nation attempted to place itself in a position to win the war should it come about. Actions led to reactions, which in turn led to new actions. The result was the deadly arms race which for a third of a century has spiraled upward in spite of negotiations aimed at achieving some degree of arms limitation or disarmament.

During and since World War II there has been a tremendous mobilization of science and technology for military purposes. We have seen the development of atomic bombs, radar, guided missiles, hydrogen bombs, missile-launching submarines, and a variety of intercontinental missiles capable of accurately delivering explosives anyplace in the world, each equivalent to several million tons of TNT. In the next few years, the quantities of nuclear explosives which can be delivered might well reach the equivalent of 300,000 million tons of TNT, well over 600 tons for each person in the two countries, and corresponding to 75 tons of TNT for every human being in the world. We have reached the time when both the Soviet Union and the United States have relatively invulnerable weapons systems capable of destroying each other as functioning nations.

Weapons systems are not static; they are constantly changing as a result of military research and development. About 125,000 U.S. scientists and engineers work on military problems, corresponding to about 25 percent of our highly skilled scientific manpower. In the U.S.S.R. it is likely that twice this number of skilled professionals is involved in military research and development. Thus, altogether some 375,000 scientists and engineers are dedicating their research skills to military problems, representing perhaps 40 percent of the world's total pool of highly qualified research people.

As the arms race gathered momentum, many Americans came to believe that communism in general, not just the particular variety espoused by the Soviet Union, was the real threat, and this conviction led to our attempts to become the policeman of the world. We became involved in war in Korea and invested heavily in the buildup of military power in Taiwan. At our initiative, the North Atlantic Treaty Organization (NATO) and the Southeast Asia Treaty Organization (SEATO) were created. In the early 1960s we became heavily involved in military activities in Indochina. Such involvements, added to the strategic arms race, resulted in an escalation of military expenditures in the early 1950s amounting to well over 50 percent of total federal expenditures for all functions. It was not until 1971 that defense expenditures fell below 40 percent of all federal outlays.

Since World War II the United States has kept large numbers of military personnel overseas, ranging from 300,000 in 1950 to more than a million at the height of the war in Indochina. In 1975 some 300,000 military personnel were still stationed in Europe and about 120,000 in Asia. Total outlays for national defense, excluding veterans' benefits, ranged from $12 billion in 1950 to $93 billion in 1976. In constant (1976) dollars, outlays peaked in 1968 at $144 billion, then gradually fell to $93 billion in 1976—which still represented 25 percent of all federal spending and about 6 percent of the GNP.

Nuclear war between the Soviet Union and the United States has thus far been avoided for one reason—the threat of retaliation. Our nuclear forces have as their primary goal the avoidance of nuclear war by making the consequences of such a war unacceptable to either party. Thus far this system has worked sufficiently well for us to assume that neither nation is likely to launch a nuclear attack intentionally. However, this approach assumes that the threat of a war started by accident or irrational decisions is negligible. We are beginning to suspect that this assumption may not be correct.

The arms race represents a substantial and continuing drain upon our resources. It diverts money and thought and effort from the solution of other serious problems, both domestic and international. It goes without saying that the expenditure of equivalent effort on such domestic problems as urban decay, crime, environment, health, or energy would have dramatic effect. Internationally, such an effort would greatly accelerate the process of economic and social development, and contribute substantially to a lessening of hunger and poverty in the world. And as we shall see, our failure to direct adequate attention to such problems is likely to increase the probability of nuclear war in the long run.

At the same time, the vicious circle in which the U.S. and the U.S.S.R. now find themselves is extremely difficult to break. It is next to impossible to place a freeze on weapons development, for scientists who deal with military matters are always conceiving of improvements to existing offensive and defensive systems. When one nation modifies a system, however slightly, this calls for a neutralizing modification on the part of the other nation. Only a comprehensive arms-control agreement could lead to a freezing of armaments levels; such an agreement seems to lie far in the future.

In addition to the difficulty of comprehensive agreements about arms control, and eventual disarmament on an international level there are large domestic groups which profit greatly from the arms race—indeed, with many of them it has become a way of life. From a purely personal—as distinct from an ideological—point of view, there are probably few officers in the Pentagon who would warmly welcome a comprehensive disarmament agreement. Equally important, weapons systems involve tremendous sums of money and large corporations. In 1975 the ten top industrial defense contractors accounted for $13 billion of defense expenditures. Altogether more than 1000 concerns, including more than 150 of the "Fortune 500" listing of the biggest industrial companies, are involved in producing or exporting weapons. In 1976, expenditures for military procurement, weapons exports, and research and development altogether amounted to about $30 billion.

The corporations involved with the arms business are sufficiently intent upon maintaining their business to have developed a substantial arms lobby which works effectively with Congress. In many cases an individual member of Congress is persuaded to vote for or against a particular measure by the numbers of defense-related jobs which are at stake in his district.

In 1960 President Eisenhower warned the American people about the dangers of the "military-industrial complex" which had emerged since World War II. The warning was well placed, but largely went unheeded. The complex today is larger and more powerful than it has ever been.

(10)

One of the more important characteristics of the growth of the American economy has been the spectacular growth of the productivity (production per man-hour) of workers in agriculture and industry. This development has resulted from the use of machines (powered by fossil fuels) combined with improved organization and management practices. Between 1900 and 1967 the production per man-hour worked increased nearly 12-fold, corresponding to an increase of about 3.7 percent annually. In the five-year period 1967–1972 the annual rate of growth of productivity dropped to 2.4 percent, and in the period 1972–1975 it was negligible. Indeed, in many areas of production, notably mining, the growth became negative. Nevertheless, in 1976 production per man-hour worked was some 13 times higher than it had been in 1900.

High productivity in the agricultural and manufacturing sectors of the economy could well have meant high levels of unemployment had a new phenomenon not entered the picture. People turned increasingly to "service" jobs, such as health care, education, government services, research and development, and entertainment. In the process the United States created the world's first service economy. At the end of World War II 55 percent of all workers were in service occupations while 45 percent were still in goods-producing industries. By 1974 more than two-thirds of all job holders were in the service sector. It may well be that by the year 2000 the proportion of workers in the services will approach 90 percent, with 10 percent of the workers producing the food and goods required to satisfy everyone's needs.

A key element in the service economy has been education. The science-based industries now represent the frontiers of economic growth, and persons who are involved with computers, communications systems, information retrieval, electronics, teaching, or health care require numerous skills. At the turn of the century only 2.6 percent of adults in the U.S. 25 years and older had graduated from college and only 13 percent had completed high school. In 1975 about 14 percent of that group had graduated from college and 63 percent had graduated from high school. During the period 1950–1974, in which total employment increased by somewhat less than 50 percent, professional and technical employment increased 2.5-fold.

Expansion of services greatly facilitated the growth of female employment. Again, during the period 1950–1974, when male employment increased by about 25 percent, female employment came close to doubling. This rapid trend has clearly led to greater independence for women.

A key element in the expansion of employment in the services has been the rapid growth in the numbers of federal, state, and local government employees. Persons who provide federal, state, county, and city services now represent nearly 16 percent of all employment, and this proportion is still growing rapidly, notably at the state and local levels. In part this is due to the heavy emphasis placed by the American people upon more access to higher education, improved medical care, and a strong defense establishment. It is also due to the fact that the entire interlocking system of mines, factories, farms, transportation and communications systems, cities, and power networks has become extremely complex and we are finding it increasingly difficult to manage.

About 6 percent of the labor force is employed by nonprofit institutions, such as private schools and colleges, foundations, labor unions, and churches. An additional 8 percent of the labor force is employed by companies such as Lockheed or General Electric, to work on projects where the entire output, whether it be missiles or research, is paid for by the government. Although such individuals are technically employed in the private sector of the economy, in a very real sense they are government employees.

When such adjustments are made, it turns out that one out of every three jobs in our present economy really is in the public, not-for-profit sector, and that about one American worker in four depends directly or indirectly upon the activities of government.

Our larger cities are becoming service economies even more rapidly than is the nation as a whole. Today, more than 80 percent of the total employment of New York City is in the service sector. As more manufacturing firms leave the city the proportion will increase still further.

In 1974, for reasons which are not understood, the United States, as well as other industrial countries, experienced an economic recession which was destined to last for several years. The recession was aggravated by the fourfold increase in the price of crude oil and by the Arab oil embargo. These difficulties led to substantial unemployment, which reached a peak of close to 9 percent of the labor force in May 1975, then fell to an average of 7.7 percent in 1976. Particularly hard hit were the poor, the young, and the less-educated. Unemployment among black teenagers ranged from 35 to 45 percent. At all ages below 65, black male unemployment was twice that of white males.

We have seen that our larger cities have substantial concentrations of minorities and the increased unemployment served to aggravate an already difficult situation. Tax revenues decreased still further in real terms, while welfare payments increased, as did crime rates.

It has been recognized for some time that the per capita cost of maintaining a city depends markedly upon the size. In 1974 cities with populations of 50,000–100,000 persons cost residents on the average $256. Cities of a million persons or more cost $737 per person. Costs per capita were higher in the larger cities in virtually all categories, but notably in education, welfare, health, and police protection. This phenomenon is explained by the fact that with increasing size there is an increase in wage rate for the same work. This in turn is explained as compensation to city residents for increased costs with size, starting with higher rents and transportation costs.

Other urban problems likewise increase with the size of the city. Concentrations of pollutants in the air over a city of a million inhabitants is approximately double that over a city of 100,000 persons. The cost of solid waste disposal per ton and the probability of a major water pollution problem are both twice as high in the large city as in the small one. Crime rates also increase rapidly with size, but this appears to be caused not so much by increasing size itself as by factors such as ethnicity, unemployment, and crowded housing. When these other factors are taken into account, the effects of size itself upon crime rates is still apparent but considerably lessened.

Thus the larger cities find themselves particularly vulnerable to the threats of both unemployment and inflation. The former is directly related to city income, crime, welfare, the outward flight of business, and the shrinking tax base. Inflation drives up costs of public services while preventing the collection of additional local taxes and the sale of municipal bonds. Increasingly, municipal workers are organized into unions with the result that wage hikes are difficult to resist and strikes occur more frequently, threatening the operation of vital services.

When we consider these problems collectively it is no wonder that the financial problems of many of our older and larger cities have become so difficult. Indeed, in some cases they verge on the unmanageable.

(11)

Thus the United States became the richest of the rich nations. When we examine what was accomplished in the course of two centuries there is much to be viewed with pride: the condition of our average citizens and their comfortable homes; their high levels of education; their ease of travel; their ready access to news, to entertainment of all sorts, to books, art, and music. We are rightfully proud of our democratic institutions and political freedoms, our scholarly and artistic achievements. We are proud of a broad spectrum of initiatives which we have taken both individually and collectively.

But as we look down the road ahead, we see signs of impending trouble. A grave uneasiness is spreading over the land, shared in different ways by the poverty-stricken of the slums of the central city and wealthy suburbanites with their swimming pools heated with once-abundant natural gas. Looking inward, many people are asking questions about both our poverty and our affluence, about unemployment and inflation, about crime, about strikes of public workers such as teachers, policemen, firemen, and bus drivers. They decry the ugliness of our cities, the noxious fumes in our air, and our wanton destruction of natural beauty. Looking outward they consider the nuclear umbrellas which can destroy us, the oil embargos, terrorism, and illegal immigration.

Many people wonder whether the violence that surged through our cities during the 1960s could return again. They realize that Vietnam and Watergate are well behind us, but they also recognize that the conditions in the central cities, particularly as they relate to minorities, are for the most part not improved. They also recognize the great personal and public hazards of excessive unemployment and inflation.

Perhaps the most important question for all Americans to ask is—how affluent are we likely to become? Clearly the "average" level of affluence will rise as poverty is eliminated and income distribution becomes more equitable. But beyond that, how affluent will the typical middle-class American family become? What will be the material prerequisites for happiness?

Quite apart from the American desire for such luxuries as rich food, swimming pools, and travel, affluence should rise considerably in the years ahead because of our great need to invest capital in city renewal, environmental clean-up, transportation, health care, education, agriculture, and industrial modernization. Such investments will place considerable demands upon our resources, for the capital needs are enormous.

We must ask: Where will we get the necessary energy and raw materials to support further growth of affluence? Will we continue to import increasing proportions of our requirements? If so, how will we pay for them? How will we protect ourselves from embargos and unreasonably rapid price increases?

If, on the other hand, we attempt to achieve a greater degree of self-sufficiency, what will this mean for the economy in terms of prices, employment, and exports? How rapidly will we move to coal and nuclear power? What will we do about the serious environmental problems associated with these energy sources? To what extent is solar energy likely to be utilized?

Another approach to self-sufficiency is conservation. Can we make do with lower levels of per capita consumption of minerals and fuels? Will we move toward smaller automobiles and perhaps a lessened need to use them? To what extent are we likely to reorganize society so that people can move between home and work on foot or bicycle? Can we operate our energy system more efficiently so that we waste less fuel? Will we recycle our wastes effectively?

We must keep in mind that numerous forces over which we have little control will drive per capita energy expenditures upward. More energy is needed to extract metal from a low-grade ore than from a high-grade one. Recycling wastes requires substantial expenditures of energy. Prevention of air pollution and pollution of streams and oceans can be accomplished only at the expense of using more energy.

Last, it must be reemphasized that American society is an enormously complex system. It is probably vulnerable to a variety of disruptive shocks ranging from war to embargos, terrorism, environmental crises, inflation, unemployment, civil disorders, and strikes. Until we really understand the system, in all of its complexity, we must always wonder whether the system is manageable. We clearly have not yet learned how to manage the economic system effectively. In spite of the fact that the economic system is man-made, it is constantly surprising us. In a sense the physical-biological system, to which the economic system is directly related and which involves the complex interrelationships between resources, environment, and our industrial network, is even more complex and may well confront us with some extremely serious shocks.

The ancient Romans were excellent managers, but their complex system got out of hand, perhaps in part because they didn't understand it. Is it likely that ours will get out of hand for the same reason?

CHAPTER III

The Newly Rich

(1)

As we have seen, the Industrial Revolution started in Britain. In time it traveled eastward to accelerate the economic expansion of Europe, which by 1815 had emerged from a generation of revolution and warfare. Although the new technology spread and factories using steam power sprang up in Western Europe, it was not until after 1870 that Great Britain faced any real industrial competition from abroad. For more than a half-century after the fall of Napoleon, Britain was the undisputed industrial leader of the world. During that period the British had a virtual monopoly in textiles, machine tools, and steam engines. British capital was exported to all parts of the world and London became the world's financial center.

For many decades Britain attempted to maintain a monopoly on its newly developed industrial skills by prohibiting the emigration of craftsmen and the export of machinery. Nevertheless, many skilled workers and manufacturers inevitably left Britain, taking their knowledge with them. In 1750 a British manufacturer settled in France, where he helped modernize spinning techniques in the textile industry. In 1789 a textile worker emigrated to America and built a spinning mill in Rhode Island. In 1799 a British carpenter moved to Belgium and began to manufacture textile machinery.

Belgium became the first nation on the European continent to become industrialized to a significant extent. Between 1830 and 1870 the nation rapidly developed its heavy industry, with considerable financial support from the government. Textile manufacture, which had been important in the Belgian economy for many years, was industrialized. But a diversity of political and social factors prevented industrialization from spreading rapidly over the continent.

The French Revolution and the Napoleonic Wars aborted French industrial progress. Germany had the natural resources needed for industrial development, but until 1871 it was a collection of separate states which often failed to cooperate with one another in economic matters. In 1848 revolutionary movements broke out spontaneously in virtually every country, and governments collapsed all over Europe. Fierce national jealousies came to the surface, as did class hatreds, and soon thereafter came yet another series of wars.

Nevertheless, between 1830 and 1850 German coal production doubled and about 1850 the mining of iron ore began to increase rapidly. Following political unification, Germany's steel production expanded greatly, and by 1900 it exceeded that of Great Britain and ranked second only to that of the United States.

France moved much more slowly. As late as 1850, more than half of France's iron production still came from charcoal furnaces. During most of the nineteenth century French industry was crippled by a poor transportation system. Because of these and other factors, France remained largely a country of farms and small businesses.

As factories appeared in Europe, towns were quickly transformed into industrial cities, most of them dirty and ugly. People moved from the farms to the cities to take jobs in the factories. In part, this movement originated in rapid population growth, which forced people off the land. It also came from the numerous attractions of the city and its potential for bestowing great wealth.

A relatively wealthy middle class of businessmen and industrialists also grew rapidly. At the same time, a large class of industrial workers emerged in the cities most of whom were poorly paid; they worked and lived under the poorest of conditions. It was in this atmosphere that Karl Marx developed his theories of communism in the mid-1800s.

The growth of large industry and a class system led to numerous social changes. Workers in many countries fought for and won the right to form labor unions and several nations began to pass laws regulating working conditions. Social legislation appeared that provided accident, sickness, and unemployment insurance for industrial workers.

During the early phases of industrialization the population of Europe grew very fast, largely because of greatly decreased death rates. The pressures which were generated resulted in the great migration from the farm to the city. Related to those pressures were those which gave rise to the mass migration from Europe to the New World, Asian Russia, Australia, and New Zealand. Approximately 60 million people left Europe during the century 1840–1940, out of which some 34 million went to the United States. The majority of these emigrants came from Great Britain and Ireland, Italy, and Russia.

This unprecedented mass movement of people had a number of causes. Perhaps most important was the fact that the new countries welcomed immigration, for many workers were needed. Second, movement had become easier. Legal barriers had been almost completely eliminated and the steamship had greatly decreased the cost of crossing the sea. Further, relatively higher wages made it possible for more people to afford the journey.

By 1880 European birth rates had begun to drop. As early as 1830 the birth rates had begun to fall noticeably in France, which happened to be the first of the European nations to undergo this demographic transition. In time, birth rates fell in other nations as well. Although the reasons for the lessened birth rates are not understood in detail, it was clearly connected with the improved general welfare. It was among those groups of people who experienced relatively high living standards that the birth rate fell most rapidly. The phenomenon was clearly related to such factors as urbanization, nutrition, infant mortality, life expectancy, and literacy.

As the Industrial Revolution continued, colonial expansion by the European powers accelerated. Africa and Asia had large quantities of much-needed raw materials and also provided vast markets where the industrial nations could sell their manufactured goods. Because of this, most of Africa and about a third of Asia eventually came under European domination. Colonialism was fortified by nationalism, which had arisen largely in reaction to the international Napoleonic system. Nationalism became a state of mind, which could be easily aroused as a unifying force and as a weapon of war. To some groups—for example, the Germans, who had long been frustrated by their internal divisions—nationalism eventually became an obsession.

From about 1870 on, new inventions and new industries appeared in Europe with increasing frequency. During this new phase of the Industrial Revolution, industry spread geographically from Britain, Belgium, and France outward to Italy, Germany, and Russia. By 1870 Germany was producing 60 percent as much steel as Britain. By 1890 Germany had become the largest producer of steel in Europe. By the outbreak of World War I the Germans were producing twice as much steel as the British. At the same time, American steel output was greater than that of Germany, Britain, and France combined.

During the nearly half-century of peace which preceded World War I, Europeans really believed themselves headed for a new level of life, in which the benefits of modern science and technology would lead to unending progress. At the same time, after about 1870 Europe lived in fear. Traditionally, the great European problems had been settled by force. By the turn of the twentieth century, standing armies were larger than they had ever been in peacetime. In addition, compulsory military service provided millions of trained reserves among the civilian population.

In 1914 Europe stumbled into a disaster from which it has still not rebounded and from which it may never totally recover. Quite apart from the three decades of human agony which World War I precipitated, technological progress for human betterment was virtually brought to a halt.

Although historians appear to agree generally about the causes of World War I, they differ in their assessments of the relative importance of those causes. Competition for colonial and economic power among European nations certainly played a role. During the 15 years which preceded the war, Anglo-German industrial competition reached considerable proportions. Added to this were two explosive pressures: the alliance systems among the great powers gave little flexibility once force was used; and tens of millions of minorities in Central and Eastern Europe were pushing their own national aspirations. Added to this were strong emotional feelings stemming from nationalism. Last, the very high level of military preparedness was certainly a contributing factor.

In the years 1914–1918 between 10 and 13 million men were killed in military action. Germany, Russia, France, and Britain collectively lost more than 6 million. About 20 million men were wounded. Countless millions of persons suffered from famine and disease associated with the hostilities.

The cessation of hostilities in late 1918 and the peace that followed left Europe prostrate. The Bolshevik regime in Russia was engaged in a life-and-death struggle for its very existence. The Peace of Paris imposed reparations upon Germany which were both unjust and impossible to collect. Indeed, the various treaties which were a part of the Peace of Paris concentrated so heavily upon purely nationalistic questions that the economic aspects of the settlement went largely neglected. Reconstruction progressed slowly, but the experiences of the war greatly accelerated social and technological change.

As a result of the war, technological innovation had heavy emphasis. Hostilities that had started with the foot soldier and the horse, ended with the truck, the tank, and the airplane. Shortages of raw materials in Germany led to the development of nitrogen fixation for the large-scale production of fertilizers, synthetic gasoline from coal, plastics, and synthetic rubber. These and other developments were destined to revolutionize the chemical industry. But the initial impacts of new industrial technologies were felt most strongly outside Europe, notably in the United States, which had emerged from the war with its economy relatively intact.

By 1922 European recovery had begun, but it was slow and uneven. In the meantime, the United States had developed a capacity for mass production and innovation that Europe could not match. Within the European framework, the countries moved forward, but in the world frame of reference they fell behind. For example, by 1928 Germany once again was the industrial giant of Europe and its production capacity was 40 percent higher than at the outbreak of hostilities. But Germany's share of world production had been cut by more than a third.

A decade of peace was followed by the Great Depression, which hit suddenly and which for the most part had been unanticipated. The crisis started in the United States, but because of the great economic dependence of Europe on America, it quickly spread to Germany and Austria. The Depression reached Great Britain in 1931 and France in 1932. Unemployment in Germany approached 40 percent of the labor force and in England 25 percent. Social unrest reached grave proportions in virtually all industrial countries. Governments were forced to intervene in their economies on a massive scale.

In a sense World War II can be looked upon as the second act in the drama which had been introduced by World War I. Following the intermission (1919–1939), hostilities were resumed with virtually the same cast playing the major roles. The primary differences between the two wars were that the second involved far higher levels of sophisticated technology and carried direct hostilities beyond the military to the civilian population on an unprecedented scale.

At the end of the war, total Soviet civilian and military deaths were estimated at 20 million. In Western Europe, deaths in the armed services were actually less than in World War I, but civilian deaths compensated for this. In Germany, nearly all the great cities were in ruins, and Hamburg and Dresden had been virtually destroyed. In Britain, most ports and industrial cities were severely damaged. In France, half a million buildings had been destroyed. A large proportion of the transport facilities of the continent had been rendered inoperable, so that goods, even if produced, could not be moved. More people died of starvation or cold in 1945 and 1946 than at any time in generations.

In the disorder and confusion which still existed in Europe in 1948, the United States set up the European Recovery Program, known as the Marshall Plan, to help the nations of Western Europe rebuild their economies. Under this plan, the United States agreed to send aid to Europe if the countries would collectively decide what they needed. Seventeen nations banded together to form the Organization for European Economic Cooperation (OEEC). In the following three years, the United States sent about $13 billion in food, machinery, and other products to Europe.

The impact of these developments exceeded by far even the most optimistic hopes of the creators of the Marshall Plan. Fortunately, a large pool of skilled laborers and managers was still available. Local ingenuity coupled with strong motivations greatly amplified the effects of the initial capital transfers. Industries and cities were rebuilt. European products began to compete once again on the world market. Agricultural productivity increased. Standards of living rose again.

Equally important, the improved European economy led to increased demands for U.S. manufactured goods and agricultural products, and this in turn accelerated the growth of the American economy. During the following quarter-century the per capita GNPs of all but the southern European nations were approaching, and in some cases exceeding, that of the United States. It was indeed a development unparalleled in history.

But in the process, the newly rich nations became dependent upon imports for food and raw materials—particularly energy. As their wealth grew, they imported increasing quantities of feed grains, particularly from the United States. As their industries grew, they imported increasing quantities of crude oil. At the same time, countries in addition to the United States were beginning to compete seriously with Europe in the export of manufactured goods.

World War II brought the downfall of Europe as the center of world power. But it also triggered an unprecedented growth of affluence as well as unprecedented cooperation across national boundaries. Indeed, one cannot help but wonder what Europe would be like today if so much human energy and so many resources had not been dissipated over two centuries by nationalistic drives and recurrent wars.

At the same time one cannot help but be concerned about Europe's future. In 1974 the combination of the recession, the increase in the price of crude oil, and the Arab oil embargo gave cause for alarm. Many wondered for how long the high level of affluence which had been achieved could be maintained. The concerns expressed were accentuated by the fact that although nationalistic feelings had been softened, in large measure they still determined the decisions of governments.

(2)

Throughout the nineteenth century and until the mid-1920s Russia remained a backward agrarian country. Following the Europeanization of Russia by Tsar Peter the Great prior to the onset of the Industrial Revolution, a tradition of science slowly emerged, but there was no significant penetration of industry from the West until about 1880. Then, European capital financed railways, factories, and mining operations to the point that by 1914 Europeans had some $4 billion invested in Russia—about the same as in the United States. Nevertheless, Russia remained predominantly agricultural with some 80 percent of the population remaining peasants.

The Russian Revolution of 1917 was one of the two major forces which shaped the twentieth century—the other being World War I. The combination of the war and the revolution destroyed the fragile industrial fabric and led to the economic collapse of the nation. As a result, 15 years passed before the production of steel, coal, and oil again reached their pre–World War I levels.

Lenin laid many of the foundations for the economy which eventually emerged under Stalin. But it was Stalin who was really responsible for the first major phase of Soviet industrialization. He focused virtually all of Russia's energy on the goal of achieving the most rapid possible industrialization, no matter what the sacrifice. He was able to extract the required massive effort only by transforming the Soviet Union into a totalitarian state which depended upon slave labor camps, police terror, and thought control.

Stalin turned to Western Europe and the United States for the advanced technology he needed. He imported huge quantities of machinery as well as thousands of Western engineers, scientists, and technicians to help design, build, and operate new plants. Large numbers of Soviet citizens were sent to the West to work in industries and learn new technologies.

The Soviet Union had established no credit, and in any event aimed at industrializing without resorting to foreign loans. Being a predominantly agricultural country, it could do this only by drawing heavily upon agriculture. A major part of the first Five-Year Plan, inaugurated in 1928, provided for substantial increases in agricultural production per laborer and per hectare by the creation of large collective farms. In this way, sufficient extra food could be grown either to feed the cities that did not produce their own food or for export to pay for the imports from the West.

The Russian farmers bitterly resisted collectivization. There were class wars in the villages which led to the deaths of the most capable farmers. Farmers slaughtered their horses, cattle, pigs, and poultry rather than give them up. Two summers of bad weather coupled with the agricultural disorders led to a deadly famine. These tremendous upheavals were coupled with the ascendancy of Lysenko's pseudoscientific political dogma and the concomitant devastation of Soviet agricultural research. Even now, nearly a half-century later, Soviet agriculture has not completely recovered from the effects of these policies.

In spite of the hardships suffered by both Soviet industrial workers and peasants, heavy industry grew at an unprecedented rate. Never before in the history of industrialization had a primitive agricultural society been transformed into an industrial one so rapidly. By the outbreak of World War II, scarcely a decade beyond the inauguration of the first Five-Year Plan, steel production had been increased 20-fold, coal production 13-fold, and oil production five-fold. Production of electricity had increased 30-fold.

The great whip which Stalin used to good advantage was the fear of defeat in another war. He was obsessed with the necessity of preparing the nation for what he regarded as the inevitability of war. Thus the production of arms and other supplies needed to wage war became an important part of Soviet industrialization.

The war that Stalin feared indeed came to pass in 1941, when Hitler sent his armies into Russia. The response was total mobilization of people, agriculture, and industry for the war effort. By the time hostilities ceased in 1945 something like 10 million Soviet soldiers had been killed or wounded in battle. Millions of noncombatant citizens had died prematurely of cold, hunger, and sickness. Much of what had been built up at such terrible cost was in ruins.

After the war Stalin pushed his exhausted nation into a frenzy of reconstruction and further economic expansion, the immediate goal being to triple industrial production within 15 years. The acquisition of massive military power, including nuclear weaponry, became a major element of the new plan. It was in those early years following World War II that the cold war was born and quickly dominated the relationships between the U.S. and the U.S.S.R.

Following Stalin's death in 1953, his successors made substantial efforts to carry out his goals, but with modified approaches. More attention was given to the desires of the average citizen with respect to housing, diet, and consumer goods generally. The base of decision making was broadened. But the highest priority was still given to military preparedness and the growth of heavy industry. By 1974 the Soviet Union had become the largest producer of steel and crude oil in the world. Its production of coal was rapidly approaching that of the United States.

It should come as no surprise that any country which had developed so rapidly prior to World War II, which suffered such great losses during the war, and which then grew with such extraordinary rapidity in the postwar years, should be spotty in its development. This has been noted particularly by international visitors who have observed that the tourist industry, the manufacture of toilets that flush and furniture that is attractive have obviously been given low priority in the Soviet system. We also see this in agriculture. But when we examine what has actually been accomplished in such a short time span, it borders upon the incredible. We are tempted to applaud the achievement loudly. Yet, when we examine the terrible costs in terms of human anguish, regimentation, and the downgrading of the free human spirit, we cannot help but have second thoughts.

Nevertheless, we must recognize the fact that the Soviet Union is now the most powerful nation on earth. It is not that her nuclear arsenal is greater than that of the United States, nor that her industrial production is so much higher, nor that her technology is more sophisticated. Indeed, when we examine the Soviet system in depth we see tremendous weaknesses, ranging from poor management capabilities to the prevalence of ignorance concerning the world, to racial antagonisms, to the repression of social and ethnic groups.

The main reason for Soviet power is that she has by now developed her technology to the point where it is bound to continue to develop further so that she can make full use of her natural resources, which are vast. For the foreseeable future the Soviet Union will be self-sufficient in minerals, food, wood, and, above all, energy. Other industrial nations, including the United States, are not likely to be in that position for a very long time, if ever.

(3)

From the early part of the seventeenth century Japan lived in self-imposed isolation from the rest of the world: only one Dutch ship was allowed to come to Nagasaki each year, and no Japanese was allowed to leave the country. During this time, after a period of prolonged civil wars, Japan was united under the Tokugawa family of shoguns, who ruled absolutely. The emperor was a figurehead.

The isolation was broken in 1853–1854 when Commodore Perry visited Japan and with a show of force opened up two ports for trade with the United States. In 1867 the emperor Mitsuhito regained his power from the shogun and under the name Meiji, which means "Enlightened Rule," launched Japan on a vigorous program of modernization. By this time, the United States was only two years out of the crippling tragedy of the Civil War. Germany was by then industrializing rapidly. But Britain was still the undisputed industrial power of the world.

Although Japan was basically an agrarian feudal society, many important industrial and commercial developments had taken place. Numerous technologies, such as metalworking, were highly developed. Above all, the Japanese had long been endowed with the willingness to assimilate new ideas and practices rapidly.

The Meiji government abolished the feudal system, modernized the government, hired European and American experts in many fields to teach Western knowledge, and sent large delegations of Japanese overseas. The government drew heavily upon Japan's social organization, deeply rooted in the family system where individuals learned discipline and the ability to work effectively within groups or organizations on collaborative efforts. In a breathtakingly short period of time Japan was in the midst of vast projects aimed at the modernization of agriculture, the development of industry, and the creation of a modern military establishment. Neither in Europe nor America had development taken place so rapidly.

Japan's success in modernization seems all the more remarkable when we consider the paucity of available natural resources. No other nation of substantial size has undergone the industrialization process starting off with so little. Only 15 percent of Japan's land can be farmed. Mineral resources are scarce. Aside from numerous swift streams which can generate electrical power, coal is the only indigenous energy resource, and even this is both difficult to mine and of poor quality. Japan had no colonies. The main natural resource consisted of hard-working, intelligent people, bound together by a social fabric which was conducive to innovation, collaboration, and rapid change.

The government encouraged the introduction of new crops and scientific methods of agriculture that would increase crop yields. Agricultural schools were established and a vast extension system was created to provide farmers with guidance and information. In spite of the mountainous terrain, the land under cultivation was extended. In the 30-year period from 1880 to 1910, cereal production increased 70 percent. Agriculture succeeded in supplying the increased demands for rice brought about by increasing population and larger per capita consumption.

The first modern textile mill in Japan was established in 1867. By 1913 the textile industries constituted by far the most important section of Japan's industrial activity, and represented an important part of her exports. Although for some time Japan was self-sufficient in raw cotton, the point was quickly reached where it was less expensive to import cotton from India, thus releasing land for other agricultural purposes.

At first the development of heavy industry in Japan was largely dependent upon the use of imported iron and steel. Considerable efforts were made to develop an iron and steel industry, but these were handicapped for some time by the fact that Japan is deficient both in iron ore and in good coking coal. In time, however, with considerable help from the government, the industry was firmly established and this led to an expansion of heavy engineering industries ranging from shipbuilding to the construction of railroad cars and power plants.

Throughout the early years of development the leaders of the Japanese government recognized that Japan was weak militarily and might easily fall prey to one or more of the industrialized colonial powers. Military defense along Western lines became the highest priority task, and expenditures on armaments soon became substantial.

During the 1880s Japan and China became rivals in Korea, leading to the Sino-Japanese War of 1894–1895, which Japan won. China gave Taiwan to Japan and also gave up claims to Korea. Rivalry subsequently broke out between Japan and Russia over Korea and Manchuria. Japan declared war on Russia in early 1904 and during the following 18 months handed the Russian land and naval forces a series of stunning defeats. Under the Treaty of Portsmouth, Russia recognized Japanese supremacy in Korea and also gave Japan the Liaotung Peninsula, the southernmost tip of Manchuria. Thus, in a short span of time, Japan had become not only a colonial power but a world power as well.

Japan entered World War I on the side of the Allies but did not fight in Europe. In 1920 Japan became one of the original members of the League of Nations and supported many measures for world peace, including reduction in the size of her naval force. But the forces of militarism were very strong and they were greatly aided by the collapse of the American economy in 1929. In a period of one year, raw silk prices dropped by a half and the export trade as a whole fell by a third. After a decade of quiescence the military quickly reasserted its authority. In 1931–1932 the Japanese overran Manchuria.

During the early years of the World Depression, the character of Japanese industry changed considerably. Heavy industries such as metals, equipment, and chemicals grew swiftly while textiles declined in relative importance. The output of pig iron increased rapidly, as did steel production. The range of finished steel products was greatly extended.

In 1937 Japan went to war with China and also signed treaties with Germany and Italy. By 1941 Japan had gone on a full wartime basis. She entered World War II when she attacked Pearl Harbor on December 7, 1941, and she ended the war when Hiroshima and Nagasaki were almost totally destroyed by atomic bombs in August 1945.

At the end of the war the Japanese economy was in ruins. She had lost her colonies and her substantial foreign investments in Manchuria and China, as well as her commercial dominance in Asia. Most of the Japanese cities had been devastated by air raids. The physical destruction of housing and industrial plants was enormous. There were severe shortages of food and raw materials. The morale of the people was extremely low.

Starting from these depths, a second Japanese development miracle took place which in its way was as surprising as what took place in Europe. By 1970 Japan had become the third greatest industrial power of the world. Her economy grew faster than that of any other large country, and not only did she recover—her real national income was by now several times larger than it had been before the war.

Many reasons for this growth have been cited. The Occupation Authority achieved fundamental institutional reforms. A program of monetary stabilization initiated in 1949 provided for a balanced budget and manufacturing production rose quickly. With the outbreak of the Korean War in 1950 the Japanese received large orders for supplies for the United Nations troops, and this started a general economic boom. In 1951, industrial production exceeded the prewar level for the first time. After the war in Korea, the U.S. continued to make substantial procurement payments in connection with the maintenance of American military establishments in Japan, so Japan's industrial output continued to expand.

After 1955 it was as though a chain reaction had been ignited. The transistor revolutionized the electronics industry. Television sets became a major item for export. The Japanese started their passionate love affair with the automobile. Soon the Japanese people themselves had become the most inexhaustible and enthusiastic consumers the world had ever seen. By 1974 per capita consumption of steel and energy was equal to that in Western Europe. In 25 years, starting from the dismal depths of wartime destruction, the Japanese had achieved the highest standard of living that they had ever known.

At the same time the Japanese were encountering new problems. The nation had become dependent upon imports for virtually all of its raw materials and a large part of its food. The U.S. embargo on soybeans in 1973 and the Arab oil embargo severely shook the country and caused many people to be concerned about the overdependence of the Japanese economy upon imports and exports. Internal problems also appeared, ranging from economic dislocations precipitated by the world recession to the dissatisfaction of youth, to pollution. Many Japanese wondered whether Japan had already passed through a Golden Age, with the road ahead being not only rocky but inclined sharply downward.

CHAPTER IV

The Poor

(1)

In 1976 about 3 billion persons—three-quarters of the world's population—lived in developing countries. In these areas, hunger and malnutrition are widespread—it is variously estimated that between 450 million and 1 billion humans simply do not get enough to eat. Malnutrition paves the way for invasion by infectious disease. Malnutrition and disease combine to give rise to high death rates with the result that life expectancy at birth in these countries is considerably less than in the industrialized ones. Birth rates are much higher, as are rates of population growth. Illiteracy is also very high (see Table 4.1).

Generally, the average per capita incomes in the developing countries are much less than in the industrialized ones. The exceptions are those countries which are for the time being large exporters of crude oil, such as Saudi Arabia and Libya, but which nevertheless have the other characteristics of developing countries such as high infant mortality, low life expectancy, high birth rates, and low literacy.

The combination of low average per capita income and maldistribution of available resources among the people has led to widespread poverty. Large proportions of the populations in the developing countries are landless and either jobless or grossly underemployed. Such persons are unable to purchase or otherwise obtain adequate quantities of food. It has been estimated that in the developing counties generally, excluding the People's Republic of China, some two-thirds of the people are "seriously poor" and about 40 percent are "destitute." It is these people, numbering some 1.2 billion in all, who are the miserable of the earth, whose short lives are filled with deprivation, disease, grief, and uncertainty.

How did such dire poverty become so widespread, particularly at a time

TABLE 4.1

Selected Characteristics of
Developing and Industrialized Countries

	DEVELOPING COUNTRIES	INDUSTRIALIZED COUNTRIES
Population (millions) 1976	2,957	1,014
Per capita GNP 1974	$ 373	$4,361
Birth rate (per 1000)	36	17
Death rate (per 1000)	14	9
Life expectancy (years)	54	71
Infant mortality (per 1000 live births)	100	21
Literacy rate (percent)	39	97
Annual rate of population growth (percent)	2.3	0.8

when a substantial part of the world was becoming richer with each passing year? Here, we cannot avoid pointing a finger at the institution of colonialism, which in substantial measure initiated the sequence of events which eventually led to the present situation. Colonies provided inexpensive raw materials for the growing industries of Europe and they provided vast markets for industrial products. This accelerated the upward spiral of wealth in Europe.

At the same time, the colonies were effectively prevented from industrializing or obtaining fair value for their resources. In the process, although some resourceful people in the colonies became extremely rich, most remained poor. They were poor, however, within the framework of a system which had evolved slowly over many centuries, which was in tune with the natural environment, and which permitted most people to live in reasonable security. There were, of course, numerous catastrophes such as famines, pestilence, and local wars. But the system was sufficiently resilient that it was able to recover from such disturbances.

Gradually, certain lifesaving features of industrial civilization were introduced to the colonies. Railroads transported food to areas where crops had failed. Relatively simple public health measures came into use. New irrigation systems were built and new agricultural technologies were introduced. In time death rates fell, and populations grew more rapidly because the birth rates did not change significantly. The vast majority of the people remained poor and the absolute numbers of the poor increased enormously.

Following World War II the combination of the new technologies with other factors resulted in an explosion of population. Rates of growth in the developing countries rose from less than 1 percent annually in the nineteenth century to more than 2.5 percent in the 1960s, corresponding to at least a doubling every 28 years. The rural areas became increasingly crowded, and the combination of shortage of land, rural unemployment, and the lure of the relative wealth and excitement of city life led to a massive movement of people from the villages to the cities. But, unlike what had happened earlier in Europe and North America, industrial and related job opportunities did not grow as rapidly as did the populations of the urban areas. Thus the cities housed increasing numbers of unemployed and underemployed people.

By 1970 about one-fourth of the persons living in developing countries were urban dwellers, but the proportions varied greatly from region to region. More than half of the persons in Latin America were living in cities; about 20–25 percent of Asians were urbanized; in Africa south of the Sahara, urban populations amounted to 10–20 percent of the population. But rates of growth of urban populations were high, more often than not amounting to more than twice the rate of growth of the population as a whole.

In the developing countries most of the rich people live in the cities and most of the poor people live in the rural areas. But within the cities, in spite of the presence of a certain amount of wealth, the great majority of the people are poor. So many poor people concentrated in such geographically small areas can generate severe political problems for governments, such that strong measures are often taken to provide the urban poor with food. Food prices are subsidized, and some countries have food distribution programs. The Egyptian government, for example, has subsidized the cost of food for many years. In 1977, when the government announced a substantial increase in food prices, rioting broke out and the government was forced to reverse its decision.

Urbanization places considerable economic strain upon developing countries. As increasing number of people move into the cities, each person remaining in agriculture must produce an ever-larger surplus of food for shipment to the cities. Larger quantities of energy are required to produce the extra food, as well as to provide essential services in the cities. If jobs are not available, the poor have great difficulty obtaining adequate food and other necessities such as fuel and housing. New jobs require the investment of capital, which is difficult to obtain, with the result that in many countries people are moving into the cities more rapidly than new jobs can be created. Vast slums emerge within and around the major urban areas.

As cities have become larger, the demands upon the rural areas, largely populated by the poor, have increased. Although the majority of the people live in the countryside, the wealth and the political power lie in the cities. As a result a new conflict has emerged, far more important than the traditional class conflicts—the conflict between the rural and urban classes.

Developing countries are usually classified by their average per capita gross national products. The Overseas Development Council, for example, uses three categories based upon an earlier classification by the World Bank: upper middle income (per capita GNP $700–$2000), middle income (per capita GNP $300–$700), and low income (per capita GNP less than $300). Table

TABLE 4.2

Selected Characteristics of
Developing Countries by Income

	LOW-INCOME COUNTRIES (PER CAPITA GNP UNDER $300)	LOWER-MIDDLE-INCOME COUNTRIES (PER CAPITA GNP $300–$800)	UPPER-MIDDLE-INCOME COUNTRIES (PER CAPITA GNP GREATER THAN $800)
Mid-1976 population (millions)	1,341	1,145	471
Per capita GNP	$ 152	$ 338	$1,091
Birth rate (per 1000)	40	30	36
Death rate (per 1000)	17	11	10
Life expectancy (years)	48	61	61
Infant mortality rate (per 1000 live births)	134	70	82
Literacy rate (percent)	33	34	65
Annual rate of population growth (percent)	2.4	2.0	2.7
Annual rate of growth of per capita GNP (percent)	1.7	4.4	4.7
Annual rate of economic growth	4.1	6.4	7.4

4.2 shows various average characteristics of these categories. It can be seen that there are enormous variations in such indices as birth and death rates, infant mortality, and literacy which appear to be related in some way to per capita income. Yet, when the statistics are examined in greater depth, it becomes clear that average income figures tend to hide important elements of the development picture.

In most parts of the world such indicators have tended to vary with each other. For example, the lower the death rate, the higher the literacy. In view of this it has been suggested that for convenience we use an index of well-being which is a composite of indices of life expectancy, infant mortality, and literacy, called the "Physical Quality of Life Index," or PQLI, on a scale of 100. The PQLIs of the richest of the industrial nations are 95 or more. The PQLIs of the developing countries range downward from about 90 to a low of 10. The average PQLI of the developing countries, weighted by population, is about 50.

One might expect the PQLI to increase as the per capita income increases, for in principle more resources can be channeled into improved nutrition, public health, and education. In general this turns out to be true, but the actual relationship between the PQLI and per capita GNP appears to be much more complicated and strongly dependent upon a combination of cultural and historical circumstances.

In Figure 4.1 we can see that five major "cultural fields" effectively describe the relationships between per capita GNP and PQLI in the developing countries. At one end of the spectrum are the nations of Africa south of the Sahara where substantial increases in the per cpita GNP are not reflected to any appreciable extent in the PQLI. One is tempted to conclude that most increased average income in Africa benefits only a small proportion of the population.

The nations of south and east Asia lie at the other end of the spectrum, where increases in the PQLI are strongly correlated with increases in the per capita GNP. In Asia, in contrast to Africa, the resources and the benefits appear to be more equitably distributed, at least from the point of view of nutrition, health, and elementary education.

The non-OPEC Arab countries and the Latin American countries form separate groups in which the PQLI is also strongly correlated with the per capita GNP, but in both groups for a given PQLI the per capita GNP is greater than in Asia. Conversely, and perhaps more significantly, for any given per capita income the PQLIs of Asian nations are higher than in other parts of the world.

It is of interest that some nations lie far outside the fields that are pictured.

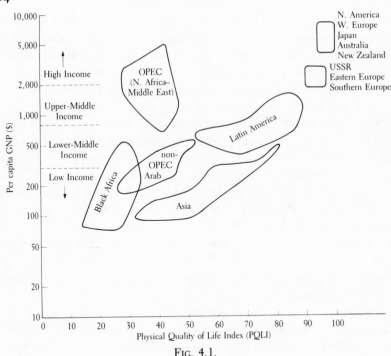

FIG. 4.1.

Notable among those in Africa are Angola, which has a very low PQLI and a high per capita income; Rhodesia and South Africa, which have higher PQLIs and per capita incomes than other black African countries; and Kenya, which has a per capita income typical of the region but an unusually high PQLI. In Latin America, Bolivia stands out as being unusually low in both per capita income and PQLI. In Asia, Taiwan and the city-states of Hong Kong and Singapore are usually high in both per capita income and PQLI. Perhaps the most interesting anomaly of all is Sri Lanka, which with a per capita GNP of only $130 has a PQLI of 83.

It is tempting to relate the observed relationships at least in part to differences in income distribution. It is well known, for example that the distribution of income (including the products of the land) in Asia is generally more equitable than in other parts of the developing world. On the other hand, it is likely that such factors as urbanization, resources available for export, elapsed time since gaining independence, and cultural traditions are also of considerable importance.

The populations of the poorer developing countries can be looked upon as being mixtures of a poor majority and a rich minority. The latter often tend to live in European fashion and have correspondingly high incomes. If the average per capita income of the poor majority is about $100 per year and if the per capita income of the rich is $5000, a mixture containing only 2 percent rich is sufficient to double the national per capita GNP. Under these circumstances the richest 20 percent of the population would share 60 percent of the national income while the poorest 20 percent would share but 10 percent. In fact, in many developing countries there are substantial numbers of persons who have far greater incomes than that used in our illustration. Further, a certain amount of "trickle down," including industrialization, gives rise to a middle class, the size of which varies greatly from country to country.

Observed income distributions in selected developing countries are shown in Table 4.3. Note how large the ratios of the shares of the richest to the poorest are for Ecuador, Mexico, and Kenya, compared with Sri Lanka. Also note how small the ratio is for the United States compared with the developing countries generally. The average characteristics of the major cultural groupings of developing countries are shown in Table 4.4.

(2)

The most important single element of individual well-being is the adequacy of nutrition. Hungry and malnourished people cannot function properly. Well-fed people are not necessarily happy, but adequate nutrition is clearly an essential component of a contented, meaningful life.

Most of the hunger in the world is in the developing countries. Lack of adequate nutrition is the main contributor to the high rates of infant mortality in those areas, as well as to the generally high death rates which stem from both epidemic and endemic disease. Malnourished people, particularly children, cannot fight disease effectively.

The incidence of malnutrition is greater in some countries than in others, but in most developing countries there are enormous inequities in food availability. It was pointed out at the World Food Conference in 1974 that in many countries, the 20 percent of the population with lowest income has only half the per capita energy intake of the top 10 percent. It is estimated that about half of the children under five years of age in the poor countries may be inadequately nourished, and so large numbers of them either die or suffer serious biological damage which handicaps them in later life.

Since World War II the goal of providing adequate nutrition for all persons has been thwarted by the constant struggle between expansion of food production and the growth of population. Between 1950 and 1975 total food production in the developing countries expanded at unprecedented rates, but popu-

TABLE 4.3

Share of National Income of Population Groups in Selected Developing Countries, Compared with the United States

COUNTRY	RICHEST 20%	2ND 20%	3RD 20%	4TH 20%	POOREST 20%	RATIO OF RICHEST TO POOREST
Argentina (1961)	52.0	17.6	13.1	10.3	7.0	7.43
Ecuador (1970)	73.5	14.5	5.6	3.9	2.5	29.40
Egypt (1964–65)	47.0	23.5	15.5	9.8	4.2	11.20
India (1963–64)	52.0	19.0	13.0	11.0	5.0	10.40
Kenya (1969)	68.0	13.5	8.5	6.2	3.8	17.90
Mexico (1969)	64.0	16.0	9.5	6.5	4.0	16.00
Sri Lanka (1969–70)	46.0	20.5	16.5	11.0	6.0	7.67
Tanzania (1967)	57.0	17.0	12.0	9.0	5.0	11.40
United States	38.8	24.1	17.4	13.0	6.7	5.79

SOURCE: John W. Sewell and the staff of the Overseas Development Council, *The United States and World Development: Agenda 1977*. Published for the Council by Praeger Publishers, 1977.

TABLE 4.4

Some Characteristics of Major Cultural Groupings of Developing Countries

	AFRICA (EXCLUDING NORTH AND SOUTH AFRICA)	ARAB STATES	ASIA (EXCLUDING JAPAN AND MIDDLE EAST)	LATIN AMERICA (EXCLUDING CARIBBEAN)
Population (millions)	295	143	2207	300
Population growth rate (percent)	2.7	3.2	2.5	3.0
Birth rate (per 1000)	47.7	47.1	39.8	38.4
Death rate (per 1000)	22.8	16.7	14.3	11.0
PQLI	25	40	50	70
Urbanization (percent)	17.5	40.0	22.4	61.5
Non-OPEC per capita GNP ($)	200	300	200	700

lation growth wiped out most of the gains. Indeed, during the period 1960–1975 population growth held average per capita increases in food production in these countries down to 0.3 percent per year. For the poorest group of developing countries, per capita consumption did not increase at all, and in the greater part of Africa per capita consumption actually fell by 10 percent.

However, as we have seen, even had per capita food production in these countries increased markedly, hunger and malnutrition would still be widespread as a result of poverty. The landless destitute can neither produce nor purchase sufficient food; in the absence of a compensating social mechanism, they suffer hunger and malnutrition together with associated diseases, bodily malfunctions, and personal indignities. Compensating mechanisms have been developed in some poor countries, for example the People's Republic of China and Sri Lanka, where serious malnutrition on any substantial scale appears to have been eliminated in spite of the fact that the individuual incomes are very low. But in the greater part of the developing world, poverty and hunger are strongly associated with each other.

In addition to population growth and poverty, a major cause of hunger involves the instability of food supplies. Vagaries of weather precipitate local or regional fluctuations in the availability and prices of food, as do heavy infestations of pests and diseases that destroy crops and animals. Indian agricultural production was severely set back by a drought in 1972–1973. The most severe famine to strike the Indian subcontinent in three decades took place in Bangladesh where much of the 1974 summer crop was destroyed by floods. The region of Africa immediately south of the Sahara known as the Sahelian Zone, stretching from Senegal in the west to northern Ethiopia in the east, suffered for five consecutive years from severe drought which led to widespread starvation.

In 1973–1974 developing countries which had come to rely heavily upon imported fertilizers and petroleum were hard hit by the rapid rise in the price of crude oil, and agricultural production suffered seriously. Instability of price and supply have their greatest effect upon the poor, who lack the resources to endure prolonged periods of shortage.

Obviously, such difficulties could be sharply lessened by the design and implementation of government policies aimed at encouraging the production of more food, making it possible to store surpluses until they are needed, and providing the logistic and social mechanisms to move food quickly from areas of surplus to areas of food deficiency. Unfortunately, in many developing countries government policies work in the opposite direction, providing disincentives rather than incentives for increased production, providing little in the way of viable mechanisms for storage and transfer or price stabilization at levels which will inspire farmers to seek the highest yields from their land at all times. Thailand, for example, has a large unrealized potential for rice production, but government policy keeps the price which the farmers receive far below the real value. At the same time the cost of fertilizer to the farmer is maintained above the world price.

Some major developing countries have placed such high priority on industrialization that agriculture has been largely ignored. In India, for example, top priority was given to industrialization while a policy of import substitution increased the prices of goods that farmers buy. As in Thailand, rice was underpriced and fertilizer was overpriced; thus, there has been little incentive for the farmer to make the additional investments that are required to take full advantage of the new high-yielding varieties. Under these circumstances, although the Indian consumers in New Delhi and Bombay pay less for their rice, they face the continuing prospect of shortages as a result of policies which have by now become well established and therefore difficult to change.

If hunger and malnutrition in the world are to be lessened significantly by the end of this century, food production in the developing countries must increase at an unprecedented rate. Considering likely rates of population growth as well as growth of per capita food consumption needed to eliminate existing malnutrition, the developing countries need to increase food production by about 3–4 percent each year, corresponding to a doubling of production in about 20 years. Only a small fraction of this increase can be obtained by increasing the area of cultivated land. Under the circumstances, the elimination of hunger depends upon very large increases in crop yields per hectare, averaging about 2.5 percent per year over the next quarter-century. Areas which are experiencing higher than average rates of population growth will require even higher increases of yield.

When we view this situation from the purely technological point of view, such large rates of increase of yield appear to be readily attainable. Even from an empirical point of view the demand does not seem unreasonably high. During the period 1965–1975 some 30 developing countries containing about 1.3 billion persons achieved the 3–4 percent annual rate of increase in overall agricultural production estimated as necessary for the entire developing world over the next quarter-century.

When we view the situation from the social and political points of view, however, the outlook is less optimistic. Such major incentives to the farmers as land reform and increased prices for their production are difficult to bring about. Land reform is opposed by the wealthy landowners. Higher prices to the farmer are anathema to the city dwellers, who must then pay higher prices for their food. In addition, further increases in crop yields require a great deal of local agricultural research and in many countries the necessary numbers of trained people and the organized structure simply do not exist. Governments generally are much closer to the problems of the city dwellers than they are to those of the peasants. In many cases they are more likely to invest scarce resources in urban services than in rural irrigation projects or facilities for grain storage.

Finally, we must keep in mind that increased agricultural yields necessitate increased utilization of energy on farms, not so much for mechanization but rather to manufacture fertilizers and to help pump adequate supplies of water. Nitrogen fertilizers are manufactured for the most part from petroleum or natural gas. Countries which do not have indigenous supplies of these resources must therefore import fertilizers, crude oil, or both.

Close to a billion people inhabit about 40 poor countries which are in serious trouble with respect to energy. Their annual bill for imports of fertilizers made from petroleum, crude oil, and cereals increased greatly following the substantial increases in the cost of crude oil in 1973–1974. This is money which they do not have, and one result has been increased debt. A more serious result has been decreased expansion in the use of fertilizers and pumped water, which means decreased expansion of crop yields.

(3)

Perhaps the most important determinant of the future of the poor countries is the course of their birth rates during the next few decades. In most developing countries death rates have already declined considerably; therefore, the future course of fertility will determine when population growth will stop and what the ultimate stationary population will be.

Stationary or steady-state populations are those in which births and deaths are in balance. A useful measure of the state of balance or imbalance is the net reproduction rate, which is the number of daughters born per woman who are likely to survive to reach childbearing age, assuming the prevailing level of mortality. If the net reproduction rate is unity, then on the average each woman would have one daughter who could be expected to live to the mean age of reproduction, and in the long run the population would cease to grow. Obviously, because some people die before they reach reproductive age and because males are born in somewhat larger numbers than females, the fertility rate, the average number of children born to a woman in a given society, is somewhat over two. In the rich countries a total fertility rate of only 2.1 children per woman suffices for replacement. In the developing countries, at current mortality rates, replacement-level fertility would correspond to about 2.6 children per woman. Typically, however, fertility rates are double this, averaging 5.3 children per woman. This fertility rate combined with the typical death rate results in a doubling of population every 30 years.

Population growth has a momentum which continues for some time after replacement-level fertility is reached. Fertility in the United States dropped below replacement level in the mid-1970s, yet we can expect about a 30 percent increase in population before we reach a steady-state. This results from the fact that higher birth rates of the past have produced a relatively high proportion of people who are currently in, or about to enter, the reproductive ages. In the developing countries, once replacement fertility has been achieved further increases of population will be even greater than in the industrial countries because of the very high proportions of young people in the populations.

At the present time the population of human beings in the world is about 4 billion. Estimates suggest that even with successful efforts in family planning there will be about 6 billion persons by the end of this century. If global replacement levels of fertility were to be reached by that time, the population would stabilize at about 8 billion, with most of the increase over today's levels in the developing countries. But were the replacement net reproduction rate not achieved until 2020, as seems more likely, the ultimate stationary populations would be well over 10 billion persons. Ninety percent of those persons would be residents of the poor countries. Clearly, the penalties for delay in substantially reducing birth rates are severe.

During the 1950s, when people first became alarmed about the explosive rate of population growth in developing countries, their crude birth rates averaged somewhat over 45 per thousand. By 1965 a slight drop could be perceived. By 1970 the crude birth rate had fallen to 42.4, and by 1975 it reached 39.0. This appears to be a truly significant lowering. But in the same period the death rate also fell, with the result that although there was a decline in the rate of natural increase, it was slight. The average rate of natural increase in the developing countries in 1969 would have produced a doubling of population in 27 years. By 1975 the doubling time had increased to 29 years. Nevertheless, we must recognize the historic importance of the fact that apparently in the mid-1960s birth rates in the developing countries started to decline, and by the early 1970s the rate of population growth had also started to fall. We must now ask whether the present trend is rapid enough.

Between 1970 and 1974 the crude birth rate in the developing countries decreased on the average about 3 points, corresponding to a drop of about 7 percent for the period. At this rate at least another 50–60 years would be required for fertility to reach replacement level. This would mean that the eventual steady-state world population would be considerably higher than the projected 10 billion persons which would exist were replacement level fertility achieved by the year 2020.

One hopes that this process can in some way be speeded up. Yet we must face the fact that we are dealing with an extremely complex process. Many economic and cultural factors are involved in the individual decisions to have fewer children. Once those factors are understood, then it might be possible for societies to take conscious action to accelerate lowering the birth rate.

Numerous studies have been made of the decline of fertility in the rich countries, a process which has taken about 150 years and which was well advanced before modern tools of contraception were available. The history of this development shows that although knowledge and contraceptive devices can accelerate the process of fertility decline, far more important is the existence of a strong motivation to have fewer children.

Fertility decline in the rich countries appears to have been sustained by a combination of coitus interruptus, abortion (both legal and illegal), postponement of marriage, and abstinence (which was never very popular). With the advent of effective technologies for conception control the process was accelerated. But even with effective technologies, the rate of decline seems to have been limited by the strength of the motivation to have fewer children. This motivation appears to have been determined by a host of factors, among them the movement from farm to city, falling infant and child mortality, increased life expectancy, increased education, changing religious attitudes, increased family income, and the changing role of women. The importance of these factors relative to each other seems to have varied from culture to culture.

The factors which can be correlated with the fall of fertility in the poor countries have been subjected to considerable study. One of the striking conclusions is that countries which launched vigorous national family planning programs back in the early 1960s have achieved the highest reduction in fertility rates. Notable among these countries are Chile, Colombia, Costa Rica, Egypt, Indonesia, South Korea, Sri Lanka, Taiwan, and Thailand. In almost all of these cases the rate of lowering of fertility appears to be accelerating. By contrast, in those countries which do not have vigorous family planning programs, fertility rates show little or no change over comparable periods of time. Major countries in the latter group include Bangladesh, Brazil, Ethiopia, Kenya, Mexico, and Pakistan.

The evidence suggests that family planning services are essential and can be effective. But other observations suggest that family planning programs can succeed only to the extent that there is a real desire—by men as well as women—to have fewer children. The intensity of this desire and the ability to fulfill it appears to be determined by a number of social and economic conditions. Among these conditions are improved nutrition and health, improved education, economic improvement of lower income groups, urbanization, and the status of women. Table 4.5 shows how the crude birth rate changed relative to indicators of some of these factors during the period 1960–1970. It should be noted in this connection that three of these indicators (infant mortality, life expectancy, and literacy) provide the basis for the Physical Quality

TABLE 4.5

Variation of Average Crude Birth Rates in Developing
Countries With Selected Development Indicators, 1960–1970

	1960	1970
Crude birth rate	46.0	42.0
Crude death rate	11.8	9.8
Life expectancy (years)	57.0	61.4
Infant mortality rate (per thousand)	80.0	68.0
Calorie consumption (per person per day)	2110.0	2310.0
Protein consumption (grams per person per day)	55.9	61.3
Literacy (% of population age 15 and over)	61.0	74.0

SOURCE: Address by Robert S. McNamara, president of the World Bank, at the Massachusetts Institute of Technology, April 28, 1977.

of Life Index (PQLI) which was discussed earlier. As might be expected under these circumstances, there should be a significant relationship between the PQLI and the crude birth rate. This relationship is illustrated in Figure 4.2, where each point represents a separate country. We see that at a PQLI of about 40 the birth rate begins to drop. At a PQLI of about 75 there is a sudden fall, the birth rate dropping about 25 percent, then continuing to decrease rapidly as the PQLI approaches 95.

It is perhaps significant that the relationship between PQLI and birth rate seems independent of culture. For example, it is nearly identical for Asia and Latin America.

Tables 4.6 and 4.7 show the variations in these critical indicators for two sets of countries, each with nearly identical per capita GNP. The data show conclusively that numerous correlations exist between the crude birth rate and a variety of indicators of social development. What has not been proved conclusively is a clear-cut cause-and-effect relationship. However, in pondering the potential impact of such factors as health, literacy, and urbanization upon fertility, it is tempting to conclude that a causal connection probably exists. Should this turn out to be true it could point the way to accelerating still further our approach to a worldwide steady-state population. Perhaps the most important lesson suggested by the data is that family planning programs seem to work, but in the absence of continuing social betterment their effectiveness is unlikely to continue into the long-range future. Such programs must be accompanied by a visible and continuing social betterment.

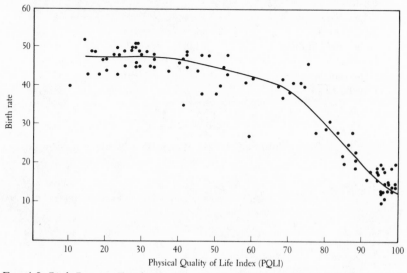

Fig. 4.2. Birth Rates in Developing Countries in Relation to Physical Quality of Life Index

There are a number of policy actions that governments might take which collectively could have major effect upon the future course of population growth. The first of these would be the establishment of population policies and programs. In 1969 about forty developing countries officially supported family planning. By 1975 there were sixty-three countries with official family planning programs. However, many governments continue to refrain from establishing population policies and goals, let alone effective family planning programs.

Beyond this, governments can take a number of actions aimed at increasing the demand for family planning services. High on the list would be sharp reduction of rates of infant and child mortality. Current rates of infant mortality are as high as they are in Africa, Asia, and Latin America because of low nutritional standards, poor hygienic conditions, and inadequate health ser-

TABLE 4.6

Selected Low-Income Countries Which Have Nearly Equal Per Capita
GNPs

	GUINEA	MALAWI	PAKISTAN	SRI LANKA
Per capita				
GNP ($)	120	130	130	130
PQLI	20	29	37	83
Birth rate				
(per 1000)	47	48	44	28 .
Death rate				
(per 1000)	23	24	15	8
Infant mortality				
(per 1000 births)	175	148	124	45
Literacy				
(percent)	5–10	22	16	81
Percent urban	19.5	6.4	26.9	24.3

TABLE 4.7

Selected Lower-Middle-Income Countries Which Have Nearly Equal Per Capita
GNPs

	CONGO (PR)	GHANA	MOROCCO	JORDAN	COLOMBIA	KOREA (REP.)	GUYANA
Per capita							
GNP ($)	470	430	430	430	500	480	500
PQLI	25	31	40	48	71	80	84
Birth rate							
(per 1000)	45	49	46	48	41	29	36
Death rate							
(per 1000)	21	22	16	15	9	9	6
Infant mortality							
(per 1000 births)	180	156	130	97	76	47	40
Literacy							
(percent)	20	25	21	32	73	88	80
Percent urban	39.8	32.4	38.0	56.1	61.8	47.4	33.5

vices. We know from experience that, given the will, such conditions can be
changed rather quickly. For example, more than 20 years ago Sri Lanka embarked upon a program aimed at improving rural health. Infant mortality was
reduced from 78 to 45 per 1000 births, and life expectancy at birth was
increased from 56 to 69 years. At the same time the crude birth rate fell from
39 to 29.

Also high on the list would be expansion of educational opportunity, particularly for women. Studies in Latin America indicate that girls who have

completed primary school average about two fewer children than those who have not. Schooling improves the opportunity of finding employment outside the home and tends to delay the age of marriage for girls. Educated men and women acquire family planning information more easily than do others, and are likely to be more careful about nutrition, basic sanitation, and other aspects of public health.

As we have seen, a key to eliminating dire poverty and, associated with it, malnutrition, is to increase the agricultural productivity of small farmers and to expand job opportunities in rural areas. The fertility of the rural poor is almost always high. Solution of these problems requires comprehensive programs of rural redevelopment including such elements as land reform, access to credit, and assured availability of water.

Achieving a more equitable distribution of income is a necessary condition for lessening poverty, improving nutrition, and lowering fertility to the level which will lead to a steady-state population. Again, this involves land reform and increasing job opportunities in both rural and urban areas, and directing more of the benefits of economic growth from the rich strata of society to the poor.

Last, there should be strong policies aimed at improving the status of women in the developing countries—socially, economically, and politically. At present, women in most developing countries do not have equitable access to education, food, or jobs. Major changes in this situation could have a profound effect upon fertility.

It is by no means clear that programs of the sort discussed will be developed in time to prevent escalation of the human population above the 8-, 10-, or even 16-billion level. At the same time, the fact that we appear to have passed a turning point in fertility in the poor countries gives us some reason to be cautiously optimistic.

(4)

Unless a developing country is quite large and well endowed with natural resources, for example the People's Republic of China, it is virtually impossible for it to carry out a viable development program without importing quantities of raw materials and machinery. Even China finds it useful to import quantities of capital goods as well as some food. In order to pay for its imports a country must either export commodities and manufactured goods of equivalent value, receive financial assistance from other countries, or go into debt.

Developing countries differ greatly from each other in their ability to pay for their imports. Altogether about 20 developing countries, inhabited by some 500 million people, are benefiting or will soon benefit from significant exports of nonrenewable raw materials, particularly petroleum. Clearly, the money obtained from the sale of these resources, if invested wisely, could accelerate development. Some of these countries, particularly those in the tropics, benefit from the export of renewable products such as sugar, coffee, timber, cotton, and cocoa.

An additional billion or so persons live in developing countries which are reasonably self-sufficient with respect to nonrenewable resources, including energy. These nations, which include China, Colombia, Mexico, and Peru, for example, were not appreciably harmed by the sudden increase in the price of crude oil imposed by the OPEC nations in 1973–1974.

Another 60 million persons live in countries, including South Korea, Taiwan, Hong Kong, and Singapore, which, like Japan, are closely integrated with the world economy almost entirely through the manufacture of goods.

However, about 1200 million people inhabit about 40 poor countries which are in serious trouble with respect to money and raw materials, particularly energy. These nations require fertilizers if they are to further increase food production, and they require energy if they are to increase fertilizer production, operate pumps for irrigation, and develop industries.

These countries, which are among those now collectively referred to as "The Fourth World," are the poorest nations on earth and prospects for future economic growth are dismal. Their annual bill for essential imports of petroleum, fertilizers and food has been greatly increased because of increased costs of crude oil. This is money which they do not have, so they must borrow. Their situation has been exacerbated by a prolonged slowdown in the economies of the industrial nations, which led to reduced economic assistance, reduced direct private investment, and reduced export earnings.

The poorest countries suffer from very low rates of economic growth. There is little chance that their per capita income will increase by more than $2 each year over the next decade. In constant dollars, the average per capita GNP of these nations increased from $110 in 1960 to $120 in 1965 and $130 in 1970. Since then it has gained no further. At the same time, the per capita GNP of all but the poorest nations has increased. In the decade 1965–1974 the average per capita GNP of the lower-middle-income countries increased at the rate of 4.4 percent each year while that of the upper-middle-income countries averaged 4.7 percent per year. This can be compared to the average per capita growth rate during the same period in the poorest countries of but 1.7 percent per year in constant dollars. Thus the same kind of fissioning process which produced the dramatic cleavage between the rich and the poor countries collectively is now producing a subcleavage between groups of poor countries.

(5)

In order for economic and social development to take place, many things must happen virtually simultaneously. Foremost among these is the accumulation of the capital which makes possible construction of industries and schools, provision of city services, development of transportation and communication networks, and expansion of a variety of rural developments such as irrigation systems, agricultural schools, experiment stations, and public health facilities. The necessary capital can be accumulated in a number of ways: through internal savings, the sale of primary commodities, the sale of manufactured products, private investments from outside the country, private loans, and economic assistance from other countries in the form of loans and gifts. Nations differ greatly in the extent to which these diverse approaches have been used.

The export of agricultural products played an enormously important role in the accumulation of capital in the United States. In Japan, the export of commodities, notably silk, was important during the early decades of development, but as her reservoir of inexpensive skilled labor increased, much capital was accumulated through the export of manufactured goods. Such exports were essential to the accumulation of capital in Hong Kong and Singapore. In the OPEC nations of the Middle East and North Africa, capital is being accumulated primarily through the export of crude oil. By contrast, in the Soviet Union and the People's Republic of China exports have played a relatively minor role in capital accumulation. In these countries, internal savings have played a predominant role, with various approaches being used to accomplish this. The Chinese, for example, have excelled in creating capital from hand labor, making use of millions of farmers during their off seasons to build irrigation and other water-control systems, roads, schools, houses, and small industries. Great planning and organizational skills are required to use this approach effectively.

The poorer the people of a country are, the greater the difficulty of accumulating capital through internal savings. If most people are living at a subsistence level, they are in no position to be taxed directly or to open bank accounts. This is particularly true if most of the work is done outside the money economy. Thus the poorest countries, which cannot accumulate significant capital through the sale of commodities or manufactured goods, have slight prospects of accumulating capital through internal savings unless, like the Chinese, they have the political will and organizational ability to transform hand labor into capital.

The paucity of skilled labor in the poorest countries makes them unlikely candidates for private foreign investment. Their very poorness mitigates against their receiving private foreign loans with reasonable terms. In these countries it is understandable that public loans and gifts from governments and international agencies loom large as ways in which capital can be made available. In 1975 the capital inflow to the poorest nations from public sources was five times greater than from private sources. But the total net flow to those countries was very small compared with the need, amounting to $7.2 billion, which corresponds to about $6 per person.

By contrast, about two-thirds of the capital flow to the non-oil-exporting, middle-income developing countries which are in the market economy was from private sources. In 1975 the total flow amounted to $28 billion, corresponding to somewhat over $40 per person. Further, the middle-income developing countries have a considerable advantage over the low-income countries in exports of both primary commodities and manufactured goods. In 1975 the value of exports from the middle-income countries amounted to $143 billion, compared with only $27 billion for the low-income countries. This explains in part why development has progressed so much more rapidly in the middle-income countries than in the poorest ones.

The debt burdens of the developing countries have increased substantially partly because of the widening gap between imports and exports and partly as a result of increased capital flows. By 1975 the total external debt of the middle-income non-oil-exporters had reached $88.4 billion while that of the poorest nations had reached $28.5 billion. The figures are summarized in Table 4.8.

The increased borrowing continued in 1976, spurred by the balance-of-payment surpluses in the OPEC nations. In particular, Saudi Arabia, Kuwait, and the United Arab Emirates have been unable to spend their oil income rapidly enough and have deposited enormous sums in major banks in the United States and other industrial countries. To keep this cash moving, the banks have been lending the funds to less developed countries. In the process, the banks have made themselves vulnerable to the possibility of substantial default as well as to pressures from the oil-exporting countries. By early 1977 the developing countries owed banks in the United States about $50 billion. The total indebtedness to U.S. and foreign banks rose to $77 billion and the fear was expressed that the banks would be forced to keep on making new

TABLE 4.8

Exports, Imports, Capital Flows, and External
Debts of Developing Countries

	LOW-INCOME NATIONS	LOWER-MIDDLE-INCOME NATIONS	UPPER-MIDDLE-INCOME NATIONS
Population (millions)	1,341	1,145	471
Per capita GNP (dollars)	152	338	1,091
1975 exports ($ billions)	27.1	37.8	104.8
1975 imports ($ billions)	32.8	48.8	114.1
1975 capital flow* ($ billions)	7.2	28.2	
1975 debt* ($ billions)	28.5	88.4	

* Excludes oil exporters.

loans in order to forestall default on the old ones. As a result, pressures were placed on U.S. banks to cut back on their foreign lending.

Since costs of imports by the developing countries, incuding petroleum, seem destined to increase still further, it is clear that the developing countries need to do something about the persistent deficits in their balance of payments. This means cutting back on their imports or expanding their exports, neither of which is easily done. Indeed, prospects for needed trade expansion are far from encouraging in spite of the fact that just six developing countries account for two-thirds of all manufactured exports to the OECD nations. The fact is that any major increase in the rate of growth of exports from the developing world requires the dismantling of trade barriers which have been erected by the industrial nations.

One of the most difficult internal obstacles to development lies with the privileged elites who exist in all countries, even the very poorest. The benefits of economic growth have accrued disproportionately to these elites and have widened the gap between the privileged and the deprived. More often than not the privileged minority likes things the way they are and will go to great lengths to keep them that way. Many import luxuries and thus lessen the resources available for development. Many export money to private bank accounts in the industrial countries. Many will happily accept substantial bribes to influence their governments to accept business contracts. Such persons often live in fear of any truly meaningful political-economic change for this might mean total loss of both wealth and prestige. Under these circumstances the elites are likely to oppose any change which appears to threaten their privileges.

Yet another hindrance to development is the expenditure of funds for military purposes. In 1974 the developing countries collectively spent about $50 billion on their military establishments, of which some $6 billion went for the purchase of arms from the industrial countries. These figures can be compared with expenditures during that same year of $37 billion for education and $10 billion for public health. Not surprisingly, per capita military expenditures increased with the per capita GNP.

In 1974 military expenditures of the poorest countries consumed about 4 percent of the GNP, an amount which they could ill-afford but which seemed necessary because of perceived threats to their security both from within and without. It is sad that this sum represented twice the amount spent collectively by these same countries on public education. In the same year, however, the combined military expenditures of the industrial countries exceeded the total gross national products of the poorest countries by 17 percent. Clearly if military expenditures in the rich *and* the poor nations were lower, development could proceed at a more rapid pace.

(6)

When we discuss the problems of development, it is convenient to talk about them in terms of money. At the same time it is important that we not lose sight of what the money is used for.

The process of development involves an enormously complex array of activities. Resources must be surveyed, analyzed, and developed; factories, railroads, and highways must be built. In the public sector, housing must be developed, educational systems must be planned, teachers and doctors must be trained; in the agricultural sector, irrigation systems must be built, varieties of new seeds must be developed, fertilizers and pesticides must be manufactured and delivered to the crops, farmers must be taught new techniques. All of these activities, which are related directly and indirectly to each other, must be carefully planned and executed as parts of a broad development plan. All of these activities require money, but they also require cadres of trained people.

Over the years planners have tended to use what is sometimes referred to as the "black box" approach to development. Here it is assumed that the primary insufficiency in the poorer countries is money and that if only we were to put enough money into a black box called the "development process," development would automatically flow out of the other end. We now have a great deal of evidence which tells us that this is not correct—that although money is an essential element of development, it is by no means sufficient unto itself. Other ingredients must be added, some of which we have come to appreciate only in recent years.

For the most part, the development policies following World War II were based upon the "trickle down" principle which assumed that accelerated economic growth at the top would eventually benefit the entire population, including the poor. All too frequently, however, development plans have been drawn up, altered, manipulated, and implemented by members of the elite who often stood to benefit the most and who were primarily urban-industry oriented. Too little attention was given to rural areas, except as the welfare of the large landowners was affected. The rural poor were for the most part ignored. In many cases, this led to increased skewing of the income distribution curve in favor of the rich minority while the absolute numbers of the poor, hungry, and malnourished grew. As a result, a number of these nations have suffered serious economic, social, and political turmoil. In the years ahead there will probably be a great deal more.

The experiences of the last three decades have led to a rethinking of approaches to development. A new understanding is now emerging which suggests that primary effort should be placed on the improvement of the condition of the absolute poor in the developing countries. It is now recognized, perhaps too late, that given the political will, poverty, hunger, and malnutrition in these areas could be alleviated in a relatively short time. At the end of the process few people would be rich; but most would have a reasonable chance of achieving happiness.

It is clear that expanded transfers of capital from the rich countries to the poor are essential if dire poverty is to be eliminated. It is doubtful, however, that a really major increase in capital flow (a factor of two, for example) could be effectively absorbed at the present time. There simply are not enough trained persons in the poorer countries who are able to make the decisions which must be made and to solve the problems which must be solved if development is to take place. Nor is there adequate organizational structure which would permit decisions to be transformed effectively into action or which would permit development problems to be solved systematically. Nor are there adequate numbers of technically trained persons who can carry out the multiplicity of tasks which are essential in even a quasi-technological society. Indeed, this appears to be a really basic limiting factor to development.

We must keep in mind that development has in fact been taking place.

Until recent years per capita GNPs have increased, even in the poorest countries. More important, the Physical Quality of Life Indices have been increasing, as can be seen from Table 4.9. Our real problem concerns the future. What will be the shape of development during the next three decades?

As we shall see, unless the process of development is accelerated, it is likely that some truly explosive situations will emerge in the near future to endanger *all* humanity, including the rich countries. It is doubtful that development will take place fast enough unless the governments of the richer countries transfer to the poorer ones as much capital each year as can truly be absorbed effectively.

TABLE 4.9

The Growth of PQLI in Selected Developing Countries

		PQLI		
COUNTRY	TYPE	1950s	1960s	1970s
Algeria	OPEC	35	38	42
India	Low-income	28	36	42
Egypt	Low-income	32	41	45
Brazil	Upper-middle-income	53	—	66
Sri Lanka	Low-income	62	77	83

SOURCE: John W. Sewell and the staff of the Overseas Development Council, *The United States and World Development: Agenda 1977.* Published for the Council by Praeger Publishers, 1977.

To start, this would amount to significantly (but not overwhelmingly) more than present levels of transfer. Within a few years the buildup on the average might be something like 1 percent of the GNPs of the donor countries. This is hardly a level of transfer designed to bankrupt the richer countries, but handled properly it could have a profound effect upon development rates. Were the rich countries today to transfer 1 percent of their GNPs to the poor countries, this would amount to about 4 percent of the GNPs of the developing nations and to about 18 percent of what the rich countries are now spending on armaments.

Equally important, however, massive technical assistance programs should be created, of far greater magnitude than any such programs previously attempted. These programs should be aimed at producing decision makers, problem solvers, managers, and other technical persons, at developing the organizational framework within which such persons can operate effectively, and at devising innovative solutions to specific development problems and bottlenecks.

It remains to be seen whether the rich and the poor nations are up to the task of collectively formulating such a program and operating it effectively. If they cannot do it, the prospects for eliminating poverty are indeed poor. The ultimate consequences could be catastrophic.

(7)

Mahatma Gandhi had a magnificent vision of how imperialism could be defeated without using violence, and how parliamentary democracy could be used to transform a poor peasant-village society into a modern, independent, industrial state. Nearly three decades after independence, the great difficulty of maintaining democratic institutions in the face of the horrendous array of social and economic problems now confronting India has become apparent.

Over the years vast wealth has been created for one group of Indians, notably private investors. A new class of government bureaucrats, often working with private investors and holding strategic positions, has channeled large sums of money to themselves. At the same time the vast majority of Indians continue to suffer the degradations of debilitating poverty. Unemployment has continued to climb. Inflation has resulted in sharply increased food costs. Population has moved relentlessly upward.

As a result of the deteriorating economic conditions, the persistent ferment among the many political groups in India intensified. In the face of the resultant turmoil Indira Gandhi began dismantling parliamentary democracy. In mid-1975 a state of national emergency was declared. Civil liberties were suspended and political opposition was destroyed by ban or imprisonment. In September 1975 a measure to amend the constitution was introduced to solidify the power of the executive branch, greatly reduce the power of the judiciary, and curtail the scope of the national legislature. The government maintained that it needed such powers to fight hunger, poverty, and disease.

It seemed that democracy was ended in the last major developing nation still subscribing to democratic principles. In fact, however, the repercussions of Indira Gandhi's actions were so great that parliamentary democracy was restored to India in 1977. Nevertheless, there were many who believed that the earlier sequence of events had been symptomatic and that Indian democracy was not destined for a long life.

Since World War II, democracy has given way to some sort of authoritarian government in a very large number of developing countries. The most popular mechanism for accomplishing this has been the military coup, which over the years has brought a considerable number of military groups into power in such countries as Argentina, Brazil, Peru, Chile, Ghana, Nigeria, Zaire, Egypt, Pakistan, Thailand, and Indonesia. To the list can be added totalitarian states which are not military dictatorships, but which are backed by the military. Examples are the People's Republic of China, the Philippines, Taiwan, and South Korea.

With the possible exception of India, parliamentary democracy is now virtually dead in the developing world, and it seems unlikely that the trend will be reversed in the very near future. We can only hope that those in power will be benevolent rather than repressive and that in time they will encourage a return to the concept of political freedom of choice. But that hope is a slim one.

CHAPTER V

Interactions Between
Rich and Poor

(1)

As we have seen, the rich and the poor nations differ greatly from each other and in a sense are worlds apart. At the same time they interact with each other in many ways, and it is these interactions which will determine the future of the relationships between these two groups of countries.

Perhaps the most obvious interactions are between those rich and poor countries which have common borders. Here it is of no small importance that each of the so-called superpowers has a lengthy common border with a major developing country. The Soviet Union shares a 7000-kilometer border with the People's Republic of China; the United States shares a 2700-kilometer border with Mexico. Of all industrial nations only the Union of South Africa, which from many points of view is still a developing country, shares with the U.S.S.R. and the U.S. the distinction of having long common boundaries with poor countries.

The relations between the Soviet Union and China have remained tense for about fifteen years and the costs to both countries have been considerable. In the 1950s China was the largest single recipient of Soviet loans, credits, and technical assistance, and was the largest trading partner of the Soviet Union. In the early 1960s political hostilities led to the withdrawal of Soviet experts, and trade between the two countries was curtailed. Since then, powerful concentrations of armed forces of both countries have been deployed along or near the border. There were serious armed clashes in 1969.

The Chinese clearly view the Soviet Union as the most serious potential threat to China today, in both political and military terms. The Russians continue to strengthen their border forces. Following the 1969 clashes they hinted that they were considering an attack on Chinese nuclear installations.

In 1964 the Chinese exploded their first nuclear device. Since then they have built up a modest nuclear force which they maintain they will not use first. Indeed, they appear to be developing strategies almost exclusively to maximize the defense of the nation, perhaps planning for limited offensive thrusts if they see their borders threatened by invasion.

The Chinese striking force apparently consists of about 100 medium- and intermediate-range ballistic missiles and about 100 medium-range bombers. They now have available thermonuclear devices which could be targeted at most parts of the Soviet Union. There is a possibility that they might have developed some tactical nuclear weaponry as well. All of this probably serves to some extent as a deterrent, particularly to any Soviet border action using conventional weapons.

It now seems unlikely that there will be any rapid improvement in Chinese-Soviet relations in the near future. Under the circumstances, the border between the two countries will probably remain a potential location for major upheaval for a very long time.

The border between the United States and Mexico presents problems of quite a different sort. It is virtually unarmed, for the two countries no longer perceive each other as threats. The major difficulty stems from the large-scale illegal crossing of Mexicans into the United States in search of jobs. Unemployment in Mexico is very high and wage scales are very low compared with those in the United States.

It is estimated that between 6 and 12 million illegal aliens currently live in the United States and a large proportion of them are from Mexico. About a million illegal workers, most of them male, flow into the United States each year, making illegal immigration a substantial contribution to U.S. population growth. The flow increased in 1977 because of the deterioration of the Mexican economy.

Estimates place the number of jobless in Mexico at about 9 million, or about 30 percent of the labor force. An additional 600,000 to 700,000 persons enter the Mexican job market each year. This number will increase considerably in the years ahead as a result of rapid population growth, and it is fully expected that the flow of illegal immigrants will increase correspondingly.

In the absence of any dramatic change in the Mexican economy, it seems likely that the United States will greatly strengthen the border patrols and make it illegal for U.S. employers to hire illegal aliens. Although such a move will be resisted by certain employers, the pressures to take strong actions are increasing.

A part of the difficulty stems from the fact that the Mexican outward migration serves as a safety valve for the Mexican economy. The persons leaving are for the most part unemployed. When they find work in the U.S., which they usually do because they are willing to work for wages which are low by U.S. standards, they often send money home to their families.

One solution to this problem would be accelerated development which is aimed at reaching the poorest parts of Mexican society. Thus far, economic development in Mexico has greatly favored the wealthy. When we couple this with the effects of pervasive corruption, inefficient industry, and the expectation on the part of local businessmen of far higher profits than are customary in the United States, the prospects of rapid economic improvement appear remote. It seems likely that millions of Mexicans will continue to be confronted by the unhappy choice of living in poverty in their own country or attempting to cross the border into the United States, with all of the risks that entails.

(2)

Weapons of war and war itself have resulted in powerful interactions between rich and poor nations. In September 1950 a United Nations armed force, consisting largely of United States military personnel, went to war against North Korea, and in November of that year the People's Republic of China entered the same war on the side of North Korea when they thought their own border gravely threatened. That war did not end until 1953. In the late 1950s the United States sent military advisors and equipment to Vietnam. In time the involvement escalated and by 1965 U.S. combat troops were involved in a full-scale war against North Vietnam which lasted until 1973. For many years the United States sent military equipment to Taiwan and stationed troops there in direct confrontation with the armed forces of the People's Republic of China.

In 1956 England and France undertook military operations in the Sinai, seeking a cease-fire between Egypt and Israel and control of the Suez Canal. In 1958 the United States sent troops to Lebanon to protect it from pro-Nasser forces and Britain airlifted troops to Jordan. In 1961 there was the Bay of Pigs incident in Cuba followed in 1962 by the Cuban missile crisis. In 1965 the United States sent troops to the Dominican Republic.

Since World War II both the Soviet Union and the United States have given freely of military equipment, training, and advice to numerous developing countries and factions within those countries as it suited their political purposes. The list of recipients is a very long one, covering most of the countries of Asia, Africa, and Latin America. A number of these were involved in violence in the form of coups, civil wars, and wars with other nations. Sometimes the Soviet Union and the United States would trade positions; one would begin providing equipment, training, and advice once the other had stopped.

A major confrontation which may well erupt again has been that between Israel and the Arab world where the military equipment used has been substantially of U.S. and Soviet origin. In a sense this is a confrontation between an advanced industrial society (Israeli technology is basically advanced European-American) and developing countries. As the arms inventories of the Middle Eastern adversaries have grown in quantity and sophistication, the military encounters have become more costly. Further, the massive transfers of conventional arms have led to the emergence of large, effective military establishments. In their respective nations these have strong voices which speak for increasing their relative military might.

It is now rather widely believed that Israel may possess somewhere between 5 and 20 nuclear weapons. Even if this is not true, it is sufficiently plausible to cause Egypt and Syria to believe that nuclear weapons are necessary for their national defense. Clearly, their motivation to acquire nuclear weapons is a strong one. In any event the Middle East might well emerge as the first nuclear battlefield.

For many years the United States and the Soviet Union have been the giants in the arms export business. In the period 1961–1975 the U.S. government sold military equipment worth $41 billion overseas. In the same period Soviet sales amounted to $27 billion. By comparison, the other major industrial countries sold relatively little. France, the United Kingdom, and West Germany together exported about $9 billion worth of armaments.

Over the years the flow of arms in international trade has increased exponentially. By 1976 total arms exports reached a record $100 billion, three-quarters of which went to developing countries. For many years major exports were confined to weapons which had been replaced by more sophisticated ones of a new generation. Now, however, the supplying nations are offering their clients their most technologically advanced weapons. Recent sales have included the Bell gunship helicopter, ordered by the shah of Iran, which can fire rockets and antitank missiles, the Hawker-Siddely "Hawk," the MIG–23 swing-wing interceptor aircraft, and the F–4 Phantom. The latter has the capability of delivering nuclear weapons. The United States has provided Israel with the Lance missile, which also has a nuclear capability.

During the last 10 years, the four major arms exporters have been primarily responsible for doubling the inventory of modern weapons in the developing countries. Included in the shipments were 17,000 tanks and self-propelled guns, 6000 combat aircraft, and 28,000 missiles.

In spite of the hopes of the original signers of the nuclear nonproliferation treaty (NPT), nuclear military technology spread to yet another developing country when India tested her first nuclear device. On May 18, 1974, India detonated a 15-kiloton nuclear explosive under the Rajasthan Desert of northwest India. Canada, which had provided the reactors which supplied the nuclear fuel for the Indian test, sharply criticized the test. There was only mild criticism from the United States. Nevertheless, studies suggested that at least seven additional countries either have or will soon have the technical capability of building nuclear weapons, including Argentina, Brazil, Egypt, Israel, Pakistan, South Africa, and Spain. None of these nations has signed the nonproliferation treaty.

In June 1974 the Nixon administration announced that it had offered to sell Egypt and Israel each a 600-megawatt reactor to produce electric power. Shortly thereafter France began negotiations to sell Pakistan a nuclear fuel reprocessing plant.

All of these developments are, to say the least, alarming. Were we to continue down this path for several more years the consequences could be disastrous.

By mid-1977, however, there was evidence that U.S. policy was changing markedly and that the Carter administration was taking a number of unilateral actions aimed at persuading other nations to modify their policies. By refusing to license the domestic reprocessing of spent fuel and by slowing the commercialization of the fast-breeder reactor, the administration hoped to help establish an international atmosphere which would discourage the proliferation of nuclear capabilities. Already by late May, for example, the French government was reconsidering its sale of a reprocessing plant to Pakistan.

On May 19, the administration announced new guidelines for arms exports. Among the restraints promised were that the volume of sales was to be reduced and that the United States would not be the first to introduce advanced weapons into an area.

The test of the effectiveness of these new unilateral policies will be in the reaction of other nations to them. Obviously, if the Soviet Union, France, and Germany continue as before, the new guidelines will have to be reconsidered. By the end of 1977 the guidelines had had little effect.

(3)

Trade with the industrial nations is an extremely crucial factor in the development prospects of the poor nations. There are many difficulties involved with the export of manufactured products, but many poor countries are endowed with renewable and nonrenewable resources which provide well over 80 percent of their export volume. Of these, crude oil is presently by far the most important export from developing countries, amounting to more than $130 billion annually, or about 60 percent of total exports. The exported crude oil originates for the most part in a group of 14 oil-rich developing nations which have banded together into the Organization of Petroleum Exporting Countries (OPEC).

The extraordinary situation in which the OPEC nations now find themselves was basically brought about by the fact that petroleum consumption in the industrial nations increased far more rapidly than production, with inadequate effort placed on the utilization of alternative energy supplies. As we have seen, a major reason for this development was price. Petroleum was so inexpensive that none of the industrial countries could afford *not* to use it.

Following the collective OPEC actions in 1973–1974, vastly increased sums of money flowed from rich countries to OPEC countries, and in particular to Arab countries (which have the most oil). In 1974 Saudi Arabia alone earned nearly $30 billion, corresponding to about $3500 for every inhabitant. About $80 billion flowed to the Arab states plus Iran, which collectively have a population of over 70 million persons.

Such large sums of money flowing to so few developing countries immediately raised numerous questions. What fraction of their new-found wealth could they spend effectively for development? How could they invest those funds which they could not spend quickly? How large would their military expenditures become? Could the vast sums of surplus money be recycled in such a way as to ease the balance-of-payments problems of the rich petroleum-importing countries? Above all, could the rich petroleum-importing countries find a way out of the trap in which they had permitted themselves to become ensnared?

The confrontation between OPEC and the industrialized nations raises the question of fairness of prices, not only of crude oil but of numerous other commodities as well. The combination of the low cost and convenience of oil led us into the energy trap. Yet why should crude oil cost so little? Should its cost be based simply upon its ease of extraction? In the days when the incremental extraction costs in the Middle East were 10¢ per barrel and the oil companies were charging $1.25 per barrel for Middle Eastern oil, the companies in effect declared that there need be little relationship between price and cost. Under these circumstances, why then was the world so shocked in 1973–1974 when the OPEC countries collectively and arbitrarily increased the price of crude oil by a factor of four?

In retrospect, the world was shocked because it was badly hurt economically by the action rather than because of any fundamental wrongdoing on OPEC's part—with the single qualification that the action was perhaps taken too suddenly. The principle of arbitrariness had already been established.

Not long after the OPEC action, the then secretary-general of the organization attended a private conference in New York. After some of the American participants had made a number of critical remarks about OPEC's action, the secretary-general asked an extremely important question. "How," he asked, "does one place a fair value on a resource which is under the ground, which is being extracted, and which will one day be gone, never to reappear?" Few persons in the room were prepared to give an answer, but most grasped the point that there was nothing magical, or for that matter even rational, about the pre-1973 price of crude oil.

Clearly, from the point of view of the consumer, the fairness of a price will be related in some way to the cost of doing business in the absence of the resource. If there were no crude oil available, hydrocarbon fuels would be obtained by conversion of oil shale or coal to synthetic fuels. If the price of crude oil were raised to a level greater than the cost of converting oil shale or coal, and if the price were predictably maintained, there is no question that conversion plants would be built in profusion in many parts of the world.

Of course, when the price of crude oil was raised so rapidly in 1973–1974 the consumer nations could not have taken any meaningful action for the simple reason that options other than accepting the increased prices (or perhaps engaging in military action) were simply not viable. A great deal of time is required to develop the necessary technology, to accumulate the needed (and substantial) capital, and to build the plants that are essential to achieve at least some semblance of energy independence.

Recognizing the effectiveness of the OPEC cartel, other developing nations have attempted to achieve the same levels of price jump for other minerals. This move has thus far not been very successful, for reasons which are understandable.

While developing nations have a virtual monopoly on exportable crude oil, the same cannot be said of other mineral commodities. When we examine those major metallic deposits which are essential for the smooth functioning of industrial societies, most exist abundantly in two or more industrial countries. Exceptions are cobalt, tin, nickel, and bauxite, in which developing countries occupy an important reserve position. While developing countries command nearly a 70 percent share of the world export market in fuels, their share of nonfuel mineral exports is less than 30 percent.

A second difference between metallic deposits and crude oil is that an elevation in price of a given metal usually opens up new reserves of lower-grade ores. Thus, although an embargo on the shipment of copper from Chile, Zambia, Peru, and Zaire to the United States would prove inconvenient, in time the needs could be met by processing local ores. The same would apply to other critical metals including iron, lead, zinc, tungsten, and molybdenum.

A third major consideration is that metals can be recycled, whereas fuels cannot. The efficiency of the recycling depends upon the price of the metal, but in principle it can be quite high.

Last, the impact upon the world economy of a sudden change in the price of metallic ores would be far less than that of a corresponding increase in the price of crude oil. The reasons for this are twofold: first, energy values far outstrip the values of metals, as illustrated by the fact that in 1975 U.S. fuel production was valued at ten times the value of all metals produced; second, relatively little processing is required to transform a barrel of crude oil into a product ready for use, such as gasoline. By contrast, the road from a metallic ore to an ingot of metal is a long and expensive one, with the result that a major increase in ore prices might result in but modest increases in the prices of ingots (on a percentage basis).

When we also consider the fact that the industrial countries themselves, and particularly the United States, Canada, Australia, South Africa, and the Soviet Union, dominate minerals production, we appreciate the relatively small leverage that the developing countries can exert on the prices of their minerals exports. At the same time we should not underemphasize the fact that many industrial countries are virtually completely dependent upon imports of certain metals. The United States, for example, imports 99 percent of its cobalt, 98 percent of its manganese, and 90 percent of its chromium. Japan and Eastern Europe are considerably more dependent upon imported metals than is the United States.

In a sense, trade in minerals is now more important for the developing countries than it is for the industrial ones. In most minerals-exporting developing countries, foreign exchange, government revenues, and employment are highly dependent upon exports. The governments themselves understandably want a reasonably high degree of predictability in the demand and the prices for their exports. That this situation is far from being realized is illustrated by the huge fluctuations in the average prices of major mineral exports from developing countries during the period 1950–1975. In the period 1963–1966, for example, prices rose about 50 percent. By 1972 they had fallen well below the 1963 level. By 1975 they had risen again by 40 percent. Under such circumstances, the exporting countries are in no position to plan meaningful programs for development. Often they are unable to maintain stable governments.

From many points of view, exports of agricultural commodities to industrial nations are more important than exports of nonfuel minerals. At present the monetary value of agricultural exports is considerably greater than that of nonfuel minerals. In addition, exports of commodities such as coffee and sugar can continue into the indefinite future. Ore deposits of copper, iron, and bauxite have finite lifetimes. But the problem of stability of price and demand for agricultural products is fully as critical as for minerals. Depending upon weather and the ravages of disease, the availability of exportable commodities goes through cycles of glut and scarcity and the prices fluctuate correspondingly.

The most important single agricultural export of developing countries is sugar produced from cane. Sugar can also be produced in the more temperate industrial countries from sugar beets, but the cost of producing sugar in the tropics is considerably less. The other important agricultural exports, however, such as coffee, tea, cocoa, and natural rubber, can only be produced in the tropics, so the developing countries do have an important monopoly. Further, the developing countries have the opportunity of expanding their agricultural exports in a number of directions, to include soybeans, off-season vegetables, tropical fruits, and cut flowers.

The developing countries are also substantial importers of agricultural products from the industrial countries, particularly the United States, Canada, and Australia. On the average, about a third of the cereals exported by the rich countries is purchased by developing countries, making up somewhat over 5 percent of their total demand. This, of course, varies markedly from year to year, depending upon weather, balance of payments, and terms of trade. At one time during the days of farm surpluses, the United States transferred large quantities of food to needy countries under concessional terms, but demands from Europe and Japan have grown to such an extent that the days of large surpluses appear to be over. This means that unless an effective international mechanism for stockpiling is created, the poorest countries will have great difficulty obtaining needed food in emergencies.

Fisheries represent an important, sometimes explosive area of interaction between rich countries and poor countries. Several rich countries, notably the U.S.S.R., Japan, and the United States, have highly sophisticated fishing technologies. From time to time their fishing boats have wandered into productive fishing grounds which developing countries, for example Peru and Ecuador, have viewed as theirs. Now that the 200-mile territorial limit for fishing has been generally recognized, this problem will be less serious.

The utilization of the resources of the open ocean, however, will present problems for the future. There is as yet no international agreement concerning the right to exploit the minerals on the sea floor. The rich countries, which have the technological capability of exploiting the sea bed, take the view that the minerals should belong to the harvester. The poor countries, which do not possess the technology, maintain that the minerals belong to all mankind and, therefore, that those who harvest should pay for the privilege of doing so. The same reasoning would apply to Antarctica should that continent's resources be exploited.

Exports of manufactured products from the poor countries to the rich ones are increasing. The extent to which this can be successful depends upon available skills and wage scales. For the most part the exported products have high labor inputs such as shoes, clothing, and certain types of electronic equipment. As labor costs have moved upward in Japan, Europe, and the United States, companies which are based in the rich countries have created subsidiaries in developing countries to produce component parts of television sets, computers, calculators, and radios. As microcircuits come into more widespread use, the demand for inexpensive, intelligent, careful, and patient workers, particularly women, is increasing very rapidly. Such work is now spreading from Taiwan and Korea (the present strongholds) southward and westward to other parts of Asia.

Again, trade barriers will probably continue to impede the flow of manufactured goods from the poor countries for a long time in the future. The importation of shoes from Brazil and Taiwan and clothing from Korea and Hong Kong results in the loss of a certain number of jobs in the rich countries and in certain financial hardships for local manufacturers. But such difficulties must be balanced against those which may arise in the absence of more rapid economic development of the poor countries.

(4)

After exports, the most important external influence on development has been economic assistance in the form of grants and loans. This has taken the form of official bilateral assistance from more affluent countries, assistance from multilateral agencies such as the World Bank, grants from private voluntary organizations, and loans at market rates made by private lending institutions.

At the present time three major groups of countries are involved in giving economic assistance. In terms of the amount of money involved, the most important is a group of 17 market-economy industrial nations, including the United States, all of which make grants and loans either bilaterally or through multilateral agencies. The group calls itself the Development Assistance Committee (DAC). The second group is composed of the wealthier OPEC countries (excluding Ecuador, Gabon, and Indonesia, which receive rather than give economic aid). The third group consists of the centrally planned economies, particularly the U.S.S.R., the nations of Eastern Europe, and the People's Republic of China. The total flows of resources to developing countries from these various sources are shown in Table 5.1.

Almost three-quarters of DAC official development assistance is handled bilaterally, with the balance passed through multinational institutions, nota-

TABLE 5.1

Net Flow of Resources to Developing Countries, 1975

SOURCE	AMOUNT ($ BILLIONS)	
DAC		
Official flows	16.61	
Private (at market terms)	21.96	
Grants by private		
voluntary agencies	1.34	
DAC Total		39.91
OPEC		5.97
Planned economies		0.88
Grand Total Net Flow		46.76

bly the World Bank Group, regional institutions such as the Asian Development Bank, and the United Nations. The pattern of bilateral aid tends to shift from year to year as political and economic relationships between individual and developing countries change.

Official contributions by DAC countries for economic assistance efforts vary considerably. Although the United States is still the largest single contributor, during the decade 1965–1975 its proportional contribution decreased steadily. During that period U.S. official development assistance increased from $3.4 billion to $4.0 billion. In contrast, the contributions of other DAC countries increased nearly fourfold, from $2.5 billion to $9.6 billion. During the same period the GNP of the United States increased substantially, with the result that the official U.S. contributions expressed as a percentage of GNP dropped from 0.49 percent to 0.27 percent. The average proportions of GNP spent by other DAC countries is now considerably higher than that of the U.S., amounting to somewhat more than 0.40 percent. Compared with ability to pay and the magnitude of the problem, these are indeed very small sums. Yet at the moment there seems to be little prospect that the contributions corrected for inflation will be increased appreciably in the next few years. Expressed in terms of the GNP, the contributions will probably continue to decrease.

Assistance is also provided through grants from private voluntary agencies such as foundations and charitable organizations supported by public contributions. In 1975 this amounted to $1.34 billion, almost entirely in the form of grants.

To all of this we must add the huge sum of $21.96 billion which in 1975 flowed from DAC countries to developing countries in the form of private export credits, direct investment, and loans. Almost all of this went to the middle-income developing countries; the share of the poorest countries was less than 6 percent. Most of this very large private capital flow to the middle-income developing countries came through commercial banks, much of it as relatively short-term loans. As we have seen, much of the money consists of oil dollars which were deposited in Western banks by OPEC countries. If for any reason the default rate should be appreciable, many of the large banks in DAC countries will be in serious trouble. It is not difficult to visualize one or more causes of default coming into play—poor performance of the local economy, falling exports, rising costs of energy, bad crop years, revolution, war, or a general worsening of the world economy. If the banks find themselves in deep trouble, the same will be true for the DAC nations.

Some two-thirds of OPEC bilateral assistance commitments is directed to the non-oil-producing members of the Arab League. Of these, Egypt receives the largest share of both concessional and nonconcessional aid, amounting to about one-quarter of all concessional and two-thirds of all nonconcessional commitments. Beyond that, substantial concessional commitments have been made to India and Pakistan to help them pay for their crude oil. It is noteworthy that the total net disbursements made by OPEC nations for assistance in 1975 amounted to 1.58 percent of their combined GNPs. This was considerably higher than the percentage of GNP spent on assistance that year by any industrial nation.

The aid expenditures of the communist nations have been very small. Communist economic aid is characterized by concentration on the public sector and tying credits to goods manufactured in the donor countries. By far the largest part of communist aid goes to other communist countries.

(5)

Since World War II, rich and poor nations have interacted with each other increasingly as a result of the spread of the global electronics communication network and the ease of travel made possible by the jet passenger plane. The interactions have positive value in that people from rich and poor countries get to know each other's cultures better and there is opportunity for better understanding. But the interactions often have negative effects as well, which may lead to hostilities.

Early in this century most people who lived in poor countries were only vaguely aware that there were rich countries. Their interactions with the cultures of industrial societies, even under colonialism, were rare and seldom more than superficial. Today, by contrast, the most remote shepherd boy in the high Andes is likely to have a transistor radio tuned to a station playing rock music. City dwellers watch television and visit motion-picture theaters to see films made in Europe or the United States. The European, American, or Japanese tourist or businessman is now a common sight in most developing countries, particularly in the cities, but even villagers see them from time to time.

Tourists and visitors on business generally stay in quarters where they can sleep, eat, and partake of luxuries, much as they would at home. Here they encounter numerous waiters, maids, houseboys, porters, drivers, and other service personnel who receive relatively little for their services. One cannot help but wonder what a waiter thinks while serving a table where the host spends more in one evening than the waiter receives in one month. It is understandable that the contrast leads to dismay and unhappiness and that petty thievery becomes a way of life in areas frequented by affluent visitors. But even more important, the local people receive a distorted impression of the cultures of the industrial countries.

Another major difficulty stems from the fact that the developing countries, most of which are totalitarian, impede the free flow of information. In many of these countries, hostility toward the Western media has grown to substantial proportions and barriers have been erected against the legitimate process of collecting and reporting the news. Indeed, a few African, Asian, and Arab states have gone even farther than the Soviet Union to isolate their societies from outside scrutiny. The impediments range from restrictions on travel to harassment and threats of expulsion.

This trend toward permitting little or no information beyond that supplied by the government unfortunately comes at a time when the Western industrial societies are reevaluating their relationships with the developing world in the light of the energy crisis, the food problem, and the general world economic situation. It seems highly unlikely that a new international economic system will be created in the absence of a reasonably free flow of information.

On the positive side, each year tens of thousands of students from developing countries enroll in universities in America and Europe. In the United States alone there are close to 100,000 such students, working for degrees in engineering, agriculture, medicine, and the natural and social sciences. There are also many professors from universities in developing countries who spend a year or more engaging in teaching and research in American and European institutions. Although the flow of students and faculty in the opposite direction is by no means as large, increasing numbers of students from industrial countries are enrolled in universities in developing countries. Similarly, increasing numbers of faculty from U.S., European, and Japanese institutions are teaching and doing research in Asia, Africa, and Latin America.

This flow of students and scholars between the rich and the poor countries is paid for by a variety of sources including governments, private foundations, receiving institutions, and often by the students and scholars themselves. The experience gained thus far suggests that whatever the source of funding—be it the Fulbright-Hayes program or a scholarship from a private university—the money is well spent, for the students and scholars live in the host country and learn about the culture which surrounds them, including the language.

Sometimes students from developing countries who work for advanced degrees in Europe or the United States suffer when they return home. They may find that they cannot engage in the kind of sophisticated research to which they had become accustomed. The equipment is too expensive, or there are no openings in an appropriate university department. Such situations are indeed unfortunate and they sometimes lead to emigration or "brain drain," in which case the young person does not contribute to the development of his or her country.

Even so, the advantages are marked. The flow of students and scholars is one of the very best mechanisms for the transfer of technology. Students and faculty who come to the industrial countries learn about certain new technologies in depth. If their programs have been planned properly, at least a portion of what they have learned will have applicability to the solution of problems in their own country. Similarly, American, Japanese, and European research workers can accomplish a great deal in developing countries by helping to build new institutions and training young people to undertake research aimed at solving local problems. The examples which have been set at the International Maize and Wheat Improvement Center in Mexico and the International Rice Research Institute in the Philippines are outstanding.

We should not conclude a discussion of the interactions between poor and rich countries without raising the question of the large multinational corporations which increasingly are becoming principal agents in the international transfer of capital, manufactured products, information, and technology. Often they are more powerful than nations and are frequently unrestrained by governments. Most such corporations were born in the rich countries, but now most have extensive operations through subsidiaries in developing countries as well. Because they can mobilize and control vast resources, their power to influence national and international affairs is substantial. The recent involvement of International Telephone and Telegraph in U.S. domestic politics, as well as in the internal politics of Chile, is a case in point.

For the developing countries, the involvement of multinational corporations in their economies can be disturbing. Often the corporations become important channels for new consumption patterns which can affect the future of the economy. In some cases the transfer of technology through the corporation hinders the development of indigenous technology. Corporations also contribute to the displacement of local entrepreneurs.

In any event, for right reasons or wrong, multinational corporations have become a major source of tension between rich and poor nations. The solution to this problem, if there is one, is by no means obvious.

(6)

Much of the current tension between the rich and the poor countries stems from the rich countries' continuing dominance of production, investment, and trade. The developing countries want to be more fully involved in international economic decision making. That is why they are demanding a "new international economic order." Those demands were obviously triggered by the success of the OPEC nations in raising and then completely controlling the price of crude oil. Clearly, the OPEC nations now have a major influence on international decisions. Other developing countries would like to influence future policies as well.

In asking for a new international economic order, the developing nations are not asking for a massive redistribution of wealth. Rather they are asking that an attempt be made, through collective bargaining, to arrive at certain understandings which can have major impact upon their future growth opportunities.

The developing countries would first like agreements involving their trade position. We have seen that the exports of about a dozen major commodities, excluding oil, account for about 80 percent of their export earnings. They would like to receive a higher proportion of the consumer price for those commodities. They would also like to establish a mechanism which would eliminate the large and sometimes disastrous price fluctuations which have plagued them for so long. Beyond commodities, they would like to see major relaxation of the present restrictions against importation of their manufactured products by the industrial countries, thus increasing the present share of the developing countries in the export of manufactured goods.

Second, the developing countries would like to see a system of economic and technical assistance created which is more binding upon the donor nations than the present voluntary system, and less susceptible to fluctuations in political goodwill. They would like to see the level of official development assistance increased considerably above present levels, and they would like some relief from their current indebtedness servicing which takes away about half of their new assistance each year.

Last, the developing countries would like the International Monetary Fund to create a new and truly international currency which would be regulated by the IMF in such a way as to facilitate growth of production and exports in developing countries. To accomplish this they would like a near-equal vote with the rich countries in the IMF.

Following upon these requests made by the developing nations, a Conference on International Economic Cooperation was held in the spring of 1977 between 16 industrial and 19 developing nations. The industrial nations offered a package which included a $1-billion special fund to help the poorest nations meet their bill for oil, other imports, and interest, as well as an agreement to set up a common fund that would stabilize certain commodity prices. They also pledged to step up assistance for the development of agriculture and to increase the financial resources of the International Monetary Fund and the World Bank in order to help poor nations meet their large balance of payments deficits.

In return, the industrial nations requested guaranteed access to oil and other raw materials, protection against arbitrary nationalization of foreign investments, as well as a continuing forum for the discussion of global energy problems.

The developing nations present did not agree with these latter requests and emphasized again the major components of the "new international economic order" as they envisioned it. Specifically, they repeated their request for debt relief and they refused to offer safeguards against nationalization of foreign investments. In addition, the delegates from the OPEC nations rejected the proposal for continuing energy discussions.

There are of course many other points of contention on which both the industrialized and developing countries would like to have agreement, but these are the major ones. Clearly, if such problems are to be resolved in the foreseeable future, unprecedented political goodwill and vision will be required.

CHAPTER VI

Food

(1)

Throughout the course of history the search for adequate and reasonably predictable supplies of food has been a dominant force. The invention of agriculture made civilization possible and its elaboration permitted civilization to spread. Today, relatively few people in industrial societies are employed in agriculture, yet the food continues to flow in seemingly limitless quantities. People in those societies are for the most part no longer concerned about where their next meal is coming from. Not having this concern, they tend to forget that civilization has been built upon agricultural foundations and that it is as dependent today upon the smooth functioning of its food system as it ever was. Should that system be seriously disrupted, industrial civilization would crumble. The people in the rich countries also tend to forget that although their supplies of food are plentiful, in the two-thirds of the world which is poor, perhaps as many as a billion persons are seriously malnourished.

We have seen that along with the fissioning process which divided the world into two cultures, the rich and the poor, there was a parallel division into two kinds of diet. The diets of both cultures are based upon cereals such as rice, wheat, and corn. In the poor countries, people usually eat these cereals directly. In the affluent countries, by contrast, where people eat large amounts of meat and other animal products, large quantities of cereals are fed to animals, which dissipate most of the food energy in the process of staying alive and ultimately return only a small fraction of the original energy to the consumer in the form of meat, milk, or eggs. In the industrial countries, for example, more than twice as much grain is fed to domestic animals as is fed directly to people. In the poor countries, people eat ten times as much cereal as do domestic animals. The average person cannot afford the luxury of eating more than small quantities of animal products.

The demand for primary foods such as cereals, then, is determined by two major factors: population and affluence. For a given level of affluence, the demand for cereals will grow in proportion to the population. As per capita income grows, demands for cereals will also increase, up to the point where people do not care for a still richer diet. In the poor countries today, per capita cereal consumption amounts to about 225 kilograms per year, while in the rich countries it amounts to about 600 kilograms per year. Directly and indirectly, the average American consumes somewhat over 700 kilograms of cereal each year, an amount that has remained fairly constant since World War

TABLE 6.1

Projected Worldwide Demands for Cereals

YEAR	DEMAND (MILLIONS OF METRIC TONS)
1970	1200
1980	1540
1985	1730
1990	1900
Eventual a)	2500
Eventual b)	7000

Eventual a) 10 billion persons living at consumption levels now characteristic of developing countries.

Eventual b) 10 billion persons living at present U.S. level of consumption.

SOURCE: For projections to 1990: John W. Sewell and the staff of the Overseas Development Council, *The United States and World Development: Agenda 1977*. Published for the Council by Praeger Publishers, 1977.

II and is not likely to increase very much in the future. Indeed, per capita consumption in the U.S. might actually decrease somewhat in response to recent findings that consumption of large quantities of animal products may cause health problems.

The total world grain consumption in 1970 was about 1200 million tons. Using present trends for the growth of personal income and U.N. population projections, total cereal demand in 1990 will amount to about 1900 million tons, as shown in Table 6.1. Estimates of ultimate demand will depend upon our assumptions concerning population and affluence. A world of 10 billion persons living for the most part as people now live in the developing countries, would require about 2500 million tons, or double the 1970 level of production. Were the same 10 billion people to live at the present American level of consumption, the demand would be 7000 million tons, or nearly six times the total worldwide production of grains in 1970. We must ask whether it is possible to produce such greatly expanded quantities of food. We must also ask what the costs of such expanded levels of food production are likely to be.

In what areas of the world can food production be increased most effectively? At the present time less than 10 percent of the total world cereal crop flows in international trade, and as we have seen it will be a very long time before developing countries can afford to purchase more than a small fraction of their food requirements. In general, food must be grown where the demand is. The exceptions are rich countries such as Japan and the countries of Western Europe, the oil-rich Arab states, and certain developing areas, such as Singapore, Hong Kong, and Taiwan, which are closely tied in with the world economy through manufacturing.

(2)

Prior to World War II, the major industrialized nations of the world were able to grow sufficient basic foodstuffs to satisfy most of their needs at the levels of individual consumption which existed at the time. But since then the situation has changed dramatically, in large measure because of the explosion of agricultural productivity in North America which has taken place since the turn of this century.

As we have seen, the explosion stemmed partly from the fact that the internal combustion engine could accomplish more work, faster, and cheaper than physical labor. Another factor was the intensive application of science and technology to improve efficiency in transforming cereals into animal products. Yet another factor was the greatly increased agricultural production per hectare.

The tremendous increases in crop yields in the U.S. have depended in part upon very large inputs of energy from fossil fuels. A recent analysis of the energy inputs to corn production indicates that while in 1945 about 0.25 calories of fossil fuel energy were utilized for every edible calorie of corn grown, by 1970 this ratio had grown to 0.35 fossil fuel calories per corn calorie. In 1970 gasoline, together with the energy required to make nitrogenous fertilizers, accounted for 60 percent of the fossil fuel energy input to corn production. In relation to other U.S. energy expenditures, the energy inputs to the agricultural sector are not large. Somewhere between 3 and 4 percent of the total U.S. energy budget is used directly and indirectly on farms.

As the demands for cereals created by growing affluence in Western Europe and Japan outstripped production, these areas became substantial grain importers, primarily from North America where about 85 percent of the production is concentrated in the United States. The exports of Australia are only about 6 percent of North America's.

The external demands placed upon North American cereal production fluctuate from year to year and depend not only upon the harvests in the importing countries but also upon the financial terms agreed to by exporters and importers. Most major regions of the world are now net importers of cereals.

In addition to the twin pressures of growing affluence and population, plant diseases and adverse weather conditions have taken their toll in crop yields in various parts of the world. As a result, the United States, which had long suffered from crop surpluses, started to bring its idle acres back into production in the late 1960s. By 1974 no government payments were made for keeping cropland idle. As reserves decreased and demands increased, food prices soared. The increases in price were accelerated in 1973–1974 by the rapid increases in the price of crude oil, which seriously limited the ability of many poor countries to buy needed food. At the same time, food aid to the poor countries was drastically curtailed.

In certain of the poor countries, such as India, which are dependent upon petroleum imports, the sudden increase of petroleum prices effectively disrupted the "Green Revolution," which basically involves cultivation of plant varieties which can benefit from large applications of chemical fertilizers and water. India must import petroleum to manufacture fertilizers and run her water pumps. Because her nitrogen-fixation capacity is inadequate, she must also import fertilizers, primarily from Japan. Her food production is inadequate so she must also import cereals. All of this places enormous strains upon her balance of payments.

Here it is important to emphasize that the "Green Revolution," which involves the use of genetically selected high-yielding varieties of cereal plants, is highly dependent upon energy inputs, primarily in the form of fertilizers, other agricultural chemicals, and irrigation. Were all of the land now being cultivated in India devoted to the new high-yielding varieties of wheat and rice, retaining at the same time labor-intensive methods of cultivation, the total national energy budget would be increased by about 25 percent for fertilizers alone. Considering the large amount of irrigation which would be necessary, a doubling of the national energy budget would not be an unreasonable requirement. But where would this energy be obtained if not from imported petroleum? And how would India be expected to pay for that energy?

Thus, food is like petroleum in that many nations—both rich and poor—have permitted themselves to become dependent upon imports. As with pe-

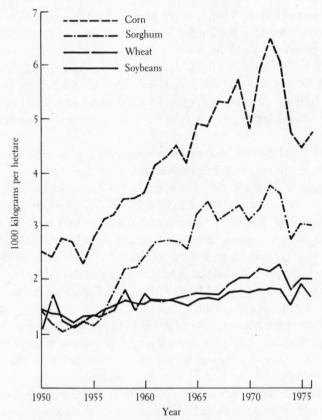

FIG. 6.1. Yield Trends for Major U.S. Crops, 1950–1976
SOURCE: U.S. Department of Agriculture, Economic Research Service.

troleum, food exports are now controlled by a relatively few countries. In both cases the importing countries are extremely vulnerable to the decisions of the exporters. And of all nations, the poor ones are the most vulnerable to major perturbations in the system.

(3)

Following World War II, U.S. farmers achieved spectacular increases in agricultural yields per hectare (see Figure 6.1). Much of the gain was due to large increases in the use of fertilizers and pesticides, irrigation systems, and improved equipment. As the yields increased, the prices of cereals fell steadily, and fluctuations were mainly the result of weather or blight (see Figure 6.2).

Crop surpluses led to the buildup of reserves and to the expansion of payments made to farmers to keep some of their land idle.

In 1954, Congress passed a remarkable measure known as Public Law 480, which made it "the policy of the United States to use abundant productivity to combat hunger and malnutrition and to encourage economic development in the developing countries" through concessional sales and humanitarian grants. Under Title I of this act, food was sold for dollars or local currencies under long-term loans, with interest rates set below commercial levels. Under Title II, food was provided on a grant basis to governments, voluntary agencies, and the United Nations Food Program.

In the 1960s huge shipments of food were sent overseas under these two titles, but by 1970 the volume of shipments was falling rapidly. In part this was due to the fact that the U.S. had accumulated very large holdings of unneeded nonconvertible currencies and decided to make concessional sales only for dollars. But the fall-off was also the result of rapidly increasing commercial exports. By the early 1970s reserves were falling and idled land was being put back into production. What had been a buyer's market had become a seller's market.

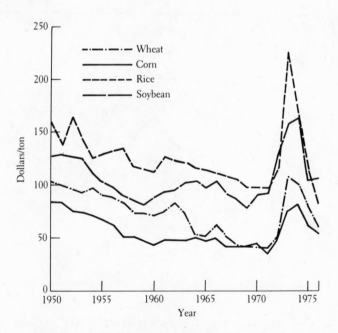

Fig. 6.2. U.S. Farm-level Prices in Constant U.S. Dollars, 1950–1976.
SOURCE: U.S. Department of Agriculture, Economic Research Service.

In the summer of 1972 the Soviet Union quietly used commercial channels to buy a large share of U.S. exportable supplies of wheat before even the
American government had any inkling of what was happening. In the summer of 1973 the United States declared an embargo on the export of soybeans
in an attempt to curb soaring soybean and food prices at home. As can be seen
in Figure 6.2, the prices of all major cereals soared in 1973. These dramatic
price increases were followed by the rapid rises in crude oil prices in
1973–1974. By 1974 all idle U.S. cropland had been put back into production and world reserve stocks of grains had dropped to 108 million tons (see
Figure 6.3). By 1976 world reserves had fallen to 100 million tons. In that
same year U.S. commercial agricultural exports were valued at $21 billion,
with shipments to needy countries under Public Law 480 amounting to only 4
percent of total exports.

In 1976, largely because of increased imports of petroleum, the United
States had the second largest trade deficit in its history, amounting to $5.9
billion. A record $32 billion was paid for oil imports that year, from which we
can appreciate how important agricultural exports have become for the U.S.
economy. In 1976 they accounted for nearly 20 percent of the value of all ex-

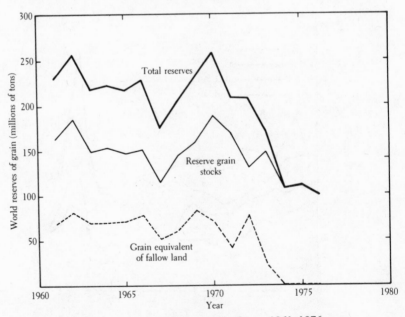

FIG 6.3. WORLD RESERVES OF GRAIN 1961–1976
SOURCE: John W. Sewell and the staff of the Overseas Development Council, *The United
States and World Development: Agenda 1977.* Published for the Council by Praeger
Publishers, 1977.

ports. In their absence the U.S. balance-of-payments deficit would have been much higher.

North American exports of grain decreased in the 1976–1977 crop year and by the summer of 1977 wheat prices at the farm were running at about $2 a bushel compared with the record $5.52 a bushel in February 1974. These changes came about in part because the harvests in the major consuming areas of the world were good. Obviously, such price instability creates uncertainty for both producers and consumers. In the absence of more effective national and worldwide mechanisms for stabilizing prices, the situation is bound to remain chaotic. At the very least, more effective stockpiling procedures are needed to smooth over fluctuations in production as well as fluctuations in outside demand.

It seems clear that for some time in the future demands for U.S. agricultural products will increase. To what extent can increased demands be met without causing domestic shortages and increased food prices?

Unfortunately, there are several danger signals which indicate that there may be trouble ahead. Most important, after many years of increasing yields, since about 1965 we have been going through a period of apparent leveling of yields for major crops (see Figure 6.1). The precise reasons for this leveling are not understood, but possible contributing factors include the cultivation of marginal soils and the greater variability of weather. The possibility exists, however, that the major cause is the lack of continued research advancement. Perhaps we are at the point where we have fully exploited what we already know and our rate of discovery of useful new approaches has fallen off. Whatever the cause or causes, the leveling of yield is a matter of grave concern and portends higher food prices in the future.

Second is the problem of increasing energy costs. We have seen that the success of U.S. agriculture depends upon high energy inputs in the form of fuel, fertilizers, and other agricultural chemicals. In the years ahead, energy costs will certainly reach much higher levels than they are today.

A third problem is our loss of considerable good agricultural land because of wind and water erosion and the salinization of irrigated land. In addition, much good land has been lost through the construction of highways and the spread of cities. This is an irreversible process.

A fourth problem is weather and changing climate. When we look back into history there is some evidence that North American weather has in general been unusually favorable for agriculture during the half-century 1920–1970. There are indications that we are now returning to a period of high weather variability, witness the extreme weather situations which developed in 1977.

A fifth problem is that heavy uses of fertilizers, pesticides, and other agricultural chemicals can cause health and other environmental problems. Restraints imposed upon the use of certain chemicals may increase production costs and result in greater variability of output.

Thus, unless new research and new policies enable us to overcome these adverse effects, the differences between our "good" years and our "bad" years will be much greater than in the past. Outside demands are also likely to fluctuate more widely, and there will be those inevitable years when outside demand is unusually high and U.S. production is unusually low. When we couple this with the virtual certainty that petroleum imports will continue to rise, thus increasing still further the importance of agricultural exports, the prospects for the American consumer are not promising. Furthermore, under these circumstances there would be little chance that food aid to the poorest countries would be resumed on any substantial scale, even for short periods in cases of grave emergency.

(4)

When nations become relatively rich they often find that it costs them less to import a basic foodstuff than to grow it themselves. This has happened many times in history. The ancient Greeks specialized in the cultivation of the grape and the olive, the products of which were traded for grain. Later they exported manufactured goods in order to augment further the food supplies that were needed for the growing population. The large landholders of ancient Rome, like those of Greece before them, specialized increasingly in cultivating the grape and the olive, with the result that grain growing declined and importation of food became essential. In Great Britain, although foodstuffs were imported, the island was basically self-sufficient nutritionally until 1875. About that time the cost of food imported from North America became less than that produced at home. Local agriculture declined and from that time on the British became largely dependent upon food imports for their survival.

Since World War II, Japan and Western Europe have become substantial net importers of food, in part because of growing affluence. In 1976–1977 Western Europe imported about 35 million tons of grain and Japan imported about 17 million tons, primarily from North America.

Japan's situation, a particularly critical one, nevertheless follows the age-old pattern. For a long period preceding 1870 the population of Japan remained fairly stable, as did food production, which was predominantly rice.

Beginning in the 1870s the total rice crop of Japan started to increase slowly but regularly, primarily because of increased yields which were obtained by more widespread use of fertilizers and by the application of genetics to the production of higher-yielding varieties. The crop more than doubled over a period of about 50 to 60 years. This increase in Japanese agricultural productivity was closely paralleled by a similar increase in Western Europe. In both cases agricultural production increased by roughly 2 percent per year, for about 50 to 60 years.

Following World War II, Japan and Europe rapidly became more affluent. People began to consume increasing quantities of animal products so feedgrains were imported in increasing quantities. Japanese preferences moved away from rice to bread made from wheat; therefore, per capita rice consumption declined and wheat imports increased.

In the 1960s the Japanese embarked upon a deliberate program to curtail domestic production of wheat and soybeans. The main reason was that they could purchase all they needed of these commodities overseas at costs considerably less than what they could be produced for in Japan. In view of the lessening demand for rice, an effort was started to curtail rice production. Imports of soybeans, a staple in the Japanese diet, increased rapidly, with the United States being the primary source of supply. It is little wonder that the Japanese were severely shocked when the United States placed a temporary embargo upon soybean exports in July 1973.

As time passed, both Japan and Western Europe lost agricultural land through the process of urbanization, as well as construction of highways and airports. In Japan particularly, land speculation is big business. Few farmers hold onto their land because they like being farmers. Rather, they are waiting until they can sell their land to developers for a very high price.

As a result of these various policies, Japan has become the most vulnerable of the major rich nations to disruptions in food supplies. The Japanese are especially vulnerable to changes in U.S. policy with the result that they are now attempting to diversify their sources of supply. For example, among other actions they are encouraging Brazil to develop a substantial program of growing soybeans for export.

For the present, however, Japan is dependent upon the availability of food from a handful of rich countries. That dependence will increase in the years ahead as affluence increases still further. At the same time, as with soybeans in 1973, the availability of food, particularly from the United States, could change suddenly. We have seen how sensitive U.S. food production for export can be to a multiplicity of external and internal forces.

There are ways, of course, in which both Japan and Europe could extricate themselves from their growing dependence upon imported food. But the costs would be high, not only in economic terms but in social terms as well.

(5)

We have seen that most of the hungry people in the world live in the poor countries. We have also seen that there are many reasons for the prevalence of hunger in those areas, such as poverty and rapid population growth. The people in the poor countries clearly must come to grips with those problems, but they must also come to grips with the problem of producing more food. Fortunately, the poor countries offer considerable opportunity for increased agricultural productivity.

In the greater part of the developing world agricultural productivity is low in terms of both production per man-hour and production per acre. The effectiveness with which solar energy is transformed into food energy in wheat or rice, for example, is usually limited by the availability of plant nutrients such as nitrogen, phosphorous, potassium, and water. Yet adding such nutrients in quantity is usually either ineffective or deleterious because the plant itself has been empirically selected over generations as one best able to survive and grow in the local impoverished environment. More often than not, the plant is unable to cope with a substantial increase in the availability of nutrients.

An obvious approach to solving this problem is to breed varieties of plants which can thrive in the local environments and which can effectively utilize large quantities of nutrients. This has been a major objective of the Mexican wheat program operated by the Rockefeller Foundation and the government of Mexico for four decades and of the International Rice Research Institute in the Philippines, established in 1960. Promising varieties of plants which have been developed by those projects have been transplanted to local environments and further modified so they can grow effectively under the local conditions.

Once this task has been accomplished, sufficient seed must be produced to permit planting by farmers on a significant scale. Fertilizers must be produced on an adequate scale and distributed. Supplementary water supplies must often be provided, either from wells or irrigation canals. Pesticides must be produced and distributed.

The Rockefeller Foundation's team in Mexico succeeded in developing a dwarf wheat which responded well to the application of very large quantities of nitrogen fertilizer, gave very high yields of wheat per hectare, and grew well in a wide range of growing conditions. Given the necessary fertilizer and water, farmers in many developing countries could easily double the production of wheat on their land. The success with wheat in Mexico was followed by the development by the International Rice Research Institute of a high-yielding dwarf variety of rice which was easily capable of doubling rice yields in large parts of Asia.

Once the productivity and adaptability of these remarkable new varieties had been demonstrated, efforts were made to introduce them into the major wheat- and rice-producing countries of Asia. The rapidity with which use of the new seeds spread was unprecedented and led to significant improvements of agricultural production in Turkey, the Indian subcontinent, Sri Lanka, the Philippines, Indonesia, and Malaysia. Between 1965 and 1972 India more than doubled its wheat production, attained economic (but not nutritional) self-sufficiency in cereals, and was able to divert nearly 2 million tons of grain to help feed nearly 10 million Bengali refugees during the civil war in East Pakistan.

But the "Green Revolution" was accompanied by a variety of difficulties. It became apparent that the solution of one problem, that of low farm productivity, could trigger a chain reaction of new problems, all crying for solutions. To obtain higher crop yields one must construct factories, locate raw materials, provide sources of energy, build highways and trucks, railroads and trains. In other words, a significant elevation of crop yields necessitates a significant level of industrialization. In many countries it also necessitates markedly increased imports of crude oil, fertilizers, and other agricultural chemicals.

As output per man-hour increases, less farm labor is needed and many of the surplus workers migrate to the cities. As nutrition improves, infant and child mortality is lowered and the rate of population growth increases. The urban areas, unable to provide adequate numbers of jobs for the migrants, become inundated by vast slum areas and the local government finds itself unable to expand community services as rapidly as people move in. On the farm, increased production strains storage facilities and distribution systems.

The history of the "Green Revolution" in India after 1972, by which time very large increases of productivity had been achieved, is worthy of study. From 1972 onward, food production stopped increasing, as did the areas devoted to high-yielding varieties of wheat and rice. This was partly due to a drought in 1972, followed by the worldwide increases in energy and fertilizer prices in 1973–1974, and poor weather conditions in 1974. But a major share of responsibility must be assigned to governmental policies.

Farm prices of cereals were kept low in order to placate city dwellers. Fertilizer prices were permitted to rise to unreasonably high levels. At the same time farmers were not able to get credit on reasonable terms in order to buy fertilizers. And when they borrowed money they were at the mercy of the village moneylenders, who charged outrageous rates of interest.

Also, personal incentives have often been lacking, for many of the farmers are tenants. Since there has been no significant government effort to achieve land reform, most farmers have little to gain by planting the new seeds which require so many expensive investments.

Even development of seed multiplication farms was neglected. Expansion of the irrigation system was very slow, in spite of the fact that the new varieties of seeds require irrigation. In unirrigated areas, farmers have been reluctant to invest in fertilizers because of the great uncertainties of rainfall.

Thus, what gave promise of being a tremendous agricultural revolution was aborted, in large part because of the enormous complexity of the problem. Indeed, this one illustration emphasizes how inextricably entwined the problems of a society are—so much so that we must necessarily consider *systems* of problems rather than isolated problems.

The Indian experience teaches us that although enormous increases in agricultural productivity are possible in the developing world, they can be brought about only if governments take vigorous actions to bring about necessary social and economic reforms. The application of existing knowledge can lead to greatly increased food production, but the political will necessary to accomplish this must be substantial.

Finally, some of the new problems which are created may turn out to be as intractable as the old ones. If a poor nation becomes dependent upon imported energy for its expanded food production, is it really better off? Once a new agricultural system is brought into existence based upon new seeds, irrigation, and heavy applications of fertilizers and other agricultural chemicals, what new kinds of vulnerabilities will it face? How resilient will the new system be once it is seriously perturbed?

While it is true that food production in the poor countries can in principle be greatly increased, there is real doubt that our knowledge will enable us to solve problems as rapidly as they are created.

(6)

In spite of such difficulties as those encountered in India, between 1950 and 1975 food production in the developing countries as a whole expanded at the unprecedented rate of about 2.8 percent per year (see Figure 6.4). This expansion was actually faster than that in the industrial countries, but as a result of rapid population growth the food intake of the average person was not appreciably improved. Looking to the future, if there is to be improvement, the developing countries need to increase food production at an even faster pace—somewhere between 3 and 4 percent per year, taking into account population increases. Such a rate of increase will be difficult to achieve, but it is by no means impossible. Research on food production can give us the technological means for improving and stabilizing agricultural yields. We are probably still far away from the ultimate limits imposed by nature upon plant productivity.

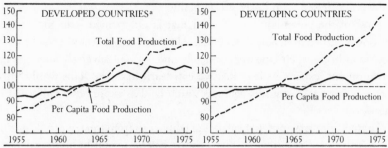

[a] United States, Canada, Europe, Japan, Australia, New Zealand, and South Africa.

FIG. 6.4. Indexes of Total Food Production and Per Capita Food Production in Developed and Developing Countries, 1955–1976.

SOURCE: Reprinted, with permission, from John W. Sewell and the staff of the Overseas Development Council, *The United States and World Development: Agenda 1977*. Published for the Council by Praeger Publishers, 1977. Data based on U.S. Agency for International Development estimates (Washington, D.C.), p. 183.

The possibility of utilizing the biological fixation of nitrogen is a case in point. As we have seen, the large increases in agricultural yields over the past 25 years, particularly in the rich countries, have resulted from the increased use of nitrogen fertilizers. These are manufactured for the most part from natural gas and petroleum, which are becoming increasingly expensive.

We know, however, that more than two-thirds of the nitrogen utilized by crops is fixed biologically by microorganisms which live in association with the plants. Nitrogen is fixed by blue-green algae living in rice paddies. Microorganisms living in symbiotic association with the roots of soybeans fix nitrogen which the plant then uses. It may turn out to be possible to induce a similar association between microorganisms and cereal grains such as wheat and corn. It may also turn out to be possible to transfer the genetic capability for nitrogen fixation directly from bacteria to plants.

Also, it may be possible to increase the efficiency with which plants fix energy through photosynthesis. Some experts believe that achievable increases in photosynthetic efficiency could result in a doubling of agricultural yields.

Improved pest management is still another area where large gains are possible. At the present time about one-half of the rice crop, which is the world's most important food, is lost to pests by the time it reaches the table.

Fluctuations in weather and climate cause the largest variations in food production. There is considerable room for improvement in estimating the effects of weather on crops and for forecasting weather and climate changes. Improved management practices for dealing with the effects of weather variability could lessen crop losses substantially.

Most of the potentially arable land that is not farmed is in the tropical regions of Africa and South America. Although we do not at present know how to cultivate such land economically and without adversely affecting the environment, experts believe that we can learn to do so. This would bring into use some three-fourths again as much land as is presently cultivated in the world.

There is little promise that catches of edible fish from the sea can be greatly increased, but it is estimated that existing catches could be more fully utilized, leading to a doubling of fish protein consumed directly by humans. Research on aquaculture could lead to even greater yields. There is reason to believe that the yield of pond fish in Southeast Asia could be increased fivefold to about three tons per hectare. Gains in production from selective fish breeding could amount to about 2 to 5 percent per year.

The pursuit of this new knowledge will not be easy. A large part of the research will have to be carried out in the developing countries, where the most serious shortages of resources for food and nutrition exist. But virtually all developing countries are far short of the scientific and technical resources they need. This means that if the job is to be done, a major collaborative effort will be required between the governments and scientists of the rich and the poor countries.

Political problems may well prevent the mounting of a global research effort of the necessary size.

CHAPTER VII

Energy

This is the most valuable raw material, it must be processed into other highly needed products, not limiting its use as fuel only. One may as well burn banknotes.
　　　　　　　　　　　　　—Dmitri Ivanovich Mendeleyev

(1)

Basically the problem of providing adequate resources for the perpetuation and expansion of industrial civilization is the problem of providing adequate quantities of energy of the right type at the right place at the right time. This is true no matter whether the resource be food, minerals, structural materials, clean air, land or energy itself.

It is often said that "It takes money to make money." Similarly, it takes energy to make energy. When our energy comes from petroleum, oil fields must be found, wells must be drilled, the oil must be pumped to the surface, then transported to the refinery where it is modified to suit the needs of the users. All of this requires energy, not only to drill, pump, and move the material, but to make the equipment, pipes, rails, trains, and cracking plants. Vast quantities of energy are required to mine and transport coal, to lay pipelines for gas, to construct and move oil tankers, to enrich isotopes and build nuclear reactors.

Today about a quarter of our energy consumption in the United States is accounted for in the mining, extraction, conversion, and transportation of fuels. As we move away from oil and natural gas toward oil shales, coal, and other more sophisticated energy sources, this proportion will naturally become larger. It is estimated that by the year 2000 more than a third of U.S. energy consumption will be for the production of energy.

As we have seen, the production of more food, no matter whether it be in the United States or India, necessitates the expenditure of more energy for the manufacture and distribution of fertilizers and pesticides and for the distribution of water for irrigation. Water itself is becoming energetically more expensive as we move it greater distances and find it increasingly necessary to remove pollutants. In some parts of the world we now obtain our water from the sea, and as this practice spreads, energy costs will increase still further.

With respect to minerals we find it necessary to dig ever deeper into the earth and to process ores of lower and lower grade. At one time in the United States we had very large deposits of high-grade iron ore. When our better grades were consumed, we moved to lower-grade ores such as taconites that require beneficiation and agglomeration to make them usable. Naturally, this requires increased expenditures of energy. An alternative is to import high-grade iron ore from other countries. This, too, results in higher energy costs, in this case for transportation.

When man first started to smelt copper he found very high-grade deposits of ore near the surface of the ground. As time passed and the easily accessible high-grade ore disappeared, he learned to process ores of lower grade and to dig more deeply into the ground. That process has continued to this day. As recently as 1900 the average grade of copper ore mined in the United States was 4.0 percent. By 1910 this had dropped below 2.0 percent, and during World War II it dropped below 1.0 percent. In 1970 the average grade was 0.60 percent and the vast open-pit copper mines were the largest holes ever to have been dug by man. Today in the United States ores containing concentrations of copper as low as 0.4 percent are being mined. The energy costs involved with moving and processing these vast quantities of materials are substantial.

How far downward in grade can we go and still obtain the metals and other substances neccessary for the continued functioning of our society? Here the answer is that *there is no limit, provided the necessary quantities of energy are available for undertaking the physical and chemical operations*. In practice, of course, there are limits to grade, below which we need not concern ourselves. Those limits are represented by the most extensive and yet the lowest-grade ore deposits on the surface of the earth: seawater and ordinary sedimentary and igneous rocks. In principle, a high level of civilization could be nourished for many millions of year by those substances. From them man could obtain all that he needs, including the energy itself. But the energy costs per capita of such a system would obviously be extremely high.

As grades of ore decrease, as other resources such as wood, water, and fertilizers become more costly and scarce, and as problems of pollution of air, water, and land become more acute, there will be increasing pressures to recycle the materials which flow through our agro-industrial network. Already we are recycling substantial quantities of iron, copper, and some other metals. In some cities paper is recycled or burned for energy. But in our society as a whole our recycling effectiveness is very low.

In the years ahead, if we behave sensibly, we will probably approach asymptotically the condition of complete recycling, where in effect we recognize that except for energy we live in a closed system. All organic wastes could be reclaimed for their water and for their chemical potential, whether it be for fertilizers, other useful chemical compounds, or energy. The metals from solid wastes could be recovered. Potentially dangerous pollutants could be isolated before they reach the atmosphere, lakes, and rivers.

All of these steps would increase substantially our energy expenditures. At the same time those increased expenditures could insure for all humanity a cleaner environment and a steady flow of the raw materials which are necessary for the smooth functioning of our complex technological society.

(2)

In view of the critical importance of energy, it is essential that the complex problems of energy availability be understood. Further, since most major energy-consuming nations now find themselves dependent upon petroleum, it is important that the life expectancy of that resource be carefully evaluated. Obviously the time that remains before petroleum is exhausted will depend on how much there is under the ground (or sea) and on how rapidly we extract and consume it.

With respect to the ultimate production of crude oil in the world, the petroleum exploration and extraction experience in the United States is vast and directly applicable to the world problem. Although crude oil production in the United States accounts today for little more than 15 percent of world production, as recently as 1950 U.S. production was more than half of the world total. About a third of all of the oil ever extracted from the earth has been produced in the conterminous United States. It seems likely that about half of the oil which can potentially be recovered from conterminous U.S. deposits (excluding shale oil) has already been extracted. By contrast, only about one-eighth of the petroleum which seems likely to be eventually extractable from deposits in the rest of the world has been recovered thus far.

It is generally believed that petroleum and natural gas are derived from organic debris that was buried in sediments under oceans and seas during the geologic past. Those sediments were subsequently transformed into sedimentary rocks; petroleum and natural gas are now found only in or adjacent to basins filled with such rocks. Sedimentary rocks are porous and the pores are generally filled with water, except when the water has been displaced by petroleum or natural gas. Under the influence of heat, pressure, and gravity, the oil and gas tend to accumulate in limited spatial regions which to some extent can be located by geological and geophysical procedures.

If one knows statistically how much petroleum is extractable from a sedimentary basin of a certain type, then by analogy one can estimate the oil content per unit volume of similar sedimentary basins elsewhere. The geographical location and extent of the sedimentary basins in the land areas of the world are now reasonably well known. Given that information, and combining it with the available extraction experience, a rough estimate can be made of the petroleum deposits in the world which are yet to be discovered.

In the United States outside of Alaska, reservoirs of petroleum have been found associated with a number of sedimentary basins, but two areas stand out as being of greatest importance. The first embraces large parts of Texas and Louisiana and extends into the Gulf of Mexico. The second is in California, embraces the Los Angeles and San Joaquin basins, and extends into the conti-

TABLE 7.1

U.S. Petroleum Situation
January 1, 1977
(billions of barrels)

Crude Oil Production (1976)	
Conterminous U.S.	2.91
Alaska	0.06
Total	2.97
Cumulative Production	
Conterminous U.S.	117.80
Alaska	0.80
Total	118.60
Proved Reserves	
Conterminous U.S.	21.10
Alaska	9.80
Total	30.90
Imports (1976)	
Crude Oil	1.90[a]
Refined Products (net)	0.63
Total	2.53[b]

[a] 39% of crude oil consumption.
[b] 46% of total petroleum consumption.

nental shelf. These areas account for well over 80 percent of the oil thus far extracted from the 48 contiguous states, and for nearly 90 percent of U.S. proved reserves outside Alaska. In 1969–70, discovery of a third major petroleum reservoir in Alaska increased U.S. proved crude oil reserves by about 30 percent.

Table 7.1 shows the situation with respect to U.S. petroleum production and reserves as of 1977. In considering the history which led to the present situation, it is important that we recognize several critical developments.

First, within the United States proper the annual rate of petroleum production increased exponentially from 1875 to the Great Depression at a rate of 8.4 percent per year. After the Depression and World War II the growth of production continued to be exponential, but at a reduced rate of increase. As can be seen from Figure 7.1 the rate of production passed through a peak in 1970 and has been decreasing ever since. The difference between demand

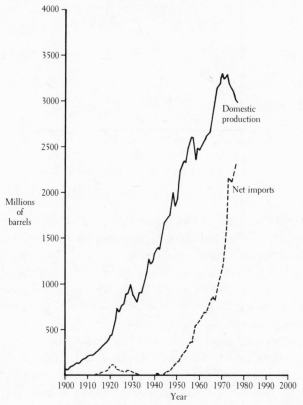

FIG. 7.1. U.S. Crude Oil Production and Net Imports of Crude and Refined

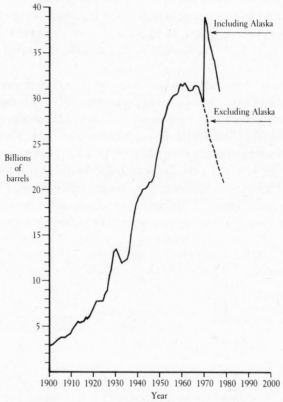

FIG. 7.2. U.S. Proved Reserves of Crude Oil (Estimates as of 12/31/Yr)

and production has been met by imports of crude oil and refined products which together in 1976 filled about 46 percent of the U.S. petroleum need.

Second, within the United States excluding Alaska, the proved reserves of petroleum, like the rate of production, increased exponentially for many years. As can be seen from Figure 7.2, the rate of increase then lessened, becoming zero during the period 1959–1967. Since 1967 the proved reserves have decreased steadily.

Third, within the United States excluding Alaska, the ratio of proved reserves to production ran in the neighborhood of 12 years for some time after World War II. Since 1963 that ratio has declined steadily, reaching about 7.2 years in 1976. This useful index represents the number of years the petroleum would last if production remained the same and no new discoveries were made. Generally it is both impractical and undesirable to extract oil from a field at a rate exceeding 10 percent per year of the remaining reserves. Extraction at a greater rate usually prejudices ultimate recovery.

When an exhaustible resource is extracted from the ground in the face of increasing demand, the shape of the production curve should look something like the recorded production curve of crude oil in the United States shown in Figure 7.1. In the full cycle, the production begins at zero and eventually returns to zero when the resource is exhausted. The technology of production requires that the early phase of production be an exponential rate of increase and the declining phase an exponential rate of decrease. At some point in between, the rate of increase of production starts to lessen considerably, eventually reaching zero as the production curve passes through a maximum.

A recent analysis suggests that the peak of discovery rate in the United States, excluding Alaska, was reached about 1957, when cumulative discoveries amounted to 85 billion barrels. The amount of crude oil which might ultimately be extracted from the ground, assuming existing extraction efficiencies, would then be twice this or about 170 billion barrels. Similarly, when the production rate of crude oil in the United States exclusive of Alaska peaked in 1970, cumulative production was 99 billion barrels. Twice this is 198 billion barrels. Such figures, of course, are only approximate; it is quite possible for the peak rates of discovery or of production to occur somewhat earlier or later than the halfway point. A more accurate approximation can be obtained by analyzing the curve of oil discovered per unit length of exploratory drilling. The data show a long-term decline in the rate of discovery with cumulative drilling and suggest 165 billion barrels as an upper limit for the amount of crude oil which may ultimately be extracted.

In any event, it makes little difference whether such estimates are high or low. The trends indicate that the United States is approaching the end of its conventional oil resources. If we assume that the production curve will be symmetrical, close to 90 percent of the extractable petroleum originally in place will have been extracted by the year 2000.

Thus, if present per capita levels of energy consumption in the United States are to be maintained, increasing proportions of the energy must be derived from other than domestic petroleum sources. Alaskan oil will help to some extent. But even the quantities which might ultimately be extractable from the North Slope would satisfy present U.S. petroleum needs for only a decade at most.

Here it must be pointed out that the figures for reserves and quantities of crude oil which might be ultimately recoverable are based upon our continuing to apply the extraction technologies now in general use. It has been estimated that although a firm figure for the average recovery of oil in the

United States is not available, about 30 percent appears reasonable. This means that about 200 billion barrels of petroleum lie unrecoverable in existing fields worked using current technologies. A dramatic improvement in extraction efficiency, perhaps made possible by greatly increased petroleum prices, would make available a supply of crude oil which is larger than any other single source within the United States. It is generally recognized, however, that this will be extremely difficult to develop and is unlikely to have a major effect upon crude oil supplies within the next decade when problems of petroleum supply are likely to become particularly acute.

TABLE 7.2

Readily Extractable Hydrocarbons in the United States[a]
(billions of barrels of petroleum liquids or liquid equivalents of natural gas)

	AS OF JANUARY 1977					1976
	CUMULATIVE PRODUCTION	PROVED RESERVES	UNDISCOVERED RESOURCES	YET TO BE EXTRACTED	TOTAL	PRODUCTION
Crude oil	119	31	61	92	242	3.0
Natural gas liquids	15	6	14	20	35	0.6
Natural gas	94	39	89	128	222	3.7
Total	228	76	164	240	499	7.3

[a] Includes Alaska and the continental shelves.

Associated with petroleum there are substantial quantities of natural gas (principally methane) and condensable hydrocarbons known as natural gas liquids (NGL) which can be extracted as liquids during the production of natural gas. The problem of estimating the ultimate quantities of natural gas and natural gas liquids which can be extracted is essentially the same as that for crude oil. In the case of natural gas, proved reserves peaked in 1967. As was true of petroleum, reserves jumped in 1970 because of the Alaskan discoveries, but have dropped steadily since then. Production peaked in 1972 and has dropped steadily since then. Indeed, during the unusually cold winter of 1977 a severe gas shortage developed.

Table 7.2 shows estimates of the quantities of petroleum, natural gas, and natural gas liquids which have been removed and which have yet to be extracted. Something like the equivalent of 500 billion barrels of petroleum appears to be ultimately extractable. Of this, nearly half has already been removed.

An appreciation of the significance of Table 7.2 is essential for an understanding of the difficult energy situation now confronting the United States. We are pushing against the upper limit of our domestic extractable hydrocarbon resources. The upward jump of reserves brought about by the Alaskan discoveries can be only temporary; reserves are destined to continue their downward path. Production of hydrocarbons will also continue downward after a brief upsurge following the completion of the Alaskan oil pipeline. There will be another smaller jump upward upon completion of several gas lines about 1980. Since U.S. energy demands are not likely to decrease during the next few years, the lessened domestic production must be compensated either by utilizing greater quantities of other energy resources in the United States, or by importing greater quantities of crude oil and other hydrocarbons.

There certainly are a number of domestic energy resources which could in principle be used to compensate for these impending shortages. The substantial quantities of oil which have been left behind in "exhausted" reservoirs have already been mentioned. U.S. resources of petroleum in oil shale are extremely large—possibly enough to last 7000 years at present rates of crude oil consumption and 3000 years at present rates of total hydrocarbon consumption. Proved coal reserves are enormous and could satisfy present U.S. energy needs for about a millennium. There are almost infinite quantities of nuclear energy which could be tapped using existing technology. Added to this, solar energy could be used for a multiplicity of purposes, including space heating and cooling, heating of water, and even the generation of power.

Where, then does the problem lie?

The problem lies largely in the "energy trap" in which human society as a whole, but particularly the rich countries, has become ensnared. The energy trap has:

1. Caused us to take extremely low energy costs for granted and to accept them as the norm to be expected for a very long time in the future;
2. Deterred the development of a broadly based industrial expertise in the use of alternative energy sources;
3. Caused us to give low priority to research programs aimed at developing alternative energy supplies;
4. Prevented us from investing adequate amounts of capital in known technological processes for utilizing alternative energy sources safely on a substantial scale.

There are of course a number of subsidiary problems, many of them of an environmental nature. There are many real and potential environmental hazards associated with the increased use of coal and uranium for power. But, in principle at least, most of these problems are soluble if we are willing to pay enough for our energy. Clearly, a large part of the environmental component of our energy problem can be directly related to our definition of acceptable energy prices.

In any event, it is highly unlikely that energy sources other than hydrocarbons will be in a dominant position in the U.S. energy picture in the next two decades. The internal combustion engine is not likely to disappear quickly. The capital now invested in equipment for utilizing hydrocarbon liquids and gases is enormous and is likely to be used to the term of its normal life expectancy. Of course, many actions can be taken to hasten the changeover from petroleum and natural gas to oil shale, coal, uranium, and the sun. But here there are two key words which are to some extent related to each other: *time* and *price*.

Major changes in primary energy sources will require substantial alterations in governmental policies including energy-pricing policies, very large capital investments, the resolution of many legal and political problems, as well as the resolution of a number of technical difficulties. It seems unlikely that these changes, urgent as they are, will be brought about very quickly, even were the changes in some way guaranteed to be profitable. But today the potential developers of a coal gasification plant or of a scheme for extracting oil from shale on a large scale or of a nuclear electric plant have no reasonable assurances of profitability, particularly when the environmental variables are taken into consideration.

Eventually, of course, there is no doubt that either the shift must be made or the U.S. perishes. The questions are: When and under what circumstances will the changes take place?

Looking to the short term—to the next 10–20 years—there seems little doubt that the United States, like Western Europe and Japan, is destined to be a major importer of petroleum products for at least another decade and probably for a considerably longer time. In 1976 imports of crude oil and refined products amounted to 46 percent of U.S. petroleum needs and to one-fourth of the combined demand for oil and natural gas. As domestic production of petroleum and natural gas falls during the next two years, imports must increase still further. The opening of the Alaska oil pipeline and of gas pipelines from Alaska will relieve the shortage somewhat. But soon thereafter imports will rise again. And imports seem destined to continue to rise until such time as the U.S. shifts clearly and on a truly large scale from natural crude oil to other energy sources. Beyond about 1990 there will be no choice, for world availability of hydrocarbons will probably be on the decline and competition for the remaining resources will be severe.

(3)

When we examine the world petroleum picture, various independent estimates suggest that somewhere between 1000 and 2000 billion barrels of crude oil can be extracted from the earth in the long run. For the purposes of this discussion we can use the higher, more optimistic figure.

World resources of natural gas (including natural gas liquids) can be roughly estimated on the basis of the U.S. experience with respect to the ratio of extractable gas to crude oil. These figures suggest that the ultimate amount of natural gas which will be extracted is equivalent in energy content to about 2300 billion barrels of crude oil. Using similar reasoning, the ultimate extractable volume of natural gas liquids would be about 440 billion barrels.

Here it must be noted that in past decades a large proportion of the natural gas and associated liquids released from the earth has been lost because of lack of adequate storage and distribution facilities. A substantial fraction of the gas has been "flared" into the atmosphere. With time, however, increasing proportions of the available gas have been marketed. In the United States today only 1 percent of the produced gas is flared. In the rest of the world, however, more than a fifth of the liberated gas is wasted in this manner.

These estimates, summarized in Table 7.3, indicate that something like the equivalent of 5000 billion barrels of crude oil might eventually be extracted from the earth as a combination of crude oil, natural gas, and natural gas liquids. About a fifth of the total has already been extracted. Another fifth is in the form of proved reserves. The remaining three-fifths is yet to be discovered.

World production and proved reserves of crude oil are shown in Figures 7.3

TABLE 7.3

Readily Extractable Hydrocarbons in the World
(billions of barrels of petroleum liquids or liquid equivalents of natural gas)

	AS OF JANUARY 1974					
	CUMULATIVE PRODUCTION	PROVED RESERVES	UNDISCOVERED RESOURCES	YET TO BE EXTRACTED	TOTAL	1974 PRODUCTION
Crude oil	300	560	1140	1700	2000	20.4
Natural gas liquids	120[a]	70	250	320	440	0.9
Natural gas	620[a]	380	1300	1680	2300	8.5[b]
Total	1040	1010	2690	3700	4740	30.0

[a] Including flared and otherwise unrecovered gases and liquids.
[b] Marketed.

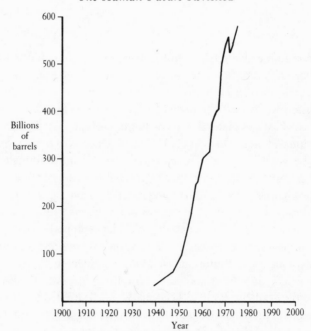

Billions
of
barrels

FIG. 7.3. World Proved Reserves of Crude Oil

and 7.4. The combination of the two curves plus the estimated quantities of crude oil and natural gas which might ultimately be extracted suggest that petroleum as well as total hydrocarbon production will probably peak by the year 2000 and possibly as early as 1990.

As the world approaches the peak of natural hydrocarbon production there will be numerous adjustments in patterns of energy consumption and in national economies. Some nations will be affected very little; others will undergo revolutionary transformations. The nations most affected will be today's major importers and exporters.

The least affected nations will be those which are at present self-sufficient with respect ot hydrocarbon fuels and which do not need to export them either for their economic survival or for their development. Among the industrialized countries, the Soviet Union is in the most favorable position. The petroleum which can ultimately be extracted in the U.S.S.R. appears to be greater than that in the United States, including Alaska, and a smaller proportion of it has already been extracted.

Among the developing countries which are not substantial exporters and which seem destined to be self-sufficient for many years in the future, China, Mexico, and Colombia are outstanding. The developing nations which are major exporters include the 13 members of OPEC and all are attempting to use their oil revenues to expedite development. As their reserves become

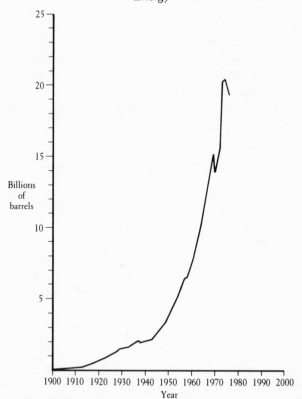

FIG. 7.4. World Production of Crude Oil

depleted they must decide how much of the remaining petroleum they intend to reserve for their own purposes.

Although the United States must clearly import increasing proportions of its hydrocarbons, and although its position does not appear to be as favorable as that of the U.S.S.R., it is in a very good position when compared with other industrialized parts of the world, and particularly Western Europe and Japan. The discoveries in the North Sea will help Europe to some extent, but there will be no respite from the need for imports. The entire industrialized world must look forward to increasing levels of hydrocarbon imports until such time as it is able to shift over to other, more abundant forms of energy.

(4)

The alternative energy resources available to us are vast. They are so very large that for as long a time as we retain our technological capabilities we need never be short of energy—even if energy consumption worldwide were to increase by another order of magnitude or two, and even if we were to speak in terms of a life expectancy for human civilization of millions of years. Our main difficulty is that all other forms of available energy are less convenient than oil and natural gas. Virtually all are more expensive than conventional hydrocarbons. Some are more difficult to extract. Some present environmental hazards. Most require extremely large installations and capital investments. Indeed, we have been greatly spoiled by the easy availability of petroleum.

TABLE 7.4

Estimated Resources of Shale Oil, Tar Sand Oil, and Coal Compared with Resources of Conventional Hydrocarbons

	UNITED STATES		WORLD	
	BARRELS OF OIL (BILLIONS)	EQUIVALENT METRIC TONS OF COAL (BILLIONS)	BARRELS OF OIL (BILLIONS)	EQUIVALENT METRIC TONS OF COAL (BILLIONS)
Conventional hydrocarbons	500	69	5,000	690
Identified reserves of shale oil	2,000	280	3,000	415
Undiscovered reserves of shale oil	25,500	3,530	340,000	47,000
Incomplete reserves of tar sand oil	30	4	750	140
Minable coal and lignite		1,500		7,600
Total		5,380		55,800

With respect to fossil fuels, there are substantial reserves of oil shale, tar sands, and coal already identified, and even greater reserves which probably exist but which have not yet been discovered. Table 7.4 shows the estimated quantities of these fuels and compares them with the estimated quantities of conventional hydrocarbons which will eventually be extracted.

The hydrocarbon in tar sands is a mixture of viscous liquids which cannot be extracted by means of wells. Techniques have been developed, however, for mining and extracting the material on a large scale and these are now being applied. As the oil from these sands belongs to the same chemical family as crude oil, it can be processed by existing oil refineries.

The principal hydrocarbon in oil shales is a solid. In most processes this solid material is converted to either a gaseous or liquid fuel and then concentrated. A number of conversion processes have been developed and, in view of the rising prices of conventional oil and gas, some of the processes appear to approach competitiveness. Yields from the shales which are considered to be reserves or potential reserves range from 10 to 100 U.S. gallons of hydrocarbon per ton. Colorado oil shale containing 30 gallons of hydrocarbon per ton is now being seriously viewed as competitive with conventional petroleum.

One of the major drawbacks to the use of coal is its sulfur content, which pollutes the atmosphere when the coal is burned. In recent years considerable effort has been directed toward developing processes which will convert coal to clean fuels. Methods now exist for converting coal to combustible gas, to synthetic hydrocarbon liquids, or to methyl alcohol. Of course, coal can also be burned directly to generate electricity, but unless the fuel is relatively free of sulfur, special provision must be made to remove the sulfur dioxide formed during combustion. In addition, the particulate matter formed by the ash must also be removed to prevent pollution of the atmosphere.

A further difficulty with the utilization of oil shales and coal is that of carrying out the mining operations on an adequate scale. Strip or surface mining is far less costly than underground mining, but in the process the topsoil together with beautiful scenery is destroyed. The task of minimizing the destruction and returning the mined land to a productive condition is both difficult and costly. In addition, huge quantities of crushed rock and other residues must in some way be disposed of, and large amounts of water are required for the processing.

On the positive side, if these problems are all solved in such a way that the products are not prohibitively expensive, the proved and suspected reserves of oil shale and coal would satisfy human needs for a very long time. However, the quantities available would by no means last forever. At present rates of energy consumption, all fossil fuels combined would last several thousand years. But both population and per capita energy demands are increasing and seem destined to continue increasing in the years ahead. Under these circumstances, the production of fossil fuels would probably peak in another 200–300 years were other sources of energy not utilized on a large scale in the meantime.

As is the case with petroleum, the most favorable known deposits of oil shale and coal are not equitably distributed around the world. The best of the known deposits of oil shale are in the United States and Brazil. But there is good reason to believe that oil shale deposits, particularly those of lower grade, should be widely distributed among the continents.

Coal, on the other hand, is quite unevenly distributed, as can be seen in Figure 7.5, where the U.S.S.R., and to a lesser extent the United States, loom as the giants of the coal world, accounting together for about three-quarters of the world's deposits.

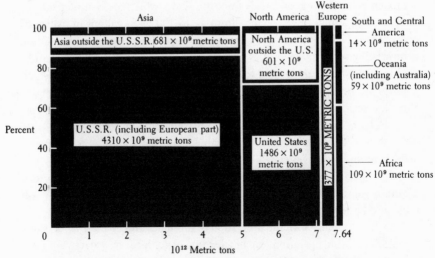

FIG. 7.5. Estimates of World Resources of Minable Coal and Lignite

One possible danger associated with the expanded use of hydrocarbons and coal lies in the fact that the carbon dioxide in the atmosphere equilibrates very slowly with the bicarbonate of the deep ocean. The deep sea turns over only every several hundred years. As a result, an eventual doubling of carbon dioxide concentration in the atmosphere would by no means be out of the question. Theoretical studies indicate that a doubling of the concentration could effect an increase of the temperature near the earth's surface by about 2°C. As will be discussed later, such a change could trigger other mechanisms, possibly leading to irreversible climatic effects.

Thus this single aspect of greatly increased consumption of fossil fuels should be monitored very closely on a worldwide basis. Any clear physical or theoretical indication of emerging adverse effects may make it advisable to lessen substantially the global rate of fossil fuel consumption.

(5)

At some time man's consumption of fossil fuels will start decreasing. It is too early to say whether this change will come about because of decreasing availability of fossil fuels in the ground, because of prohibitively high costs of mining and conversion, or because of adverse environmental effects. But even before we reach that time, it seems probable that we will be using nuclear or solar power, or perhaps both, on a very large scale. In addition, there are other energy sources which can be tapped.

Hydropower is by no means yet being fully utilized. If we assume the present observed average rate of flow which is available 95 percent of the year, something like 10,000 billion kilowatt hours could be generated each year worldwide. About 13 percent of this is already being utilized. With present technology about 4 billion tons of coal would be required each year to generate that power—a little over half the present world energy demand.

In some parts of the world tides can be harnessed, but the potential does not seem to amount to more than a few percent of the potential of hydropower. The power which can potentially be generated by wind appears to be even smaller than the generating capacity of the tides.

Geothermal resources could prove important in many parts of the world, including the United States. There are wide variations in resource estimates, even in the United States where the geology of thermal areas is reasonably well known. The highest of the U.S. estimates suggests that an electrical generating capacity of 400 billion watts based on geothermal resources could be developed in the western United States by 1995. This would correspond to the rate of electrical generation from the expenditure of about 1.4 billion tons of coal annually. This is close to, but smaller than, the present annual U.S. energy budget.

Although the estimate cited for the U.S. is probably optimistic, it nevertheless seems clear that geothermal energy might be a very important supplement to other energy resources, at least over a period of 50 to 100 years. This is particularly true when we consider the relatively nonpolluting qualities of the resource.

When we look at the entire heat content of the earth's crust, as distinct from thermally active locations, a different picture emerges, for tremendous quantities of energy are available in principle—enough to last for over a million years at present rates of consumption. But the technical difficulties are enormous. At this stage, no real conclusion can be drawn as to whether or not geothermal energy can be exploited on a truly large scale. If it can be so exploited, it must be considered along with fission, fusion, and solar energy as one of mankind's primary long-term energy options.

Electricity is now being produced in many parts of the world from nuclear fuels, and nuclear reactors of the present type, which feed primarily upon U–235, will undoubtedly grow in number. The total amount of energy which is likely to be produced by such reactors is in the long run resource-limited. As only about 1 percent of the total energy available in the uranium is utilized, the quantities of uranium needed are large. Quantities of uranium which can be obtained for $30 per kilogram or less are no more than a million tons. Perhaps an additional 5 million tons could be obtained at costs under $100 per kilogram. Probably, as long as we adhere to nuclear technologies which make use of such a small fraction of the total energy available, the spread of nuclear power will be limited by the cost of uranium. Costs greater than $100 per kilogram lead to power costs which are too high to consider seriously.

On the other hand, it now seems likely that breeder reactors will eventually be available. These will feed upon plutonium, derived from the most common isotope of uranium, U–238, releasing as much as 60 percent of the available energy. From a technological point of view, such reactors might be in operation by the early 1990s. It is also possible that breeder reactors using thorium (which is more abundant than uranium) will be available around the turn of the century.

The deployment of fast-breeder reactors will have a profound effect upon the uranium supply problem, for even very expensive uranium can be viewed as economic. When uranium costing as much as $1000 per pound can be used from the economic point of view, vast reserves of uranium, as well as thorium, can be identified, although they would not have been seriously considered under current conditions. To take an extreme case, it has been demonstrated that about 30 percent of the uranium and thorium in an average granite is situated in such a way that it can be washed out of the pulverized rock using dilute acid. Considering the energy cost of quarrying, pulverizing, and treating a granite in this way, the energy "profit" from a ton of average granite is equivalent to about 15 tons of coal.

But there are huge outcrops of granites in various parts of the world which contain considerably higher than average concentrations of uranium and thorium. The energy potentially available from such rocks in the United States is thousands of times larger than that of all oil shales and coal combined.

Thus the fast-breeder reactor gives man access to a supply of energy which can last literally for thousands and perhaps millions of years. But there are numerous problems which must be solved. There are problems of reactor safety—plutonium dispersed in the atmosphere can be lethal. There are problems of waste disposal—huge quantities of radioactive by-products will be generated. Last, but by no means least, there are problems of preventing plutonium from falling into the hands of unscrupulous persons. Not much plutonium is needed to make a bomb of substantial explosive force. Indeed, the very fear of such problems may lead to lengthy delays in the use of breeder reactors for power generation.

Beyond the fast breeder lies fusion, perhaps first by reacting deuterium with tritium. It is not as yet technologically feasible to achieve this on a large scale, but there are signs that this may eventually be achieved. However, contrary to popular opinion, this does not open up new fuel reserves which are much larger than those offered by fission. In fusion involving tritium the supply of lithium (from which tritium is made) is the limiting factor.

The potential supply of solar power and heat is practically unlimited. Its effective utilization suffers from the fact that it is of relatively low intensity, variable in its availability, and not available in any one location for the entire day. In spite of these difficulties, however, the prospects for its use on a large scale seem reasonably hopeful. Already it is in use to some extent in some regions of the world for heating water and for space heating. It seems likely that such uses will spread fairly rapidly. Numerous investigations are now in progress on the possibilities of generating electrical power by concentrating the energy with mirrors, by using thermocouples or photoelectric cells, and by using biological processes.

With nearly 25 percent of the energy consumed in the U.S. being used to heat and cool buildings, this particular aspect of solar energy is receiving high priority. The University of Delaware's solar house has now been in operation for some time and the best systems tested there have provided at least 70 percent of the heating and cooling needs of the building.

In the power area, studies are being made of arrays of reflectors which concentrate heat onto a receiver located atop a central tower. Here a fluid is heated to high temperature which in turn drives a turbogenerator. In the photovoltaic area (direct conversion of light to electricity), major efforts are being made to lower installation costs. The Energy Research and Development Agency hopes eventually to reduce the capital cost of an array to about $500 per kilowatt of installed capacity.

Still another approach to the generation of power from the sun is to grow plants and then generate the power either by combusting the plant directly or by processing it to produce a useful fuel. Electricity has long been generated in some areas by burning wood. At present the Brazilians are planning a massive program for the production of alcohol from sugar cane. The alcohol would be economically competitive with the gasoline which the Brazilians must now produce from imported petroleum.

Solar energy is concentrated in the oceans in the form of thermal gradients between cold water at great depth and the warmer surface waters. Studies suggest that substantial quantities of power could be generated by making use of these gradients in deep tropical waters. Solar energy is also concentrated in the winds of the atmosphere and experience suggests that considerable power could be generated by arrays of windmills.

Thus, although great difficulties can be anticipated, it now appears that man need never suffer from a shortage of available energy. He will be faced by considerably higher costs than he has experienced during the Golden Age of petroleum and natural gas. He will be confronted by environmental problems that are far more difficult to solve than those presented by oil and gas. But to compensate for these difficulties he has available far more energy than he can use even in the foreseeable long-range future, when presumably his total energy needs will be far greater than they are today.

(6)

In the history of society's utilization of energy there has been a sequence of replacement of one energy resource by another, brought about in part by technological change. Wood was displaced by coal, and coal was in large measure displaced by crude oil, then by natural gas. Each of these transitions has involved the replacement of one dominant energy source by another, which then became dominant, only to be displaced by yet another fuel. Energy from nuclear fission is usually cited as the most likely candidate for replacing oil and natural gas, with fission in turn eventually giving way to some virtually infinite and relatively safe energy source such as solar radiation or nuclear fusion. This ultimate energy source has been dubbed "solfus."

There are many reasons, however, for doubting that the future will be as simple as the past. In the first place, it is by no means clear what future energy demands are likely to be. In the second place, although nature has endowed us with vast energy resources, none is devoid of serious technological and sociological problems, all of which must be resolved if the resources are to be effectively utilized.

With respect to total basic energy demand, one can take the conservative view that the world population will stop growing when it reaches 10 billion persons and that per capita demand for energy will stop growing when it reaches the average of that of the rich nations today—the equivalent of about 6 metric tons of coal per person per year. This would give a total energy demand of about 60 billion tons of coal annually—nearly ten times the present world consumption. We could also take the ultraconservative view that all nations can learn to use energy more efficiently and that living patterns can be adjusted so that ultimate per capita energy needs will be reduced, perhaps by as much as a factor of two. This would give a total world demand of about 30 billion tons of coal annually. For many reasons it seems doubtful that world demands could be stabilized at much less than this in the absence of a catastrophe, which would, of course, result in a world energy demand close to zero.

On the other hand, we have seen that the energy costs of maintaining the status quo in the present rich countries will undoubtedly rise because of the increased energy that must be used to extract necessary raw materials, to recycle used materials, and to combat pollution. These requirements could easily triple the current per capita needs in the rich countries and give rise to an ultimate world energy demand equivalent to 180 billion tons of coal annually.

From a radical point of view, the reclaiming of seawater and arid lands could well result in a doubling of the 10 billion persons suggested by present demographic trends. To go further, there is little reason for us to suppose that in the long run an expenditure of the equivalent of 20 tons of coal per person each year (twice the present U.S. level) would really satisfy human wants. An ultraradical futurist might well say (and for plausible reasons) that human beings could not possibly achieve their full potential unless they were each allocated the equivalent of 100 tons of coal each year.

Thus, ruling out catastrophe, we see that estimates of eventual world annual levels of energy consumption ranging from the present equivalent of 7 billion to 2000 billion tons of coal are all plausible, depending upon how conservative or radical our outlook might be.

Although these estimates do not tell us precisely when solfus will take over as our major fuel, they do tell us that when we view the energy situation in historical perspective, the road to solfus, like the road to catastrophe, is not a very long one. And, like the road to hell, it is paved with good intentions. We must recognize how critical it is for us to travel that road carefully.

It seems essential that we keep all of our future energy options open by developing and gaining experience from each of them. The difficulties presented by coal and shale are considerable. Fission may prove to be a dead end in more ways than one. Geothermal power may be impracticable on a truly large scale. It may turn out that we can't afford the capital costs of nuclear power. And fusion may be impossible to achieve in a practical way.

The needs of nations will differ considerably, at least in the short run. Europe and Japan may need nuclear power on a large scale while the United States is powered by coal and shale and the U.S.S.R. is still powered by oil. And the diverse energy sources themselves are more useful for certain applications than for others. As time passes, crude oil, natural gas, oil shale, and coal should be increasingly reserved for chemical use as distinct from the production of heat and power. Nuclear energy is particularly suited for power production and solar energy for heating and cooling. We must attempt to achieve the maximum flexibility with the mix of energy sources available to us.

Thus, it appears that success with respect to the foreseeable problems of energy lies in diversification rather than specialization. In the short run, we must recognize that there is no single solution—even if we admit that in the long run solfus is the answer.

CHAPTER VIII

Global Changes

(1)

From the time man first appeared upon the earth he has had a profound effect on the patterns of life around him and on his physical environment. The use of fire enabled him to burn vegetation covering extremely large areas of land. As he improved the effectiveness of his hunting technology, he drove numerous species of animals to extinction.

With the invention of agriculture, man's effect upon the environment increased dramatically. Deforestation, slash-and-burn agriculture, and erosion changed the nature of many landscapes and living systems. As pressures upon the land increased, the terracing of vast ranges of mountains changed the appearance of many regions. One of the more impressive sights for the visitor to China today is the seemingly endless sequence of mountains, all terraced from bottom to top—a vivid testimonial that man's actions can be a major geological force.

Mines, roads, and cities each contributed to the changing landscape, as did man's rubbish. Ancient cities have been unearthed which appear literally to have been buried in their own garbage. Irrigation schemes made deserts bloom, but they also led to catastrophe. Faulty irrigation practices eventually led to the conversion of much of the Tigris and Euphrates valleys to desert as the result of salt accumulation. Overgrazing and poor cultivation practices probably contributed over the millennia to the expansion of the Sahara Desert.

Over the centuries the changes wrought by man's actions were enormous, but they took place extremely slowly. People would die in a world which appeared virtually identical to the one into which they were born and in which their parents and grandparents lived before them. But when small annual increments of change are multiplied by centuries and millennia of time, the cumulative change can be very large.

After the invention of the steam engine, the rate of change was greatly increased. Man became a global geological and ecological force on a time scale of years instead of centuries. Indeed, the earth's surface, oceans, and atmosphere are now being transformed by industrial man more rapidly than they have ever before been changed by natural forces on a global scale.

The average person in the United States consumes each year over nine tons of nonmetallic substances such as stone, sand, gravel, cement, clay, salt, and phosphate rock. To this must be added about ten tons of fuels and about one ton of steel and other metals. To this we must also add the quantities of materials which must be moved and processed in order to obtain the metals. To satisfy our needs for copper, for example, about five tons of ore must be processed for every person in the United States. Altogether something like 50 tons of materials must be removed, quarried, mined, and processed each year for every person. This is several thousand times the global per capita rate at which rock is disintegrated, dissolved, and carried by the rivers into the oceans.

Industrial man's wastes are scattered over the countryside, dumped into rivers and oceans, and spewed into the atmosphere. At first these actions produced nuisances which were primarily local in nature: dirt, smog, and smells in the cities, the killing of fish in rivers and estuaries, localized changes of temperature and rainfall patterns, changing ecology as the result of urbanization and highway construction, destruction of natural beauty. But as time has passed and as the intensity of man's actions has increased, many of the effects have spread over large regions and have crossed national boundaries. Indeed, it now seems clear that the activities of industrial man are producing changes in both the atmosphere and the oceans which are having a profound effect upon all mankind.

(2)

Of our several environments—land, water, and air—the latter is the most sensitive to human activity. In part this sensitivity stems from its smallness: there is only about one kilogram of air for every square centimeter of the earth's surface, while there are some 180 kilograms of water.

Our atmosphere is a gas which shrouds a rotating earth. The friction with the earth's surface causes the atmosphere to rotate also, but unevenly. It is heated during the daytime and cooled at night and the amounts of cooling and heating vary from season to season. As a result of the combination of the earth's rotation and the changing patterns of heating and cooling, the motions, temperature, and pressure of the atmosphere at any point on the earth's surface are constantly changing. The situation in a particular locality as it changes from day to day we call "weather." The changes that occur seasonally, from year to year, from decade to decade, or from century to century we call "climate."

Climate, like weather, is constantly changing. Today we have "permanent" ice around our poles. When we look back over the past 500 million years, this situation has persisted no more than 15 percent of the time, leading us to the conclusion that we are in a colder-than-usual period. On a much shorter time scale, however, we are in a warmer-than-usual period. The last glaciation reached its climax some 15,0000 years ago. Since then the glaciers have receded and conditions have become warmer. If the behavior of climate in the future conforms to that of the past, we are due for another glaciation, perhaps a few thousand years from now, and possibly considerably sooner.

We know that climate, like weather, is determined by the interactions between the earth's motion, the sun's radiation, the land, oceans, ice, and atmosphere. The interactions themselves are extremely complex and phenomena such as volcanic activity and fluctuations in the energy output of the sun, which are not necessarily periodic, complicate the picture. Because of these complexities, an adequate mathematical model of our climate system has not as yet been developed.

Nevertheless, we do understand something about the factors which affect climate. Although we cannot yet confidently predict natural climatic changes, we can estimate what the effects of certain phenomena, including man's actions, upon climate might be. Indeed, our knowledge is sufficient to tell us that man has already significantly affected the climate over vast areas of the earth.

In order to obtain some concept of the tremendous complexity of the factors which affect weather and climate, it is useful to examine the kinds of things that happen when sunlight strikes the earth. Some of the radiation is absorbed in the atmosphere, and of this, some is reflected back into space. Some of the sun's ultraviolet radiation produces complicated chemical reactions in the stratosphere. Much of it is absorbed by the ozone layer. Infrared or heat radiation is absorbed by carbon dioxide and water vapor and then radiated in all directions. Of the radiation which reaches the earth's surface, much is reflected by snow, ice, clouds, oceans, and land. A large part is absorbed and then radiated in a different form. Some of this is in turn reflected back to earth by clouds, dust, water vapor, and carbon dioxide.

Water is evaporated from the oceans and continents and rain falls upon both in proportions which are dependent upon the outlines and topographies of the continents. Where the temperature is cooler, water turns to ice and rain turns to snow. When snow and ice are formed on the average more rapidly than they melt or evaporate, ice accumulates and the pressures cause it to flow like water, only more slowly, and we experience the phenomenon of glaciation.

The heating and cooling of the atmosphere, oceans, and land areas, coupled with the rotation of the earth, produce ocean and air currents which change seasonally. They also change from year to year, from decade to decade, from century to century, and from millennium to millennium, dependent as they are upon the multiplicity of factors which determine their behavior. In addition to these short-term factors, over geologic time the intensity of solar radiation has probably varied, the continents have drifted, the earth's axis of rotation has shifted, and the earth's orbital geometry has changed.

These diverse phenomena have interacted to produce tremendous variations in climate. We know very little about the earth's climate prior to about 550 million years ago when the first complicated living organisms to possess protective or supporting structures appeared upon the earth. These are preserved in the fossil record. As has been noted, during the greater part of the time since, the climate has been much warmer than at present and indeed the polar regions have been ice-free in both hemispheres. There appears, however, to have been a widespread glaciation about 300 million years ago which lasted perhaps 30–50 million years.

Reliable temperature records, which are obtained by studying the ratios of oxygen isotopes in fossils, are available for the last 200 million years. The ratio of oxygen isotopes in shells has been found to depend upon the temperature at which the calcium carbonate which makes up the shell material is deposited. The results indicate that both poles were well above freezing (8°–10°C) during the greater part of this period and the average temperature of the tropics was between 25° and 30°C. The subtropics appear to have extended considerably poleward from their present locations.

During the past million years there have been a number of very cold periods in which glaciers have spread over large continental areas, particularly in the Northern Hemisphere. A reconstruction of the temperature record of the last 400,000 years in the Caribbean, as calculated from observed ratios of oxygen isotopes in fossils found in sediment layers, is shown in Figure 8.1. The chart shows a clear succession of major ice ages followed by warming periods at intervals of about 100,000 years. Within these cycles there have been alternating subperiods of relative coolness and warmth which have lasted about 20,000 years. Periods between glaciations typically have spanned about 10,000 years. The interglacial period in which we find ourselves at the present time has already lasted about 10,000 years. Perhaps significantly, the several thousand years during which agriculture and urban civilization have existed coincide with the present interglacial period in which the average temperatures have been warmer than any experienced in nearly 100,000 years.

With the help of computer models, it has recently been convincingly demonstrated that changes in the earth's orbital geometry have been the fundamental cause of the succession of ice ages during the past half-million years. When the models which successfully explain past ice ages are used to forecast the future, they tell us that the long-term trend over the next several thousand years is toward extensive glaciation in the Northern Hemisphere. It must be noted, however, that this forecast does not take into account the possible effects of man's action upon the world climate, which could be considerable.

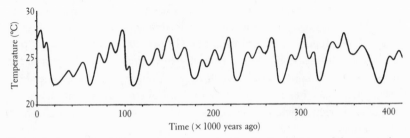

FIG. 8.1. Generalized Temperature Curve for the Surface Water of the Central Caribbean Sea

During the ice ages huge quantitities of water were stored in the ice sheets and sea levels fell. During the warm periods sea levels rose. During the last ice age, some 20,000 years ago, the sea level was about 100 meters lower than it is today. In previous interglacial periods sea levels have risen at least 15 meters and perhaps as much as 80 meters above the present level. Thus the area of the continents which lies above water has changed considerably on a time scale of 10,000 years or so.

The large continental ice sheets disappeared from Scandinavia about 7000 years ago and from northern Canada about 5000 years ago. At that time mean temperatures were 2°– 3°C warmer than they are today. The Arctic Sea ice had receded well north of its present position. The Sahara and the Near East were considerably more humid than they are today and supported considerable natural vegetation.

In the millennia which followed, climate continued to vary but for the most part it was cooler, especially during the period 950 to 400 B.C. This was followed by a warming period which peaked during the early Middle Ages (A.D. 800 to 1200), when the mild conditions permitted the Vikings to settle

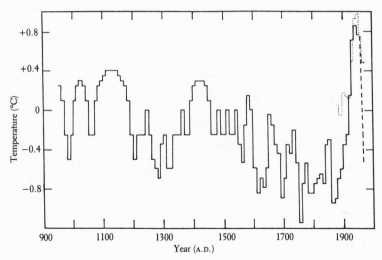

FIG. 8.2. Reconstructed Mean Annual Temperature for Iceland

in Iceland and Greenland and explore the coast of North America. At that time annual mean temperatures in southern Greenland must have been 2°–4°C above present averages.

The mean annual temperature in Iceland during the past millennium has been reconstructed from the historic records of the duration and extent of sea ice on its shores. Because of Iceland's location and its sensitivity to temperature change, climatologists regard it as a good indicator of what is happening over the entire Northern Hemisphere. The results, shown in Figure 8.2, show the generally warm period which ended about A.D. 1200. Particularly noteworthy is the "Little Ice Age," which lasted for three centuries from about A.D. 1600 to A.D. 1900. During that period winters were much colder than they have been in recent years and glaciation in such mountainous areas as Switzerland and Alaska was more extensive.

Early in this century the temperature started to rise in the Northern Hemisphere and by 1930 it had reached a level of warmth which had not been experienced in the entire millennium. The temperature continued to rise and passed through a maximum in the early 1940s. Thereafter the temperature decreased rapidly, as can be seen in Figure 8.3, apparently leveling off or perhaps starting to rise again in the 1970s.

Mountain glaciers in the Northern Hemisphere receded significantly during the warming period. Since the onset of the cooling phase there have been some glacial advances. The extent and duration of ice in many locations ranging from Wisconsin to Iceland and Scandinavia confirm the general temperature trend. Indeed, a variety of observations, including long-term instrument records of winter temperatures in New England and Europe, strongly support the conclusion that the three warm decades, 1930–1960, probably constituted the most climatically anomalous period of the millennium.

Although the cooling trend at high northern latitudes has been severe, the opposite appears to be the case at high latitudes in the Southern Hemisphere, where a warming trend appears to be underway. The consequences of these developments for mankind are extremely difficult to assess. Obviously, lower temperatures can have substantial effect upon agriculture simply by shortening the growing season. But the changing patterns of atmospheric and oceanic circulation which are associated with the lowered temperatures will be crucial. In the long run they will determine the geographic and seasonal patterns

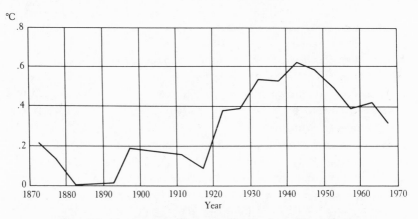

FIG. 8.3. Temperature Change in the Northern Hemisphere

of rainfall and temperature, and will determine as well the variability of the weather. Weather variability is a much more important factor in agricultural production than either a cooling trend or a trend in precipitation. It is when temperature and rainfall deviate greatly from normal that crop yields are lowest.

(3)

On the southern fringe of Africa's Sahara Desert is a desolate region called the Sahel. This is a broad band of arid land that extends nearly 2000 miles from west to east, and in it some 25 million people coax a meager living from the soil. The average rainfall in the Sahel has declined since the early 1960s. Late in that decade the area was hit by a drought which persisted for several years. In large areas of six nations, wells dried up, crops failed, pastures disappeared, millions of domestic animals perished, and thousands of people died. The level of Lake Chad fell dramatically. Flows of water to dams in Nigeria, Ghana, and the Ivory Coast appreciably lessened, with serious consequences for electric supplies. The drought spread from the Sahel to Sudan and Ethiopia.

The rains returned to the Sahel in 1975, but some scientists believe that the relief is only temporary. They point to the overgrazing which has resulted from increased population of both people and livestock and which has led to accelerated soil erosion. The original open woodland of thorn bush has been destroyed and replaced in part by man-made desert.

Other scientists contend, however, that although overgrazing is a contributing factor to the disasters, the primary cause is the changing pattern of world climate. They see the decline of rainfall in the Sahel as part of a much larger pattern of shifting climatic zones. Most notably, North Africa is getting wetter, the Sahel is getting drier, and the Sahara is moving southward at the rate of several kilometers each year. Fluctuations are superimposed upon this long-term trend. Thus, in this view, although the drought might be temporarily eased from time to time, the long-term trend will inexorably reestablish itself.

The Sahel is part of the monsoon belt, where during May to October the winds move from the sea over large land areas, bringing torrential rains. During the rest of the year the winds, now dry and hot, blow in the opposite direction. In 1972 the monsoon rains failed extensively from Africa to Sri Lanka, India, and Bangladesh. The changing world climate may cause them to fail with increasing frequency in the future. In view of the fact that a substantial proportion of the world's people live in the monsoon areas and depend upon the monsoon rains for their survival, this is clearly a situation which should be monitored extremely carefully.

Droughts in India were frequent early in this century. But as the world became warmer, the frequency of droughts decreased dramatically. The climate during an interval of 30 years between 1935 and 1965 was unusually favorable for agriculture and, perhaps in part because of this, the population of India grew very rapidly during that period. As we have seen, the trend since 1968 appears to be in the direction of increased drought, which is a particularly grim prospect since the population of India is now more than double what it was at the turn of the century.

The United States, too, might be facing important climate changes in relation to agriculture. For nearly two decades (1956–1973) the weather varied so little that conditions for grain production were extraordinarily favorable. Indeed, this gave rise to an attitude of complacency concerning the effectiveness with which the new agricultural technologies could reduce the hazards associated with variable weather conditions. In the minds of farmers and government officials alike, weather ceased to be a significant factor in grain production.

The year 1974 brought many shocks. The weather that year deviated greatly from the norm. There was an unusually wet spring over most of the corn belt, followed by drought in the Great Plains. This was followed in turn by an early frost. These events combined to produce a greatly reduced crop, leading to a further reduction of the already meager world reserve of cereals.

The year 1976 brought still another shock: an unprecedented drought in England and on the European continent. The weather in the midwest and eastern part of the United States during the winter of 1976–1977 was the most severe ever recorded. It appeared that weather variability had returned to the Northern Hemisphere with a vengeance. If so, we can look forward to substantial fluctuations in harvests in the years ahead.

All of these developments raise many questions about the world's agricultural future should the cooling trend continue and should the weather become more variable. Unfortunately, our understanding of weather and climate and the ways in which the many factors that influence them operate is pitifully small. Major efforts are now being made to simulate the global weather picture, using elaborate mathematical models and large computers. But much work must be done before such a complicated phenomenon as the drift of climate can really be understood. Nevertheless, the evidence suggests that we are in truth dealing with a major climatic change that may well have a profound effect upon the availability of food in much of the world during the next few decades.

Is it possible, as some scientists have suggested, that we are entering another glacial period? Or are we in a less serious situation and returning to another "Little Ice Age"? Or does the warming of the Southern Hemisphere indicate that our globe as a whole is entering a new warming period? Again, our ignorance is vast and much research remains to be done.

(4)

Why has the earth experienced such an endless succession of climatic changes over the years, decades, centuries, and millennia? It has been pointed out that a system as complex as that made up of the rotating solid earth with its continents, oceans, atmospheres, clouds, snow, and ice can fluctuate ceaselessly, all by itself, even were the external inputs such as solar radiation completely fixed. This being so, it should be possible to develop a mathematical model of the system, then examine the adequacy with which the model fits the facts. If there are discrepancies, then one can search for external causes such as variations in solar radiation which might explain the discrepancies. Unfortunately, in order to solve the complex mathematical relationships with the tools now available it is necessary to ignore many details, with the result that one is never really certain how closely the model resembles reality.

In spite of these difficulties, however, it might well be that climatic changes which have resulted from external causes are so pronounced that they can be identified either observationally or theoretically. This seems to be the case, for example, with volcanic dust. Clouds of volcanic dust obstruct the inward passage of solar radiation more effectively than they obstruct the outward passage of the longer wavelength terrestrial radiation. For example, after the eruption of Mount Agung in Bali in 1963, direct solar radiation reaching the surface of the earth dropped suddenly by nearly 2 percent. Under these circumstances, it is believed that during periods of higher than average volcanic activity the temperature at the earth's surface falls.

The quantities of dust injected into the atmosphere by volcanic activity is considerable. It has been estimated that the gigantic Krakatoa explosion of 1883 ejected about a million million tons of lava, dust, and mud, two-thirds of which fell back to earth within a radius of 35 kilometers while the remainder stayed in the atmosphere, settling slowly over a period of several years. Within a month this mass of fine dust had spread over the Southern Hemisphere. By the end of three months it veiled the entire earth.

Of course, an eruption of the size and force of Krakatoa probably does not occur on the average more frequently than once each century. Nevertheless, since 1890 there have been between 120 and 200 volcanic eruptions each decade north of latitude 30°S, and collectively these appear to have injected sufficient dust into the atmosphere to have had a marked effect upon the radiation balance.

Abnormal weather has followed a number of major explosions. The year 1816 has been called "the year without a summer" and this followed the eruption of Tambora in Java in 1815. There were severe winters following eruptions of Vesuvius in 79 and 1631, Heckla in 1636 and 1694, Petee in 1902, and Katmai in 1912. Perhaps significantly, volcanoes were remarkably quiescent in the period from 1920 until the Agung eruption in 1963 and much of this period coincided with the decades of abnormal warming of the Northern Hemisphere.

In spite of these rather remarkable apparent relationships, volcanic dust cannot explain the downturn in temperature following 1945. Some scientists believe that the downturn has resulted from man-made dust partly of industrial origin and partly caused by mechanization of agriculture, slash-and-burn practices, and overgrazing. Others believe that the downturn has resulted from an actual decrease in the energy output of the sun.

Studies of variations in solar intensity suggest that the intensity of solar radiation is more than 2 percent lower when there are no sunspots as compared with periods of moderate sunspot activity. If this is the case, and if indeed there is a quantitative relationship between sunspot activity and solar radiation intensity, there might be a correlation over the centuries between sunspot activity and climate. Indeed, the relative absence of sunspot activity during the period 1650 through about 1700 coincides with the unusually cold weather which persisted during the same period.

Thus it might well be that the general nature of climatic change over the past several centuries can be explained by the superposition of the effects of volcanic dust and changing solar radiation upon the "natural" pulsations of the climate system. Then we must add the effects upon climate of human activity.

Man unintentionally affects weather and climate in many ways. In the past such activities as deforestation, irrigation, slash-and-burn agriculture, and overgrazing have undoubtedly contributed to local climatic changes, if not to global ones. Rainfall over and downwind from cities is greater than in surrounding areas because of the ejection of particulate matter. But large as these changes have been over the millennia of urban civilization, they are small when compared with the changes being wrought today and in the decades ahead due to our accelerated technology, our increasing use of energy, and our rapid growth of population.

(5)

One of the major ways in which man is likely to change his climate in the future is through the combustion of petroleum and coal. The primary product of that combustion is carbon dioxide which, although a minor constituent of the atmosphere, exerts a major influence upon the earth's radiation balance.

Carbon dioxide shares with water vapor and ozone the ability to absorb and radiate infrared radiation. They behave in the atmosphere as a pane of glass behaves in a greenhouse. Solar radiation falls upon the glass. Most of the radiation passes through the glass and is absorbed by the ground and plant materials. The infrared radiation is absorbed and reradiated in all directions. The heated earth and plant materials radiate the absorbed energy as infrared energy which in turn is absorbed by the glass and again reradiated in all directions. The net result of all of this is that the space beneath the glass becomes warmer than it would have been had there been no glass between the sun and the ground. Increasing concentrations of atmospheric constituents such as carbon dioxide have, then, the "greenhouse effect" of increasing the temperature at the earth's surface. Of course, the situation is complicated by changing atmospheric circulation patterns.

Prior to our modern industrial age our atmosphere contained on the average about 285 parts per million of carbon dioxide, which is in chemical equilibrium with the much larger amount of dissolved carbon dioxide in the oceans. The latter is present largely in the form of the bicarbonate ions. Since man started to burn coal and petroleum at a substantial rate, large quantities of carbon dioxide have been injected into the atmosphere and in time this should come into equilibrium with the oceans. But as matters stand, equilibration is achieved rather slowly—on a time scale of about 300 years. As a result, the carbon dioxide concentration in the atmosphere is now about 330 parts per million—some 15 percent higher than it was in preindustrial days. Projecting present trends of energy consumption, we can expect a carbon dioxide concentration of some 600 parts per million sometime late in the twenty-first century. This would be more than double the normal concentration and would almost certainly give rise to a substantial global temperature increase. Indeed, it is estimated that an increase in carbon dioxide concentration to 600 parts per million would increase the mean global temperature by about 2.5°C above the present level. Such a change would undoubtedly give rise to substantial changes in patterns of circulation and precipitation.

This raises an important question: If carbon dioxide is so important to the earth's radiation balance, why has the Northern Hemisphere been getting colder? A reasonable answer might be that we are in the middle of a rapid natural cooling period and that the carbon dioxide is likely to keep the earth from getting as cold as it might otherwise have gotten. In this view we might expect to pass through a minimum temperature around 1985, following which the temperature will increase rapidly, exceeding the 1945 maximum by the year 2000 and then going to much higher levels. Such a projection is shown in Figure 8.4.

In reality, of course, increasing carbon dioxide simply adds yet another variable to an already very complex system. The ultimate effects of the resultant warming upon climate, when we take into account changing precipita-

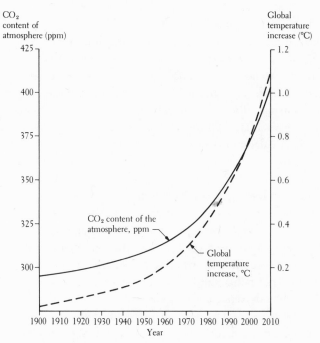

FIG. 8.4. Global Temperature Increases and Atmospheric CO₂

tion patterns, melting of ice, and the consequent changing circulation patterns of both atmosphere and oceans, are impossible to forecast on the basis of our present state of knowledge.

In addition to carbon dioxide, man's activities inject into the atmosphere large quantities of dust which, like volcanic dust, could change the radiation balance. The dust generated by human activity arises in part from slash-and-burn agriculture and in part from industrial activity such as combustion of coal, the manufacture of cement, and the production of steel. The activities associated with mechanized agriculture also generate large quantities of dust, as does intensive grazing in arid and semiarid regions. Most of this dust injection takes place in the Northern Hemisphere. Measurements of dust particles in Greenland ice and on glaciers in the Caucasus indicate that there has been a sharp rise above what might be called the "natural" level of man-made dust following about 1940.

Finally, through the process of burning fossil fuels, man injects substantial quantities of heat into the atmosphere. This is very small when compared with the sum total of solar energy which falls upon the earth's surface (about 0.01 percent), but the generation of this "unnatural" energy gives rise to intensities of energy liberation at specific locations which are far greater than those generally experienced in nature. And the fact is that industrial energy use, which is rising rapidly, already amounts to about 10 percent of the total energy involved in photosynthesis worldwide.

Our knowledge of meteorological processes enables us to say that the creation of these islands of energy activity—in the form of cities or of individual power-generating complexes such as that in the Four Corners area of the United States—can affect the weather locally and even regionally. As the complexes become larger and more numerous they may well affect atmospheric circulation patterns and therefore climate worldwide.

(6)

In 1974 it was reported that the propellant gases used in aerosol spray cans, such as those used for hair sprays, deodorants, or insect repellents, might result in the destruction of the ozone in the "ozone layer" which exists in the stratosphere and which protects terrestrial life from the damaging effects of the sun's ultraviolet rays. If true, this represents an extraordinary example of the potentially dangerous effects of human activities upon the atmosphere.

Ozone, which is made up of three combined oxygen atoms instead of the two which are combined to make up a molecule of ordinary oxygen, is continuously being formed at high altitude by the action of sunlight. The sun's rays of short wavelength decompose oxygen molecules into free oxygen atoms and those atoms in turn combine with oxygen molecules to form ozone. The action of sunlight also destroys ozone, primarily indirectly, by creating intermediate substances with which the ozone reacts. The ratio of the rate at which ozone is produced to the rate at which it is destroyed depends upon the presence of "catalysts"—namely atoms or molecules which react with the ozone but which are regenerated in a "catalytic cycle." Thus, even small concentrations of the right substances can give rise to considerable ozone decomposition.

Most propellants used in aerosol sprays are compounds of carbon, fluorine, and chlorine known as chlorofluorocarbons and usually referred to by a widely used trade name, Freon. These gases are also widely used as refrigerants as well as for other industrial purposes. Their remarkable inertness makes them particularly suitable for these purposes. They are harmless to living organisms. Human tissue is not hurt in any way by direct exposure to those particular chlorofluorocarbons.

But the very inertness of chlorofluorocarbons enables them to travel freely from the home to the stratosphere. They do not dissolve in water, so rainfall does not wash them away. They do not react rapidly with gases in the lower atmosphere, so that, once released, they slowly diffuse upward into the stratosphere.

Ultraviolet light in the stratosphere dissociates chlorofluorocarbons causing them to release free chlorine atoms. The latter are extremely effective catalysts for the decomposition of ozone. Further, there is no evidence of a reaction that would either remove the chlorofluorocarbons before they reach the stratosphere or remove the active chlorine from the stratosphere once it is formed. In other words, once the active chlorine is in the stratosphere, it remains there and continues its work of decomposing ozone for a very long time. Its concentration seems destined to increase for as long as chlorofluorocarbons continue to be used on a substantial scale.

In order to have an effect on the ozone layer, chlorofluorocarbons must diffuse upward into the stratosphere and this takes time. The delay between emission of the gases in the home and their maximum effect in the stratosphere seems to be in the order of 10–20 years. Even were we to stop using aerosol sprays tomorrow, the effects of those already used would continue to increase for at least another decade. And the effects would persist for several decades beyond that.

Two committees of the National Academy of Sciences have independently studied the potential dangers involved with the increasing use of chlorofluorocarbons and have recommended that their use as propellants (but not as refrigerants) be phased out. Even so, it seems likely that their use will continue to increase for some time in the future. Calculations indicate that were the manufacture of chlorofluorocarbons to continue increasing at the current rate, the zone layer might show a 15 percent depletion by the year 2000.

What would be the effects upon human beings were the ozone layer significantly depleted? Unfortunately, because of our inadequate knowledge, the estimates embrace a wide range of possibilities.

A clear effect of the depletion of the ozone layer would be an increase in the incidence of skin cancer, particularly were human beings not to take actions which would compensate for the increase in ultraviolet radiation. A 5 percent depletion of ozone which would result in a 10 percent increase in radiation might cause an additional 20,000–60,000 cases of skin cancer each year worldwide. Fortunately, most such cancers are curable. Most could be prevented by application of modern chemical creams which screen the ultraviolet.

The problem of the effect of ultraviolet radiation upon natural ecosystems is far more complex. It is known that such radiation can have genetic effects which are by no means negligible. It is also known that intense ultraviolet radiation is detrimental to plants and can be lethal. But the overall effects of an increase of ultraviolet intensity of, say, 20 percent upon an ecosystem are extremely difficult to estimate. The effects might be very small; but they might be substantial. In any event, the effects would be global.

Finally, chlorofluorocarbons can also have an effect upon climate. Like carbon dioxide, they absorb strongly in the infrared and thus would contribute to the alteration of the radiation balance of the atmosphere. It has been estimated that continued injection of chlorofluorocarbons into the atmosphere at the 1973 rate would result in another 50 percent increase in climatic effect caused by the expected carbon dioxide increase over the remainder of this century.

Several years before aerosol sprays were looked upon as a potential threat to the ozone layer, there was considerable debate concerning the vulnerability of the layer to emissions from the supersonic transport. It was pointed out that nitric oxide is an effective catalyst for ozone decomposition and that the amount of this substance in the stratosphere may be increased significantly if supersonic aircraft were to become an important part of air transport in the years ahead. Nitric oxide is produced when air is heated to the very high temperatures characteristic of jet engines. The engines of supersonic planes flying at altitudes near 20 kilometers would deposit the nitric oxide close to the layers of maximum ozone concentration. It has been estimated that a fleet of 500 Boeing SSTs, each flying at an altitude of 20 kilometers for seven hours every day, would result in an average ozone reduction of 16 percent in the Northern Hemisphere. Smaller reductions of ozone are calculated for the Concorde and the Tupolev 144 because they are smaller planes and fly lower.

Nuclear explosions in the atmosphere provide yet another mechanism for the destruction of ozone. Large quantities of nitric oxide are created when the air is heated by such explosions, and in the case of thermonuclear explosions the hot air with its high concentration of nitric oxide rises into the stratosphere where it can accelerate the destruction of ozone. It has been estimated that a nuclear exchange between the great powers equivalent to 10,000 megatons of TNT would increase the nitric oxide concentration in the stratosphere some five- to 50-fold. Ozone reduction in the Northern Hemisphere might be in the range of 30–70 percent. Perhaps 60 percent of this reduction would be restored as a result of natural atmospheric processes within two to four years. Although such figures are awesome, it is nevertheless clear that from the point of view of their long-term effects upon the ozone layer, aerosol spray cans collectively seem mightier than the thermonuclear bomb.

Last, the ozone layer is subjected to an assault which in the long run may be more ominous than any of those thus far discussed. The same nitric oxide produced by jet planes and nuclear explosions, which catalyzes the decomposition of ozone, is also produced in the stratosphere by oxidation of nitrous oxide, which is produced by bacteria in soils and ocean waters from nitrites and nitrates. Thus far the quantitative aspects of the production and flow of nitrous oxide in the atmosphere are not well known. If most of it is now produced in the oceans, it is unlikely that man can strongly affect that aspect of nitrous oxide abundance which is produced biologically. On the other hand, if biological production of nitrous oxide in the soil turns out to be of paramount importance, man's use of agricultural fertilizers may turn out to be a critical matter.

At the present time most nitrogen fixation takes place biologically, with a lesser amount being fixed as a result of processes like lightning and combustion. Today, fertilizer manufacture accounts for about 15 percent of all terrestrial nitrogen fixation. But in view of the extremely serious shortage of food in the world, industrial production of nitrogen fertilizers is increasing very rapidly. It is not unreasonable for us to expect another fivefold increase in fertilizer consumption in the next 25 years. Under those circumstances, nitrogen fixation by man would about equal fixation by nature, with the result that the injection of nitrous oxide into the atmosphere by denitrifying bacteria would also be greatly increased.

We can hope that chemical reactions in the atmosphere will prevent all but a small part of the nitrous oxide from reaching the stratosphere where it would be converted to the effective catalyst, nitric oxide. Should this not happen (which is quite possible) we would find ourselves in the unenviable position of being "damned if we do and damned if we don't." Increased fertilizer use is needed if we are to grow more food. But the increased fertilizer usage itself might decrease the concentration of ozone in the protective ozone layer.

Nitrous oxide also can affect climate, for it too absorbs strongly in the infrared. It is estimated that a doubling of its concentration in the atmosphere would result in a rise of global temperature by about 0.7°C.

The problem of the vulnerability of the ozone layer may turn out to be relatively easy to handle; but it could be a disaster. Our major difficulty is that our knowledge is too limited relative to the scope and intensity of our actions.

Even should the problem turn out not to be as serious as it now appears, there are lessons to be learned from this experience. First of all, our natural environment is extremely complex. Second, our knowledge of that environment is inadequate—so much so that we can easily paint ourselves into a corner. Third, we are confronted by a global problem which requires a global political solution embracing *all* nations. Fourth, although we are now aware of the problem of ozone vulnerability, there are undoubtedly many other global environmental problems which will arise from man's actions and inactions and which will eventually rise to the surface of our consciousness.

(7)

To what extent can man intentionally modify his weather and climate on a substantial scale? In the 1950s it was demonstrated that in special circumstances precipitation could be induced by seeding clouds with tiny crystals of silver iodide which serve as condensation nuclei for ice formation. Although there has been considerable exaggeration concerning the state of the art, some progress has been made. Under special conditions rainfall has been increased, cold fog has been dispersed, and hail has been suppressed. There is good reason to believe that one day we will be able to modify hurricanes.

Our growing ability to modify weather creates problems of a dimension not previously experienced. If we produce rain in one location, another location usually will be deprived. Under these circumstances, domestic understandings are difficult enough to achieve. But what about international arrangements? At present there are no significant international agreements concerning weather modification other than to refrain from using the new technology as an act of war. Although this understanding is important, it is inadequate.

Many schemes have been proposed to modify climate on a large scale. One suggestion, for example, is to eliminate the ice which covers much of the Arctic Ocean to an average depth of two to three meters. Were this ice removed, the climate of the northern polar regions would become much more moderate, with mean temperatures running some 10°–15°C warmer than at present. At the same time, winters would probably be more snowy and conceivably this could start another glaciation of northern Canada and Europe. In any event, there would certainly be important climatic changes throughout the Northern Hemisphere were such a project implemented.

One approach to the removal of the ice would be to spread black particles of soot over the ice by cargo aircraft. The lowered reflectivity would cause the ice to disappear in a few years. Another approach would be to dam the Bering Strait and pump water from the Arctic Ocean into the Pacific, thus drawing warm Atlantic water into the Arctic and raising the surface temperature sufficiently to melt the ice. Still another approach would be to detonate thermonuclear devices in the Arctic Ocean to fragment the ice and stir the water. The process of melting could be accelerated by diverting rivers which at present flow into the Arctic Ocean, thus slowing down the rate of growth of pack ice in the winter.

Who would benefit from such a major project? Presumably property owners in the northern regions, for the limits of agriculture would be extended northward as would the limits of wooded land. Mining and exploration activities would be easier. New cities could be created. Such a project would almost certainly be of interest to the Soviet Union, Canada, Scandinavia, Iceland, and the United States (the latter because of Alaska). Because of Greenland, Denmark would be doubly interested.

Who would be the losers? It is difficult to answer this with any confidence, for the simple reason that our knowledge of the complexities of weather and climate is so very limited. We are not in a position to assess how the patterns of air circulation and precipitation over the greater part of the Northern Hemisphere would change. Yet, change would be virtually certain and the probability is that the changes would result in tremendous agricultural dislocations. Were the dislocations to take place in areas of high population density such as India or China, the resultant famines could be of unprecedented magnitude.

People live in those parts of the world where they can survive. For most people, this means that they are located close to where food can be grown. It is in those areas where we find the world's highest human population densities. It is the people who live in those areas who are particularly vulnerable to any major climatic change. They would probably be the major losers were there a substantial program to improve the climate of the northern regions.

To be sure, there are abundant examples throughout history of major engineering projects which have produced both winners and losers. Whenever a major dam is constructed, people must be relocated. More often than not the people of the country have benefited, but most dams have been of slight consequence to humanity as a whole. Again, mistakes in judgment have led to misery, but the misery has generally been confined to a small geographic area. When we engage in projects which are aimed at changing the climate over an entire hemisphere, mistakes in judgment or decisions which are made on the basis of inadequate knowledge can lead to disaster for a large proportion of humanity.

There have been numerous other proposals aimed at changing or stabilizing the climate of a particular region or of the entire globe. One possibility would be the deliberate injection of fine particles into the atmosphere in order to produce a cooling effect to counteract the heating effect of carbon dioxide. There is also a proposal to tow icebergs from the Antarctic to Australia, South America, the Middle East, and California to provide an additional source of fresh water, as well as a scheme to melt parts of the Greenland ice cap to generate hydroelectric power. Another would create a vast system of freshwater lakes in the Amazon basin.

None of these ideas is ridiculous. A number of the goals might be desirable. But we don't know enough about the ocean-atmosphere system to be able to say what is predictable and safe and what isn't. In any event, no plan for large-scale, man-made climatic change should be implemented until we are able to forecast with reasonable accuracy what the consequences of the change will be. And even were we in possession of a reliable mathematical climatic model (which is unlikely in the foreseeable future), there clearly would have to be a general global consensus as to the goals as well as the actions to be taken. Agreement among the rich countries without a parallel agreement among the poor ones would be insufficient.

(8)

Looking to the future, it is obviously not possible to forecast with any degree of certainty what climate will be like during the next few decades. Nevertheless it is possible to construct a sequence of future climatic changes which many climatologists would consider plausible.

1. From a long-range point of view, by which we mean a time scale of several thousand years, we appear to be entering a new glacial epoch. Under normal circumstances in the absence of human activity, mean temperatures could be expected to fall eventually about 5°C below those of the present, but they would do so extremely slowly, amounting to an average drop of only about 0.05° per century.

2. The warming trend which took place in northern latitudes during the period 1920–1940 was probably of natural origin, possibly brought about by a combination of a paucity of volcanic dust in the atmosphere combined with increased solar activity.

3. The cooling trend in northern latitudes during the period 1940–1970 cannot be explained on the basis of the volcanic-dust/solar-activity model. It is tempting to conclude that the cooling has resulted from dust injected into the air of the Northern Hemisphere because of increased mechanized agriculture combined with rapidly expanding industrial activities.

4. In the meantime, the combustion of fossil fuels has been increasing exponentially, so the concentration of carbon dioxide in the atmosphere has risen significantly. It is estimated that the higher level of carbon dioxide concentration in the atmosphere has brought about a mean global temperature

which is some 0.3°C higher than it would have been had carbon dioxide not been added. This may well reach a 0.8°C elevation by the turn of the century. Although the carbon dioxide is generated primarily in the Northern Hemisphere (where most of man's industrial and agricultural pursuits are located) unlike particulate matter which mixes across the equator very slowly, carbon dioxide mixes very rapidly so the effects are global. The same consideration applies to trace quantities of gases such as chlorofluorocarbons and nitrous oxide which may also be contributing to a global temperature increase.

5. The outlook for the next few decades, then, is for a generally increasing global temperature, with fluctuations brought about by natural causes superimposed upon the curve of rising temperature, and perhaps with a continuing cooling in the northern latitudes for awhile brought about by the presence of increasing quantities of particulate matter in the atmosphere.

6. With our present state of knowledge it is not possible to forecast what rainfall patterns would be like under these unprecedented circumstances. We can say with confidence that the rainfall patterns will be substantially different from those of today, but we cannot say in what ways.

7. When we combine the possibility that climatic change may be unusually rapid during the next few decades with the indications that we have returned to a period of substantial weather variability, we see that world agriculture might well be faced with enormous problems leading to decreasing and fluctuating harvests in the remainder of this century. In the face of rapidly growing food demand, all of our technological genius may be required to avoid disasters.

8. Considering our grossly inadequate knowledge, it would be premature to attempt to lessen worldwide rates of combustion of fossil fuels. But the nations of the world may one day in the not-too-far-distant future have to face up to this possibility.

CHAPTER IX

Vulnerabilities

As an individual can form no conception of personal death, so neither can nations. While individuals readily realize the inevitability of death in the greatest of men or a world of them, they cannot comprehend their own extinction, though their hours be ever so pitifully few. So it is with nations; and though the most insignificant of them can complacently witness the death-throes of the greatest of world empires, they are utterly unable to comprehend the possibility of a similar fate.

—Homer Lee, *The Valor of Ignorance*

(1)

How vulnerable is the world system of rich and poor countries to disruption from either internal or external forces? What are the major dangers? What kinds of shocks could so perturb the complicated systems of such countries as the United States or Japan, or groups of countries such as Western Europe, that they would stop functioning? What kinds of steps might be taken to decrease vulnerability and increase resilience?

As we have seen, traditional peasant-village cultures are basically not vulnerable to disruption. Although the villagers are likely to be poor and malnourished, each village is nevertheless reasonably self-sufficient. Individual villages are vulnerable to forces such as weather or disease, but large systems of villages are less so and have built-in mechanisms for recovery. Cities in such cultures have traditionally been far more dependent upon the villages than the villages have been dependent upon the cities.

This situation is now changing, particularly as ever-increasing proportions of the populace become city residents and as villages become increasingly dependent upon such industrial products as fertilizers, pesticides, and water pumps. Nevertheless, were Bombay, New Delhi, Calcutta, and Madras suddenly destroyed by some catastrophe, life would probably go on in India much as it has for the last millennium. Of course, there would be major dislocations, but they would not be fatal to society as a whole. The villages for the most part would survive. Indeed, the unfortunate U.S. experience in Indochina testifies to the resilience of peasant-village culture even under extremely destructive circumstances.

By contrast, an industrial society such as the United States, consisting of a vast, complex, interlocked network of mines, factories, communication, transportation, and power systems connected to the outside world by supply lines for raw materials, would appear to be vulnerable in a multiplicity of ways. India is composed of some 500,000 villages all loosely coupled. The United States is essentially a single unit.

The resilience of this enormously complex system is largely untested. Germany showed considerable resilience during World War II to the effects of Allied bombing, yet since the war industrial society has become far more complex than it was then. After the war Europe and Japan recovered rapidly but outside help played a major role.

In recent years parts of the system have failed, but repairs have generally been quickly engineered. There are numerous redundancies which prevent stoppage of the system as a whole when parts of it fail. But we know little about the amount and kinds of disturbance that the system can tolerate and still remain functioning sufficiently to repair itself.

(2)

The possibility of all-out thermonuclear war is the most serious danger confronting industrial civilization today. Such a war could reduce our complex technological society to a condition from which recovery might not be possible. The poor countries in their misery would inherit the ruins of the rich.

We have seen that both the United States and the Soviet Union have built up enough strategic nuclear striking capability to destroy the military and economic power of any nation which might strike first. These systems are now sufficiently automatic that should either the U.S. or the U.S.S.R. launch a strategic attack upon the other, the attacking country as well as the country attacked would almost certainly be destroyed.

The sheer numbers of delivery vehicles and nuclear devices which have been discussed seriously in the Strategic Arms Limitations Talks (SALT) speak for themselves. In late 1974 a joint U.S.–U.S.S.R. declaration enunciated the need to work for an agreement under which side would be limited to 2400 strategic nuclear-delivery vehicles, including strategic bombers, land-based intercontinental ballistic missiles, and submarine-launched ballistic missiles. Within this number, each side would be limited to 1320 missiles equipped with multiple independently targetable reentry vehicles (MIRVs). Such vehicles can carry several separate warheads on a single booster. Included is a guidance system which permits each of the warheads to be delivered against a separate target. Under such an agreement the actual number of deliverable thermonuclear warheads would be enormous. It appears that the U.S. and the U.S.S.R. can look forward to a period of many years in which strategic nuclear arsenals contain tens of thousands of thermonuclear weapons. Already the United States can deliver about 8500 such weapons and the number is likely to be increased substantially in the next few years.

What would be the targets for all of these missiles? There are no more than 100 cities in each country "worthy" of destruction. The remaining missiles would be aimed at missile and air bases, wherever they might be, at transport and communications centers, and at power stations. We are now at a point in the arms race where a nuclear exchange involving the equivalent of some 30,000 million tons of TNT is possible. Under the SALT agreement, as visualized, an exchange in the future might be even ten times greater.

That the Soviet Union and the United States can annihilate each other is self-evident. But if such an exchange were to take place, a large part of the rest of the world would be severely damaged as well. If the detonations were confined to the Northern Hemisphere, the Southern Hemisphere would be damaged far less—but the damage would by no means be negligible. In the north, however, nations other than the targeted ones would suffer from extremely high levels of radioactive fallout plus a tremendous increase in ultraviolet radiation. The latter would result from a substantial decrease in the concentration of ozone in the stratosphere brought about by the explosions. Ozone shields the earth's surface from ultraviolet radiation. A decade or two would be required for the ozone to be replaced by normal stratospheric photochemical processes and in the interval there will have occurred severe worldwide effects on climate and agricultural production. In addition there will have been considerable mutagenesis of pathogenic viruses and microorganisms as well as numerous deaths from intense sunburn and elevated incidence of skin cancer. When we add these physical and biological effects to the political and economic disruption which would be brought about in virtually all areas of the world, it is difficult to see how a high level of industrial civilization could survive, at least in the Northern Hemisphere.

Conceivably, South Africa and Australia could survive as industrial states, but even this would be questionable. The former might well collapse under the weight of her internal social problems; the latter might cease functioning simply as the result of extremely severe economic and social shock.

It is accepted as axiomatic that the huge strategic weapons systems possessed by the U.S. and the U.S.S.R. deter war between these two powers. To a certain extent this is probably true—but it will be true only for as long as people behave rationally. As we so well appreciate when we read history, rational behavior is by no means inevitable. There will always be those who are willing to destroy everything if they cannot have their own way. And here we must keep in mind that it is now easier to destroy the body of a nation than to destroy those who have the responsibility of defending it. Although 300 megatons might have to be dropped to destroy the missile bases surrounding Tucson, a single 10-megaton bomb could transform the Los Angeles basin into an inferno of flame—totally destroying the city and its inhabitants.

Were large-scale nuclear military capabilities to be forever confined to the United States and the Soviet Union, one might imagine a long-range stabilization of the system with reasonably adequate built-in safeguards against accidental triggering. Unfortunately, it is virtually impossible to protect oneself completely from human error. The technological complexity of intercontinental missile systems renders human or mechanical accident a finite possibility. Further, the system could conceivably be triggered by the willful efforts of a third nation.

If either the Soviet Union or the United States wished to precipitate a war, that war could not be avoided. We are faced, however, with the additional possibility that our two nations may become involved in a war which neither wants. We came very close in 1962. It can happen in the future as the result of any number of possible destabilizing influences or actions.

With careful planning and by the use of self-restraint, the United States and the Soviet Union can perhaps avoid for a time a war that neither nation wants. But nuclear military technology is spreading. For some time the United Kingdom and France have possessed the knowledge as well as modest offensive capabilities. China and India, the two most populous nations on earth, are now members of the nuclear club. What will happen when such weapons are also possessed by Japan, Germany, Israel, Iran, South Africa, Egypt, Brazil, Argentina, and Chile? The long-range prospects for stability, indeed, appear remote.

One of the more difficult destabilizing phenomena in recent years has been the increasing frequency of armed conflict on a substantial scale. Although there are no longer official declarations of war, some 97 wars, both international and civil, were waged in the quarter-century 1945–1969. This can be compared with 24 wars fought between 1900 and 1941. On the average each war fought in the 25 years up to the end of 1969 lasted for nearly three years. The persons killed in these conflicts numbered in the tens of millions and the theaters embraced some 60 countries in Europe, Asia, Africa, and Latin America. There is no sign of any decrease in the frequency of armed conflict. Indeed, in 1974 some 14 wars were underway.

A potentially destabilizing effect would be the tactical use of nuclear weapons in a war. The possibility of using such weapons was seriously discussed during the war in Vietnam, and the U.S. has not denied the possibility of their use should hostilities break out again in Korea. A policy of greater reliance on tactical nuclear weapons for both deterrence and defense in Europe is receiving increasing attention in the United States.

The U.S. now maintains something like 7000 tactical nuclear warheads in Europe, intended for use by artillery, surface-to-surface and surface-to-air missiles, and a variety of tactical aircraft. Most of the systems are capable of using conventional warheads as well as nuclear ones, and NATO envisages at least an initial nonnuclear response to a nonnuclear attack. But in the event of aggression, would the response remain nonnuclear? Probably not, for the systems as presently deployed are vulnerable to the threat of unauthorized use. The situation is further complicated by the introduction of the neutron bomb into the nuclear arsenal.

Several tactical nuclear wargames and studies have led to the conclusion that the costs of such a war fought in Europe would be high even were cities themselves not involved. The studies indicate that as many as 20 million Europeans might be killed—a number which could escalate to 100 million if the cities were involved. Under such circumstances, how convinced would we be that such slaughter would not trigger an all-out strategic nuclear war? Again, we should not depend too much upon the hypothesis that human beings will usually behave rationally.

The expanding volume of international trade in sophisticated armaments is yet another destabilizing influence. Modern delivery systems of the most up-to-date design are being sold or given by industrial countries, notably the U.S.S.R. and the U.S., to developing countries. In 1974 the transfers amounted to nearly $4 billion. Since tactical nuclear weapons are increasingly being looked upon as essential elements of nonstrategic arsenals, it seems but a matter of time before such weapons are transferred to selected countries such as Egypt, Iran, and Israel. Or perhaps those countries, as well as others, will produce their own. In any event, we must keep in mind the fact that sophisticated delivery systems require inputs of far greater technological complexity than do the warheads to be carried. We must also keep in mind the fact that as the use of nuclear power spreads, the potential availability of weapons-grade nuclear explosives will expand. And once tactical nuclear weapons are exploded in anger, it will probably be only a matter of time before strategic nuclear weapons are also exploded in anger.

A danger of no small proportions stems from the fact that the United States now exports considerable quantities of nuclear materials and equipment. Since these exports already contribute about $1 billion to the U.S. balance of trade they cannot easily be stopped. Making matters worse is the trend toward selling fuel-processing facilities that offer substantial opportunities for diversion of nuclear materials into weapons production. Unfortunately, some countries which are most interested in power reactors and fuel-processing facilities—for example, Argentina, Brazil, Egypt, Iran, Israel, Pakistan, South Africa, South Korea, and Taiwan—are also suspected of being interested in acquiring nuclear weapons.

In April 1975, the Federal Republic of Germany agreed to sell a full array of nuclear reactor and fuel technology to Brazil, including a fuel-reprocessing plant and a facility for enriching uranium. The estimated value of the sale was $8 billion and would give Brazil the full technological potential to build nuclear weapons. The United States immediately requested talks with West Germany, France, and other exporting countries for the purpose of channeling the nuclear export competition in less risky directions. But Europeans are resistant to a ban on selling reprocessing plants, reasoning that countries that want them will eventually, like India, build them by themselves.

The International Atomic Energy Agency was created in part to inspect nuclear facilities as a safeguard against diversion of nuclear materials for weapons purposes. Unfortunately, however, the inspection system itself, as well as its coverage, is grossly inadequate.

The nuclear nonproliferation treaty, which was agreed to by the U.S. and the U.S.S.R. in 1968, was designed to prevent the spread of nuclear weapons capabilities. The original concept was that countries in possession of the technology would agree not to help anyone else obtain either the technology or the weapons. Adhering countries which did not have nuclear weapons would promise not to try to acquire them. Thus far, that treaty has not been signed by three members of the nuclear club—France, China, and India. Nor has it been signed by about half of the countries which do not as yet possess nuclear weapons, including Argentina, Brazil, Israel, and South Africa. Egypt and South Korea have signed the treaty but have not ratified it. Iran has ratified.

In the light of these developments, it seems most unlikely that proliferation of nuclear weapons capabilities will be halted in the near future. As the number of nuclear nations increases, the probability that nuclear weapons will be used in anger increases as well.

(3)

We have seen that the industrial countries have become dependent upon petroleum for their primary energy source. For the time being the U.S.S.R. is self-sufficient, although even her large reservoirs of crude oil are destined to dry up in a few decades. However, virtually all other advanced industrial nations are at present dependent upon imports of crude oil for their survival. Canada and Australia are currently the only exceptions. This growing dependence of most of the rich countries on the precarious flow of crude oil from the Middle East, North Africa, Nigeria, Venezuela, and Indonesia represents the second great vulnerability of industrial civilization.

What would happen if the flow of crude oil from these countries to the industrial nations were suddenly cut off? What would happen if there were another sudden major increase in the price of crude oil? In late 1973 and early 1974 the rich countries had a taste of the consequences when the price of crude oil was increased fourfold and the Arab oil-producing nations cut off crude oil exports to the United States as well as to other nations they deemed to be overly friendly to Israel. In spite of the fact that the U.S. at the time imported only one-third of its crude oil, and only a part of that from the Middle East, the impact was sensational, sending waves throughout the entire economy. Although the actions of the oil-exporting nations probably did not in themselves bring on the worldwide economic recession which followed, they almost certainly made a substantial contribution.

It is important for us to recognize that there is a great difference between an instantaneous transition to a new situation and a gradual evolutionary change. As we have seen, when we view the energy situation from a purely technological point of view, the problems are solvable. The combination of coal, oil shale, nuclear energy, and solar energy can in principle satisfy human needs reasonably safely for an extremely long time. But if this transition is to be made, a great deal of technology and money must be injected into the system. Many tens of billions of dollars must be invested if there is to be adequate plant capacity for the conversion of oil shale and coal to synthetic crude oil and if the land which is mined is to be restored to usefulness. Additional tens of billions of dollars must be invested if electricity is to be generated on a large scale from coal and nuclear energy without undue atmospheric pollution and with a minimum danger of accidents. The efforts needed to make full use of solar energy for heating homes, offices, and water are equally substantial. None of these changes can be made quickly, although all are technically feasible.

At the time of the energy shock in late 1973, the third of U.S. petroleum needs met by imports corresponded to about 15 percent of total energy requirements. Of the imports, only about a quarter came from the Arab countries of the Middle East and North Africa. Thus, immediately prior to the Arab embargo less than 4 percent of U.S. energy demands were being met by imports of Arab petroleum. Yet, the embargo resulted in a substantial economic disruption in spite of the fact that it was of short duration. The U.S. fortunately had reasonably adequate reserves of crude oil in storage and in transit.

Prior to the embargo about a third of U.S. imports of crude oil came from Canada and another third from the Middle East (including Iran) and North Africa, the balance being divided among South America, Nigeria, and Indonesia. Since the lifting of the embargo the pattern of imports has changed. Canada has started a program of curtailing exports to the United States, saving her reserves for her own use. With Canada phasing out her exports, we find the U.S. becoming completely dependent for her imports on a group of countries all of which are potentially antagonistic, most of which are potential candidates for civil strife, and some of which lie in areas of possible future hostilities.

Of course, the Middle East and North Africa are regions of particular concern because of the close relationship between the United States and Israel. By August of 1974 U.S. dependence upon those areas had dropped from a third to a quarter. Even so, this is enough to cause severe dislocations if the flow were stopped. On the other hand, Europe is dependent upon the Middle East for 70 percent of its oil and Japan receives 80 percent of her crude oil from the same region.

It is not difficult to visualize a series of circumstances which would rock the economies of Europe, Japan, and the United States. A collective embargo of long duration aimed primarily against the United States, but possibly also against Europe, and even Japan, is by no means out of the question. A partial embargo involving only the Arab countries is even more probable. Destruction of the major Middle Eastern petroleum production and transportation facilities as a result of a major conflagration is certainly imaginable. Such actions could be triggered by any one of a number of plausible sequences of events.

When we look away from the Middle East the crystal ball becomes more cloudy, but there appears to be little room for complacency. Both Nigeria and Indonesia have experienced tremendous internal upheavals in recent years. The hostility of Latin America toward the United States is growing.

If the United States were cut off from supplies of crude oil from one or more of these areas, would she take military action? The pressures for her to do so would be considerable, yet the risks would be tremendous. The oil producers with their increasingly sophisticated weapons systems would certainly be able to carry out a "scorched earth" policy and make it difficult to produce or transport crude oil on any substantial scale for many years to come. Even more dangerous would be the possible involvement of the Soviet Union, which would probably side with any or all members of OPEC.

Within the framework of the cold war, which in spite of détente still goes on, major dislocations of the economies of the industrial nonsocialist countries would obviously work to the advantage of the Soviet Union. It is doubtful that she would discourage, and indeed it is plausible that she would encourage, OPEC actions against Western Europe and above all the United States. In view of this it seems reasonable for us to expect that the U.S.S.R. would take strong measures to deter military action on the part of the U.S. or other countries. At one end of the spectrum of possible Soviet actions, she could extract a high political price from the West for staying out. At the other end of the spectrum, she could intervene militarily under the protection of her nuclear umbrella.

In 1962 the U.S. and the U.S.S.R. had direct nuclear confrontation over the question of Soviet missiles in Cuba. Important as that issue was, the problem of crude oil supplies for the West renders it insignificant. A confrontation between the Arab world and the West over supplies of crude oil could well be the trigger which starts the nuclear arsenals of the U.S. and the U.S.S.R. moving in their long-planned trajectories.

In a lecture at the University of Edinburgh in late 1976 Saudi Arabia's oil minister said he suspected that the International Energy Agency was aiming to ensure that Arab oil could never again be used to further the Arab cause. "If this indeed proves to be the real aim," he said, "then the IEA and the Arab world, and perhaps the whole of the Western and developing worlds, will be set upon a collision course that can only lead to the destruction of everyone." He added, "If the situation in the Middle East erupts again, none of the countermeasures will be able to defeat oil once it is used as a weapon."[1]

What would happen if an extremist group took over Saudi Arabia? Such an action would by no means be implausible. At the same time it would certainly increase the likelihood of U.S. military intervention. Correspondingly, it would also increase the likelihood of Soviet intervention.

Europe, Japan, and the United States are not likely to extricate themselves from this extremely difficult situation unless they achieve a substantial measure of independence from the need for petroleum imports. Yet there is no in-

[1] *Los Angeles Times*, November 29, 1976.

dication that the necessary actions will be taken in time by any of the nations involved.

In the case of the United States, which is less pressed than Japan or the nations of Europe, there are growing indications that the necessary actions may well not be taken in time even to avoid the ultimate dislocation—the peaking of world petroleum production—let alone in time to avoid the enormous political and economic pressures which threaten us long before world production actually passes through its maximum.

By 1976 the U.S. depended on imports for 42 percent of her petroleum needs. A great deal of energy could be saved by increasing taxes on gasoline and large automobiles, and by providing incentives for improved home insulation and for utilizing solar heating. The United States is the world's largest waster of energy, yet there is little indication that she is switching to a new conservation ethic.

The switch to coal is impeded by the substantial costs of making the mining and burning of coal environmentally acceptable. The capital costs of producing synthetic crude oil from either coal or oil shale are very high, with the result that no company in its right mind is about to invest the necessary capital in the absence of guarantees on the part of the federal government as to the purchase price of the product.

The switch to nuclear energy is impeded by a mystique which has evolved over the years concerning its safety. Clearly there are dangers, some of them serious. But in our modern world we are surrounded by a multiplicity of dangers, many of them far more serious than those associated with the use of nuclear power. And the problems associated with the generation and use of nuclear power are probably solvable if we are willing to avoid cutting corners and to pay enough for the power that is generated.

The only way the United States and other importing nations can protect themselves against major energy dislocations is to develop options which are truly viable. If such options are to be developed and put into operation on a meaningful scale, the entire price structure of our various energy resources must be reexamined and drastically altered. Ideally, the revised price structure and associated guarantees would make oil shale and coal competitive with crude oil and natural gas (both domestic and imported) for the production of liquid fuels and petrochemicals. Nuclear power (fission) would be made competitive with coal for the generation of electricity. Solar energy would be made competitive with fossil fuels for space heating and cooling. In this way, all of our major near-term energy possibilities would be developed and utilized on a substantial scale.

In the absence of such major actions, the oil-importing industrial nations will remain extremely vulnerable to the actions of the major oil-exporting countries. And this vulnerability can in turn lead to actions and reactions which could be disastrous.

(4)

The third vulnerability of industrial nations, with the major exception of the U.S.S.R., lies in their growing dependence upon the importation of nonfuel minerals. At the present time the United States is completely dependent upon imports for chromium, tin, manganese, and the metals of the platinum group. She imports about 90 percent of her nickel and aluminum ores, 85 percent of her asbestos, and 80 percent of her cobalt. More than half of her zinc requirements are met by imports. She now imports about a third of her requirements for iron ore. Most of the exporting countries are developing countries, and virtually all of them have considered emulating the example of the OPEC countries by increasing considerably the prices of the ores which they export. In 1974 Morocco substantially increased the price of her exported phosphate rock. Jamaica and other bauxite-exporting countries increased the price of that mineral considerably. In general, however, the exporters of non-fuel minerals have not been able to organize themselves and bargain as effectively as has OPEC.

When we look at the flows of metal ores, concentrates, and scrap in the world, we find that the European socialist countries are relatively self-sufficient and that the major importers (as with petroleum) are Western Europe, Japan and the United States. Three-quarters of all these exports have their origin in developing countries, tl e balance originating in Canada. It is reasonable for us to suppose that as Canada's requirements for raw materials increase, her exports, particularly to the United States, will lessen. This has already happened in the case of her petroleum exports. Thus, unless something new is injected into the picture, the present major importers of ores are destined to become almost completely dependent on the developing countries for their external sources of supply.

What is more, the developing countries themselves want to make use of their own ores. The Venezuelans would rather export finished steel products, or at least steel ingots, than iron ore, and they are planning to develop an integrated steel industry. Similarly, Australia and India are the two largest single suppliers of iron ore to Japan and both have been endeavoring to build up their own steel industries.

We know that there is a great deal of iron ore in the world, but for the most part, like petroleum, it is not where the present demand is. In time, the present importing nations will become increasingly subject to the same kinds of political uncertainty which we see today with respect to petroleum. How soon will Canada and Australia start curtailing their own exports? How will the attitudes of Liberia, Venezuela, India, Brazil, Peru, and Chile change with time? To what extent might they collectively and suddenly disrupt the rhythm of production in the major importing countries? The same questions can be asked with respect to virtually all mineral commodities, whether ores of iron, aluminum, copper, cobalt, chromium, or manganese.

At the same time we have seen, as with crude oil, that it is not really necessary for most industrial nations to become as vulnerable as they are to threats of disruption of their supplies of raw materials. The situations with respect to iron, aluminum, and copper in the United States provide specific examples.

The United States has vast quantities of iron, aluminum, and copper ores of reasonable, yet relatively low grade. Often it costs less to import ores or metals than to process the lower-grade domestic materials. The use of the latter requires considerable capital investment as well as substantial expenditures for equipment and energy.

Were the availability of imports suddenly curtailed on any substantial scale, it would not be possible to shift over quickly to these lower-grade deposits. The necessary scales of operation and capital investments would simply be too vast. Thus, as with petroleum, the United States is vulnerable to major disruptions in the supplies of a variety of mineral commodities and is likely to remain vulnerable for many years in the future. Even so, the United States is much less vulnerable in this respect than either Western Europe or Japan.

All of these areas can decrease their vulnerability in a variety of ways. Pricing is an essential element of lessening import dependence. Major advantages and guarantees should be given companies which invest the tremendous capital necessary to develop and process low-grade ore deposits. There should be adequate financial incentives to encourage the recycling of scrap. There should be incentives to build consumer items so that their life expectancy will be greater than that of their counterparts being built today.

Such major changes in our ways of doing business are not likely to come about quickly, even if we resolved to bring them about. The vulnerability of the United States, Western Europe, and Japan to disruption in their supplies of mineral imports is likely to remain high for many years. As in the case of crude oil, this vulnerability could lead to disastrous actions and reactions.

(5)

The fourth major vulnerability of the rich industrial countries, and one of the greatest for the world as a whole, lies in the world food situation. We have seen that the countries of Western Europe have become net importers of cereals, now importing some 20 million tons annually. Japan's imports have increased steadily and are now about equal to those of Western Europe. The Soviet Union, faced by the desires of its citizens for a diet richer in meat and also suffering from erratic agricultural production, imports large, but highly variable quantities of cereals. In 1972 those rich regions of the world which are net food-importing countries obtained 10 percent of their cereals from abroad, also primarily from North America. Altogether the rich exporting nations, primarily the United States, Canada, Australia, New Zealand, and South Africa, exported nearly 40 percent of their total cereal production.

Exports and imports of soybeans, which supply substantial amounts of crucial protein, are even more concentrated than those of cereals. The United States has become the principal supplier of this important foodstuff and in the early 1970s provided over 90 percent of world soybean exports. Soybeans are a dietary staple in Japan and over 90 percent of the Japanese requirements have been filled by the United States.

As we have seen, Japan has become the most vulnerable of the major rich nations to disruptions in her food supplies. She is dependent upon the availability of food from a handful of rich countries and this dependence will increase in the years ahead as her affluence increases still further. At the same time, the availability of food, particularly from the United States, could change suddenly. An obvious possible cause for change would be a shift in political relationships between the two countries. Although at present there is a real symbiosis between Japan and the United States, history tells us that these relationships can change quickly. But beyond that, other factors could be even more important.

As discussed, the United States, at least for the next decade, will be extremely vulnerable to a sudden fluctuation in the availability of crude oil. Since U.S. agriculture is highly dependent upon crude oil for agricultural chemicals and mechanical power, our ability to export food will depend upon the continuity of crude oil supplies. A complete cutoff of overseas supplies of crude oil, for example, could result in a complete cutoff of exportable agricultural commodities.

But, as has been emphasized, the flow of energy is only one part of the agricultural picture. Climatic change could be disastrous. In the short term, a sudden major fluctuation such as a widespread drought can substantially decrease the quantity of food available for export. In the long term, a major climatic trend extending over a period of a few decades could have critical repercussions. Thus, to the extent that the United States is vulnerable to such perturbations, Japan is even more vulnerable.

Western Europe is less vulnerable than Japan to major fluctuations in the availability of food, but she also is in a very difficult situation and, like Japan, she is highly dependent on North America. If, for any of the reasons discussed above, there were a sudden curtailment of food shipments to Western Europe, the economic dislocations would be substantial and the political ramifications could be disastrous.

The Soviet Union, with its large area and diversity of soils, is basically self-sufficient with respect to her food needs. But her affluence has been growing more rapidly than has her agricultural production. During the decade 1963–1973, per capita consumption of cereals (both direct and indirect) increased by nearly a third.

The Soviet Union has not yet been able to organize the agricultural sector of her economy in such a way that her potential for agricultural production is even remotely realized. Superimposed upon the problem of organization is the problem of weather. A good deal of the agricultural production of the U.S.S.R. is in marginal lands where crop yields can vary greatly from year to year. During fiscal year 1972 the U.S.S.R. imported 4.3 million tons of grain. In the following year this jumped to nearly 20 million tons. One year later cereal imports dropped back to 4.4 million tons. Later they again rose.

Imports of cereals by the Soviet Union are primarily utilized to provide a diet which is richer, particularly in animal products, than could be provided by her indigenous agriculture. The Soviet people have become accustomed to this richer diet, and if imports were curtailed for any reason there would be considerable discontent although widespread hunger and malnutrition could undoubtedly be avoided. We must keep in mind that even in 1973, when the imports of cereals by the Soviet Union were at an all-time high, they represented only about 12 percent of her total cereal consumption.

In 1972 about 40 percent of the cereal exports of the rich exporting countries went to developing countries and filled less than 10 percent of the total cereal demands in those areas. Small as that percentage was, for many of the countries involved the shipments were critical. Unlike the rich countries, which in an emergency can restrict meat consumption and thus release cereals for direct human consumption, the poor countries have very little flexibility. If shipments of cereals from the rich exporting countries to the poor countries were sharply curtailed, considerable suffering would probably result, particularly in the cities.

In the early 1960s between 25 and 30 percent of the agricultural exports from the United States were transferred overseas under the terms of Public Law 480 which, under special circumstances, permits sales of agricultural products for foreign currency or for dollars on long-term credit. Basically the law created a mechanism for providing food to the poor countries and at the same time disposing of U.S. agricultural surpluses. In the mid-1960s, as U.S. surpluses began to diminish and as demands for cereals in other rich countries increased, transfers under Public Law 480 began to drop, reaching 13 percent in 1970 and 3 percent in 1974. Most transfers of U.S. cereals overseas to rich and poor countries alike are now accomplished through commercial sales.

One can imagine circumstances in which shipments of cereals to poor countries under concessional terms might be completely stopped and in which commercial shipments would also be severely curtailed. If severe drought or blight in the U.S. were to coincide with unusually poor harvests in the U.S.S.R. and China, the price of grain would increase substantially, conceivably beyond the reach of many of the poor countries. Most exports would be purchased by the rich importing nations and by certain of the poor countries, such as China, which are able to pay in hard currency. Should such a situation coincide with poor harvests in the monsoon areas, notably the heavily populated Indian subcontinent, in the absence of adequate mechanisms for the international transfer of substantial quantities of food for compassionate reasons much suffering and starvation would result. Such a development could well precipitate political and social turmoil which could in turn trigger international conflict.

As we have seen, a sudden perturbation in the availability of crude oil could have a similar effect. Prices of exports would increase and their availability would decrease. In view of the fact that many poor countries depend upon substantial imports of petroleum and fertilizers to maintain their agricultural production, their domestic production would fall, precipitating the unhappy developments described earlier.

The consequences of such major perturbations would be even more serious were the timing of the energy perturbation linked (intentionally or unintentionally) to the period of poorest crop yields. On the other hand, the consequences would be greatly lessened were there truly substantial reservoirs of cereals available on an international basis and were the poor countries generally to achieve a greater degree of agricultural self-sufficiency.

It seems unlikely, however, that either of these developments will be brought about rapidly. By 1976 world grain reserves had dwindled to 100 million tons, corresponding to about 25 days of annual grain consumption. Even under the most optimistic circumstances, several years would be required to build reserves up once again to a level greater than 200 million tons. As we have seen, the task of increasing agricultural production in the poor countries to an adequate level is a formidable one which, given all goodwill internationally, would nevertheless require several decades to bring to completion. In the absence of that goodwill and the concomitant help, the task verges on the impossible for most countries as they are presently organized.

The vulnerability of the United States to major perturbations in the world agricultural picture can be appreciated when we examine the critical importance of agricultural exports to the U.S. balance-of-payments picture. In 1971 agricultural exports accounted for about 17 percent of the dollar value of all U.S. exports. The proportion rose to a high of 24 percent in 1973 and fell to 22 percent in 1974. Had it not been for agricultural exports, there would have been substantial balance-of-payments deficits in all of those years, increasing from $9.1 billion in 1971 to $24.5 billion in 1974. Thus a major perturbation in U.S. agricultural production would undoubtedly have profound economic, social, and political repercussions within the United States as well as overseas. Were the United States to lessen its dependence upon imported crude oil the situation would not be so dangerous, for crude oil represents a sizeable proportion of the dollar value of U.S imports. But as we have seen, this lessened dependence is not likely to be brought about very quickly.

(6)

As was stressed in Chapter VIII, the human species lives in, and is an intimate interacting part of, an extremely complex system which we now call the "environment." The atmosphere and oceans are in constant motion, sometimes being heated, sometimes being cooled, always interacting with the rotating earth, the sun's rays, and with each other. For billions of years prior to the emergence of humans on the earth scene there was a ceaseless pulsation involving changing circulation patterns, temperature, rainfall, ice cover, and sea level. These changes have taken place on many time scales, some long and some short.

Although we understand many of the broad outlines of this complex network, we do not really understand the system in detail. One of the important questions which confronts us is whether such changes can take place on a large scale so rapidly that we are unable to cope with them.

In the days when most humans were food gatherers, changing climate was not a critical matter for humanity as a whole. Being nomads and therefore mobile, people could always move from a region of drought to one where water was more plentiful. In those days, population densities were low so the flexibility for movement and adaptation was high. But with the invention and spread of agriculture and animal domestication, which gave rise to very high population densities, this flexibility has decreased considerably. Indeed, one of the most difficult of the problems associated with the recent drought in the Sahel (the region in Africa just south of the Sahara Desert) was the mass flight of thousands of people from the countryside into the cities where they could not adequately be taken care of, and across national boundaries in frantic search of the wherewithal to remain alive.

For the most part, particularly in peasant-village cultures, people live where water is available—and usually that means they live close to rivers or where there is adequate natural rainfall. The huge population densities which have emerged on the Indian subcontinent are able to subsist there thanks to the well-established pattern of monsoon rains. What would happen if that pattern were to change dramatically over a period of years? Would hundreds of millions of hungry, frightened people attempt to migrate to the cities, as they did during the drought in the Sahel, only on a vastly larger scale? The suffering and chaos that would ensue can only be guessed at.

Also, how vulnerable are the rich countries to rapid climatic change? Can we imagine changes which might take place sufficiently rapidly that in spite of our plant-breeding proficiency we could not keep up with the changes? Can we imagine a sequence of events which would lead to agricultural catastrophe in North America, Europe, and Japan?

When we look at the sweep of earth history we must answer that such circumstances are certainly imaginable. But then we must ask whether such circumstances are even remotely probable.

Were another ice age to come upon us gradually we can easily imagine industrial society adjusting to the changes. Agriculture would move slowly southward and in time certain cities might be abandoned. But civilization itself need not be destroyed as a result of the changed circumstances. When we examine the major climatic changes that have taken place during the past 100,000 years, it would appear that the rates of change have indeed been sufficiently slow to make such adaptation possible. This is by no means a certainty, but the evidence makes it appear likely.

Unfortunately, we cannot view the present and the future simply as extensions of the past. The growth of human population and affluence has added yet another dimension to the picture. We are pouring vast quantities of carbon dioxide and particulate matter into the atmosphere. Our outpouring of energy into the atmosphere is rapidly increasing. We have seen how our protective layer of ozone might be disrupted by any of a number of human activities. As time passes and as human activities intensify, what are the combined effects of those activities likely to be? Could we be bringing about a global climatic catastrophe?

We simply do not possess sufficient understanding of the complexities of our atmosphere-ocean system to be able to answer this question. In the absence of that understanding we must look upon the climatic effects of human activities as representing a potential vulnerability to human society of substantial magnitude. We know of countless systems in nature in which causes produce effects which are in proportion to the causes, but at a critical point the effects completely outstrip the causes in magnitude, like slowly stretching a rubber band up to, then just beyond, the breaking point. The earth's atmosphere could well be such a system, but unfortunately we don't really know what combination of circumstances might cause it to snap.

(7)

We have seen that an industrial society such as the United States is a large, integrated system of mines, factories, farms, communication and transportation systems, and interlocking power networks. To a certain extent the system is vulnerable to accidental disruption simply because it is composed of so many variable and often fragile parts. At the same time, however, the system contains within it sufficient alternative pathways that in the absence of significant outside interference, whether it be a natural or deliberate perturbing force, it is highly unlikely that the system as a whole would be critically disrupted. Nevertheless, it is noteworthy that significant parts of the system have failed in the past as the result of accident.

On the evening of November 9, 1965, shortly after 5:00 P.M. an electric power failure blacked out all of New York State including New York City, all New England states except Maine, and parts of New Jersey, Pennsylvania, and the Canadian provinces of Ontario and Quebec. The affected area had a population of 25 million persons. The first difficulty appeared in Ontario, quickly spread to the New York Niagara area, and then fanned out, striking New York City some 10 minutes later. Power was restored gradually to much of the area over a period of a few hours, but in New York City, which was particularly hard hit, power was not fully restored until 14 hours after the failure. Coming as it did during the rush hour at the end of the working day, there was tremendous confusion as all electrical services stopped. Lights went out; subways, trains, and elevators came to a halt; TV and radio stations went off the air; airports stopped operations. Fortunately, there was no major blackout-caused disaster, although there were some incidents of vandalism and looting. The crime rate during the blackout was actually lower than normal.

In 1977, twelve years after the Great Blackout, New York suffered a second one of considerably longer duration. This time there was looting, burning, and violence on a massive scale, particularly in the slums.

Ten years after the Great Blackout a pump broke in a plant that filters the water supply of Trenton, New Jersey. The breakdown caused an estimated million gallons of water to back into the filtration plant, rupturing pumps and pipes and causing general damage. During the several days that elapsed before repairs could be accomplished, the 250,000 residents of the area were without regular water service, business and industries were closed, and a fire alert was declared. Tank trucks carried water to hospitals and other areas of critical need until some water could be pumped from nearby communities.

These disruptions were "natural" in the sense that apparently they were not caused by deliberate human effort. At the same time, neither disaster resulted from what we would call a "natural catastrophe" such as the earthquake which destroyed San Francisco in 1906. The New York blackout and the failure of the Trenton water system are examples of what might be termed "natural systems failures." As industrial society becomes increasingly complex and still more highly interlocked, its vulnerability to such natural perturbations within the system will increase still further. However, it should be emphasized that the real wonder is not that such dramatic breakdowns take place, but rather that they are so rare.

When we add the element of deliberate human actions to the possibility of natural failure, the vulnerability of the system as a whole increases enormously. Strikes represent one category of such actions. In the United States in recent years there have been major work stoppages ranging from strikes of garbage collectors in New York to nationwide strikes of steel, railroad, and automobile workers. Each in its own way disturbed the system as a whole, some more seriously than others. Even more ominously, in 1975 policemen and firemen in San Francisco went on strike, leaving the city virtually unprotected. This action was repeated by policemen and firemen in Kansas City, and more recently in Dayton, Ohio.

The effects of strikes in Europe have been even greater than those in the United States. Italy and France have been beset by general strikes as well as specialized ones. A major postal strike in Italy brought communication by letter virtually to a standstill. In November 1973, 18,000 engineers and other skilled workers in England refused to stand by for sudden electrical power breakdowns and imposed a ban on overtime in a protest over pay. This action, coupled with labor disputes in the coal industry, resulted in a declaration of a state of emergency by the British government on November 13. Subsequent slowdowns by coal, railway, and electrical workers coincided with the Arab oil embargo, and the resultant crucial energy shortage prompted the government to establish a three-day work week for most industry and businesses. There were numerous unplanned blackouts, commuter train service and the delivery of coal were seriously disrupted, and stringent measures were taken to reduce domestic energy demand. The state of emergency was not ended until March 11, 1974.

In the early days of the labor movement in the United States strikes were intended to bring pressure upon employers to come to terms with the workers' demands, and for the most part only the striking workers or the employers or both were hurt in the process. As industrial operations became larger and more integrated with each other, strikes increasingly perturbed the system as a whole and eventually came to affect seriously the general public. Simultaneously, as industrial productivity increased due to the introduction of increasingly sophisticated technologies, the actions of fewer and fewer persons were required to bring huge operations to a halt. Modern oil refineries and electrical power plants, for example, are now so highly automated and computer-managed that very few workers are required to keep them operating. As time passes and as our technology becomes even more sophisticated this trend will continue, and the labor of but a small minority of the U.S. population will be required to keep extremely critical elements of the U.S. system of mines, factories, transportation, and communications systems functioning.

Table 9.1 shows the percentages of the entire U.S. labor force involved in activities which are particularly critical for national well-being. We see that a work stoppage by only 0.1 percent of the labor force would bring to a halt all pipeline transport of petroleum and natural gas, all water systems, and all garbage collection and sewage treatment in the nation. An extension of the work stoppage to include 1 percent of the labor force could bring to a halt all petroleum refining, coal mining, oil and gas extraction, and fire protection. A spread of the stoppage to embrace 5 percent of the labor force could add all air and rail transport, mining (in addition to coal mining), steel production, and police protection, as well as all electric and gas utilities. Obviously, a work stoppage by 5 percent of the labor force could bring the economy to a complete stop, but actually by very careful selection within the mining, utilities, industrial, and transport sectors, much less than that would be required. Cessation of work by a very small number of workers in but a few carefully selected strategic areas of activity could paralyze American society.

The "natural" vulnerability of industrial society to disruption can be magnified by the process of decay, brought about in large measure by failure to invest sufficient capital in the system as well as failure to protect earlier investments with adequate maintenance. Numerous components of the U.S.

TABLE 9.1

Percentages of U.S. Labor Force Engaged in Activities
Particularly Critical for National Existence
(1974)

ACTIVITY	PERCENT
Pipeline transport	0.02
Water, steam, and sanitary employees	0.07
Petroleum refining	0.17
Coal mining	0.18
Oil and gas extraction	0.31
Fire protection	0.31
Air transport	0.39
Mining (other than coal)	0.54
Railroad transport	0.63
Steel production	0.65
Police protection	0.70
Electric and gas utilities	0.73
Telephone communications	1.06
Truck transportation	1.27
Total	7.03

network are now strained to the bursting point and there are many parts of the system, for example some of our cities, which are likely to break down for lack of proper care. Such possibilities represent a major vulnerability of all industrial societies.

Fortunately, the system contains a certain redundancy which permits the use of alternative pathways to bypass damaged or clogged components. In spite of this duplication, which has grown haphazardly with the system, its adequacy in the case of certain major dislocations is questionable.

To the "nonviolent" vulnerabilities we must add those which could be brought about by sabotage and terrorism. The very complexity of modern machines makes them, as well as the people associated with them, extremely vulnerable to willful acts of destruction. The airplane is an obvious example. In the 1960s the hijacking of airplanes became commonplace and it was soon recognized that substantial steps were needed to lessen the likelihood that a hijacker would be able to accomplish his mission successfully. The steps that eventually evolved turned out to be largely successful, and hijacking was considerably reduced.

But the costs were high. Millions of dollars were spent on a multiplicity of security systems. Millions of travelers had to learn to live with a new set of inconveniences ranging from inspection of luggage, to personal searching, to interrogation. Not the least of the inconveniences was the lost time.

Although hijacking of planes has diminished in importance on the world scene, largely because of the stringent security precautions, other forms of terrorism have increased markedly in recent years. Countless government officials, diplomats, members of wealthy families, and business executives have been kidnapped. Passengers in airline terminals have been massacred. Bombs have been planted in government buildings, factories, offices, theaters, and restaurants. In the period 1970–1974 there were on the average about 40 significant incidents of international terrorism each year. The frequency of national incidents, of course, has been much larger.

More than 2000 actual or attempted bombings were reported in the United States and Puerto Rico in 1975. The bombings killed or injured nearly 400 persons and resulted in property damage of about $30 million. Of the bombings, 89 were attributed by the director of the Federal Bureau of Investigation to "terrorist activity."

The number of active terrorists has increased substantially in recent years and includes a broad spectrum of political extremists, criminals, and even some lunatics. Although many terrorist activities appear to the average observer to be mindless and irrational, we must remember that terrorism in its most refined modern form is a new kind of warfare which is designed to impress people more than it is designed to kill them. In a world in which virtually all nations have large military establishments, it is a technique for bringing one's cause to public attention and of stimulating action, with minimum likelihood of an encounter with conventional military forces on any substantial scale. In an age of "nuclear umbrellas" and large military establishments which are capable of engaging in large-scale conventional as well as nuclear warfare, the balance of military power is shifting away from armies to small armed groups. Terrorists have clearly demonstrated that small groups, properly armed and motivated, can achieve disproportionately large effects.

Recent terrorist successes have stemmed in part from new societal vulnerabilities which have emerged as a result of rapid technological change. The successes have also stemmed from the effectiveness of the electronic news media in reaching huge audiences worldwide. Up to now, however, the toll in lives and property damage as the result of terrorist activities has been very small when compared with the general worldwide volume of violence. But this situation might well change dramatically in the years ahead.

In the first place, terrorists are becoming more sophisticated. Their ability to disrupt will increase considerably as they learn more about such things as the computer programs of the electric utilities and the special vulnerabilities of many of our transportation and communications systems. The power of terrorists to disrupt society, using conventional weapons and conventional capabilities for infiltration, will undoubtedly increase considerably with time.

Second, the effectiveness of the weapons which are available to terrorists is increasing rapidly. In part this stems from extremely effective research and development programs, particularly in the West, aimed at counteracting the superiority in manpower of certain countries. Major weapons such as anti-aircraft-missile launchers have now been miniaturized to the point where they can be carried and operated by individuals. These highly destructive and easy-to-operate weapons, undoubtedly to be produced on a large scale, will sooner or later be available to terrorists. Recently a modern antiaircraft gun was used in Canada to achieve a million-dollar robbery of an armored car. Even more sophisticated approaches will follow.

As tactical nuclear weapons multiply in number and the use of nuclear energy for power becomes widespread, nuclear explosives and radioactive materials will become more easily available for terrorist activities. We are probably not far distant from the time when the threat by a terrorist group to destroy a major city can be both believable and effective for the achievement of the group's objectives.

Some recent studies of terrorist activities have stressed that the groups involved have for the most part not been particularly interested in killing large numbers of people or even of paralyzing society as a whole. Rather, they have been interested in achieving their immediate objective, whether it be the extraction of a large sum of money or publicizing a particular political point of view. It has been pointed out that no attempt has thus far been made to poison a city water supply or to engage in bacteriological warfare. But times change and terrorists vary in their levels of rational behavior. Even in recent years humanity has suffered the presence of presumably intelligent individuals who would welcome the extinction of civilization rather than suffer a society which does not come up to their personal standards of perfection.

(8)

Quite apart from those forms of terrorism which have political roots, conventional crime of nonpolitical origin and the terrorism associated with it are also increasing rapidly in the industrialized countries, particularly in the cities. In the quarter-century between 1950 and 1975 in the United States the crime rate (number of crimes committed per unit of population) increased some fourfold. In 1974 there were some 10 million reported serious crimes. The actual number of serious crimes might well have been many times greater than that. About 90 percent of the reported serious crimes were for burglary, larceny-theft, and motor vehicle theft. Crimes of violence against persons such as assault, murder, and rape accounted for the remaining 10 percent, or some million reported cases.

Nations appear to differ considerably in their crime rates. The evidence suggests that increases in crime are associated with the rate of social change. In this view, the rapid but differing rates of social change in industrial countries have led to increasing yet differing rates of crime. Until quite recently crime rates in the United States appear to have led those in the rest of the industrialized world. In 1966 the U.S. murder rate was more than twice that of Canada, Japan, and Sweden, and about five times larger than the rate in Great Britain. But crime rates are now increasing rapidly in other countries and the rate in West Germany now appears to be about the same as that in the United States, although the distribution of crime by type is different. The crime rate in France increased threefold between 1963 and 1974 and now appears to be approaching that of West Germany.

In the United States in the period 1970–1974 the reported rate of serious crimes increased by 27 percent to 41 per 1000 residents. In the cities the average rate of serious crime reached 52 per 1000, with the rates in the larger cities ranging upward to more than twice this. The crime rate in the cities was 44 percent higher than in the suburbs, and more than three times greater than in the rural areas.

In substantial measure crime is both a cause and an effect of the decline of America's cities. As we have seen, for many years the major cities have been losing population to the suburbs and rural areas, chiefly in the group of middle-income families which are solid taxpayers and which possess technical and professional skills. Left behind are the poor, the badly educated, the unskilled, and the unemployed. Proportionately far more blacks than whites are included among those remaining.

The sense of danger to family is generally regarded by urban residents as the major problem of the cities and as the principal reason for their wanting to leave. Families with children cite next the school situation in the cities, referring to the deteriorating quality of the education and to their fear of schools in which there are high proportions of blacks.

Thus, in the United States a process of social and economic fissioning has been taking place, not unlike what has taken place among the world's nations, leading to the emergence of rich and poor cultures. In this case the rich for the most part live in the suburbs and rural areas, and the poor, a high proportion of them black, have inherited the central cities.

Poverty, crime, and narcotics addiction are closely related. Heroin use is rising, particularly among the poor, offering escape from a seemingly intolerable existence by providing a temporary feeling of joy and relief. Continued use leads to addiction and soon the addict's chief goal is getting more heroin—which is expensive. Many addicts turn to crime to get the large amounts of money required to support the habit. Indeed, heroin addiction appears to be a major contributing factor to the high crime rates in the central cities. (This is not to suggest that the suburbs are without drug problems. They are experiencing increasing addiction to heroin and other drugs, perhaps in part because of boredom and frustration.)

In the United States another contributing factor to the rising crime rate appears to be the increasing availability of firearms. In the period 1960–1975 about 70 million firearms were produced domestically or imported. Of these, about one-third were handguns, the balance being rifles and shotguns. A recent survey made in California[2] indicates that about one out of six adults reports that he has, or has access to, a handgun in working order. This works out to 2.5 million in California alone, and nationwide to perhaps 25 million persons. It has been suggested that there are more firearms in American homes than in the combined armies of the United States, the Soviet Union, and Europe. Further, the number of privately owned arms appears to be increasing, in large measure because of fear. In the California poll, half of those who now have guns said they had acquired them within the last five years. Of the respondents who did not have access to a gun, 7 percent said they intended to acquire one in the near future, which would increase the number of privately owned guns by another 50 percent.

Not all of the guns lie idly in drawers and closets. About 10 percent of the owners said they had used guns to protect themselves or their property. Deaths from handguns in the United States have increased 50 percent in the past 10 years. A recent analysis of a six-year, 60 percent increase in homicides in New York discloses that the increase is attributable primarily to "deliberate" murder, as opposed to the unpremeditated, spontaneous kind.

It is of interest to compare the frequencies of serious crimes in the United States with those in Great Britain. A distinguished English police official noted that in 1970 "there were sixteen thousand murders in the United States and one hundred and sixty-seven in Great Britain. In 1974, there were more murders in Detroit than in the whole of Great Britain; there were almost as many robberies in Washington, D.C., as in England and Wales. And there

---

[2] *Los Angeles Times*, June 9, 1976.

have been nearly fifty times as many rapes annually in the United States as in Great Britain." He added, "I truly believe that the concept of violence in America is promoted by the fact that you are an armed society."

The officer was quick to point out, however, that guns are only a part of the reason for the enormously greater level of violence in America than in England. He cited heroin and racial, socioeconomic inequality as other major factors for the great differences.[3]

In San Francisco crime soared at a staggering rate in the 1960s, with an emphasis on homicide and rape. In 1974 racial tension was transformed into systematic terror as a gang of black cultists shot down more than a dozen whites. The following year about 100 teenagers robbed and beat terrified passengers on two San Francisco streetcars and then roamed through at least ten other buses and streetcars as bystanders watched helplessly and the drivers fled in fear.[4]

No matter where we turn we see increased violence in the central cities, ranging from robbery to senseless murder. Gangs of teenagers have gained strength in Los Angeles, New York, and Detroit. In 1976 during a rainstorm black Chicago gangs preyed on stalled motorists, robbing some and shooting others. A week earlier black drivers and passengers were attacked in white areas of the city. In the schools each year 70,000 wounded teachers required medical treatment.

Few persons will forget the senseless destruction and looting which took place in the 1960s during the massive riots which erupted in the slums of Los Angeles, Detroit, Newark, Cleveland, and Washington. Statistical projections suggest that the increase in violent crime in recent years is a forerunner of still greater violence in the years ahead which will erode still further the thin veneer of civilization which barely covers the central parts of most of our larger cities today. We must ask: To what extent can our cities survive such insults to their complex and fragile systems?

(9)

The economies of the capitalist industrial nations are extremely complex systems made up of numerous components and a diversity of linkages between them. As in the case of climatic change we can identify many of these components and their interactions. But also, as in the case of climate, the develop-

---

[3] *New Yorker Magazine*, May 31, 1976, pp. 25–26.
[4] *Los Angeles Times*, November 16, 1975.

ment of a truly satisfactory, comprehensive mathematical model is extremely difficult. As a corollary, forecasting the economic futures of the industrial nations which operate within the framework of a "free economy" is a task of extraordinary difficulty. In a very real sense economic forecasting is even more difficult than climatic forecasting, because in the former case human behavior, and related to it institutional behavior, is involved, which is not easily predictable.

The conventional wisdom is that there are four main elements which make it possible for a nation to produce goods and services: natural resources, capital, labor, and technology. People and institutions invest money in land, mines, factories, and communications and distribution systems. Laborers construct and operate the systems. The income received by the investors and the laborers is used to purchase the products of the system as well as to invest in expansion. However, outside of this system of production, distribution, and consumption, an increasing variety of services are needed to improve human well-being, provide for "national security," and develop new technologies. Thus we have cadres of teachers, medical personnel, civil servants, scientists, entertainers, soldiers, and salesmen, among a host of others, who provide the services we need (or think we need) and who must be paid in some way. Sometimes they are paid directly by laborers from their wages and by capitalists from their profits. More often they are paid indirectly, through taxation. In substantial measure, however, workers in the services are paid directly or indirectly by each other.

Historically, the interactions between all of these factors have led to surges, both upward and downward, in economic activity, rate of growth, employment, and prices. A major downward surge led to the disastrous Great Depression of the 1930s. Another led to a marked decline in economic growth in the 1970s. In the latter case, increased unemployment has been accompanied by rapidly increasing prices, which we call "inflation." For the most part, these recent developments caught the industrial world by surprise.

We are probably in for many more surprises. Quite apart from the fact that we don't really understand the complex interactions within the economic system, we nevertheless know that foreseeable developments in the future are likely to have profound effect upon the system as a whole. It is generally admitted that another widespread depression leading to massive unemployment is possible. It is also generally admitted that historically high inflation rates are likely to be characteristic of free economies for a very long time. There are serious doubts that capital expenditures can be raised to a level to ensure a pace of long-term growth which will reduce unemployment to acceptably low levels.

Of all of the changing characteristics of the free-market economies, one of the more disturbing is the high general level of inflation. Increases in prices have characterized Western society for a very long time, and there have been periods in the past, notably during and immediately following major wars, when inflation rates have been particularly high. However, for the most part, rates of price increases have been sufficiently low to be manageable. But in 1972–1973 the inflation rate in the United States jumped to 6 percent and in 1973–1974 to well over 10 percent. The situation in Great Britain has been much worse. There the inflation rate reached 6 percent in 1968, jumped to 8 percent in 1971, and entered the truly dangerous realm of two digits in 1973.

The inflation profiles of nations differ greatly from each other. At present the United States is on the low side and Great Britain on the high side. But high or low, there is little disagreement that the levels of inflation which have characterized the 1970s undermine the foundations of the free-market economies. Continuation of such rates for only a few years could lead to disaster.

Some groups, notably labor and big business, have learned to live with inflation. Business takes inflation into account in its planning and pricing, and passes the increased costs along to the consumer. In many countries wage contracts are tied directly to the cost-of-living index, so that as prices increase, wage increases come automatically. Even the Congress of the United States has now tied its salaries to the cost-of-living index, thus placing an official stamp of approval upon the inflation mentality. But there are large groups of individuals who are in no position to secure such automatic increases of income, persons living on fixed annuities for example, and it is they who pay the greater share of the cost of the inflationary trend.

Tying wages to the cost-of-living index, once it becomes the rule rather than the exception, can create enormous instabilities leading to an acceleration of the inflationary trend. Beyond that, there are a number of trends which will undoubtedly lead to additional inflation in the years ahead. The cost of raw materials, which is in a very real sense arbitrary, has already increased considerably and seems destined to increase much more. Pollution control will add to the costs of goods and services. If food production lags behind the demand created by increasing affluence and population, as seems likely, prices will increase still further. As populations grow and societies become more complex, public services must expand. Many governments lack the resources to pay for the services, so the needed money is printed, leading to still further inflation.

Obviously, inflation is by no means the only threat now confronting the capitalist economies. High on the list are the related problems of economic growth, unemployment, income distribution, and balance of payments. Some serious students of the U.S. economy maintain that unemployment cannot be reduced much below the high levels characteristic of 1975–1976 in the absence of accelerated growth of the gross national product in real terms. It is also maintained that the large numbers of people who do not now share in the nation's wealth, particularly the poor who live in the cities, are destined to remain poor unless the rate of economic growth increases. On the other hand, some serious students of the economy maintain that we are nearing the end of our long period of sustained substantial growth. They point to the constraints imposed by our decreasing resource base, environmental problems, and growing affluence and population. Growth, they say, will stop.

In a sense, both groups are correct. Clearly at some time, probably soon, growth measured in terms of such elements as resource consumption per capita must stop. A major question confronts us given zero growth in per capita consumption: Will we be able to substitute increase in quality for increase in quantity and in this way provide the means for people to earn their livelihood? Will we be able to improve substantially the efficiency of resource utilization and at the same time channel more human effort into badly needed services?

Thus far, rapid economic growth has blinded many Americans to the inequities of income distribution in their society. For the most part, the poor and middle-income groups have benefited from the growth, but not at the expense of the rich group, which has also benefited. The poor are better off than they were before, but relative to the rich they are still very poor. It is remarkable how our definition of poverty changes from decade to decade.

Given a stationary or even a slow-growing economy, the problem of income distribution may well become explosive, particularly if slow economic growth is coupled with high levels of unemployment and inflation. Such a situation would contain both the powder and the fuses for massive social and political upheaval.

(10)

One of the more critical of the economic and social problems in the United States, as well as in other industrial nations, is that of the decline of the cities. As we have seen, people have been leaving the central cities for the suburbs and smaller settlements in large numbers but in demographically uneven proportions. Those leaving generally have been from the middle and upper economic classes. Those remaining have been the less educated, the poor, and the unemployed. Those remaining are far less able to pay taxes yet their presence places greater demands upon city services and welfare.

Our largest cities, such as New York, Philadelphia, and Chicago, are products of nineteenth-century transportation and industrial technologies. Raw materials were brought in and finished products were shipped out by ship and by railroad. Industries were concentrated near the docks and terminals because of the difficulties of transportation between the terminal and the factory. Now, however, with trucks having replaced horse-drawn wagons, such central locations are no longer necessary. Industries are better off outside the central cities where more land is available at lower prices. Further, changing technology now makes it possible for many industries to operate out of several small, dispersed plants rather than out of large factories in the central cities.

The increased cost of doing business in the larger cities has resulted in an accelerating exodus of companies to the suburbs and to the smaller cities. In the period 1970–1974, when jobs in the U.S. as a whole increased by more than 9 percent, available jobs in large cities shrank, in some by as much as 18 percent. Unemployment in the cities is high, particularly among blacks. As still more companies move away, taking with them their middle- and upper-middle-class employees, unemployment will increase still further, as will crime.

Ironically, the larger a city is, the greater is the cost per resident of maintaining it. In cities of a million or more inhabitants, all services combined, including police and fire protection, sanitation, and education, cost more than twice the average expenditure per capita of all American cities. Also, the average local debt per resident is greater the larger the city. The per capita indebtedness of cities of a million or more inhabitants is more than twice that of the average of all U.S. cities.

Thus, most of the larger cities find themselves in a vicious circle. There is a net migration of population to the suburbs, stimulated in part by the outward movement of industry, and by increasing crime rates together with decreasing quality of education. Although there is movement of population into the cities, the rate of emigration exceeds the rate of immigration and, even more critical, the average income and educational level of those moving in is less than those moving out. As a result of these changes, by 1973 the median family income in the suburbs was nearly 25 percent higher than the median family income in the central cities. By 1974 the average central city was over 22 percent black and the unemployment rates were appreciably higher than the national average. In the central cities as of 1974, nearly one-third of the unemployed were black and some 10 percent of the families were living on public welfare. As a result of such changes the local governments clearly need more income, but they are caught between rising demands for city services and growing resistance to tax increases. This leads to a continued rise in crime rates, further deterioration of the quality of education, and further acceleration of the rate of exodus of the middle class.

In a sense our cities are becoming concentration camps for poor people. Obviously, the poor are not required by law to remain in the vast urban slum areas in which they find themselves. But the fact of the matter is that for the most part they have no practical way of leaving.

Even in the absence of further inward migration of the poor, the populations of the slums seem destined to increase because of high birth rates among the poor. Thus, as the total population in the central cities continues to decrease, the proportion of the poor and poorly educated seems destined to continue its upward course until perhaps 80 percent of the population will be black or Latin. Most of the English-speaking white minority will be affluent, without children of school age, and they will live in relatively luxurious and secure surroundings.

As the tax base and the median income goes down, the larger cities will have increasing difficulty paying old debts and securing new loans. In 1975–1977 New York City came close to financial collapse. Other cities on the brink of insolvency include Jersey City, Newark, Detroit, and Buffalo. San Francisco now finds itself in a precarious position in part because of its high salary scales for municipal workers and in part because of strikes of police, firemen, transportation workers, and garbage collectors.

Even in the absence of a major perturbation such as a sharp increase in unemployment, most large cities appear to be in deep and worsening trouble. Yet, as we have seen, the likelihood of a major economic perturbation is by no means negligible. This could lead in turn to tremendous civil strife which could make the urban riots of the 1960s seem like minor disorders.

(11)

In various parts of the world certain chemicals, electronic equipment, and other industrial products are manufactured which represent an insignificant fraction of total world industrial production but which are nevertheless indispensable to the smooth functioning of society. Technological and economic circumstances have not infrequently caused the production of a number of critical products to be concentrated in the hands of a few nations and corporations. Nowhere is this development more apparent than in the steroid pharmaceutical industry, the products of which range from drugs used in the treatment of illness to oral contraceptives. At present, only two pharmaceutical companies—Schering in West Germany and Roussel in France—are responsible for the bulk of the totally synthesized oral contraceptives in the world outside the People's Republic of China.[5]

At one time Mexico had a near monopoly on the production of steroid intermediates. A species of yam abundant in Mexico is particularly rich in diosgenin, which in the 1940s was the most versatile of all steroid raw materials. The Mexican government made the exportation of this chemical prohibitively expensive, thus encouraging the establishment of an advanced steroid-manufacturing industry in Mexico. From the 1950s to the early 1960s well over half of all steroids manufactured in the world originated in Mexico, either as finished product or advanced steroid intermediates.

The situation changed significantly when the Mexican government started to control, then nationalized, the collection of the yams. The cost of diosgenin rose rapidly, thus stimulating the development of alternate pathways for steroid chemical production. A variety of other agricultural raw materials from various parts of the world are now used, but more significantly, total synthesis of steroids for oral contraceptives, starting with relatively simple chemicals, is now an economically competitive process. This has been a gigantic achievement and represents one of the most complicated and lengthy synthetic processes employed anywhere in the chemical industry. The complexity of the process is such that total synthesis is now confined to two companies in Western Europe, and even partial synthesis is achieved by only a handful of companies in North America and Europe. Economic competitiveness depends in no small measure upon high volume of production.

The prognosis for the yam-based steroid industry in Mexico is now quite poor. In the near future most multinational pharmaceutical companies will probably cease steroid production in Mexico because production elsewhere will be more economical. In the end Mexico's steroid output will be entirely for internal consumption, compared with only 10 percent today. Because of the lowered level of total production, unit costs will be much higher than they are at present.

Thus, the brief history of the steroid chemical industry has ended in the probable disintegration of important agricultural and chemical industries in a developing country, and in enormous and growing concentration of the means of mass production in two rich countries. It is essential that we inquire about the ultimate significance of these changes, for analogous ones will un-

[5] I am indebted to Professor Carl Djerassi for bringing this situation to my attention.

doubtedly take place in other areas of industrial production. Unfortunately, this trend toward centralization and its ultimate consequences have not been examined thus far in any depth.

Were the production of steroid contraceptives in Germany and France suddenly to stop, for whatever reason, the consequences would be disruptive but by no means catastrophic. But when we add to this picture the possibility of sudden disruption of other equally small, essential, yet complex and highly centralized industries, many questions arise. "For want of a nail a shoe was lost" is an often-quoted piece of children's doggerel, and in the story this ultimately leads to the loss of the war.

How many "nails" do we have in our industrial inventory?

(12)

Throughout history contagious diseases have disrupted human societies, often in the form of epidemics. Plague, or the "Black Death" which struck Europe in 1348, apparently killed about a third of the population in its first onset, and kept returning in the fifteenth, sixteenth, and seventeenth centuries. London was particularly hard hit in 1664–1665 when tens of thousands of persons died and two-thirds of the population of the city fled to escape the contagion. After 1666 there was no epidemic of plague in London, or for that matter in the rest of England. Indeed, there was a striking retrocession of plague in the greater part of Western Europe, and by the mid-eighteenth century the disease had virtually disappeared in the West. The long history of plague on the continent came to an end in 1841 with an isolated outbreak in Turkey.

In the spring of 1918 an influenza epidemic appeared in the United States. Within four months it had spread around the world, killing relatively few persons, mainly young adults. Although the dead from this pandemic numbered in the tens of thousands, the number was sufficiently small on a worldwide basis to cause little notice.

In the latter part of August 1918, the virus apparently mutated and epidemics of unprecedented virulence exploded in three widely separated port cities: Freetown, Brest, and Boston, all of them involved with the transport of troops to Europe. As the fall and winter progressed the new virus spread to virtually all parts of the world, leaving in its wake millions of dead. By May of 1919 the disease had ebbed. By Christmas of that year it had returned, but with reduced strength.

By the time the epidemic had run its course the disease had infected about a quarter of the U.S. population and had killed well over 500,000 persons.

Worldwide, at least 20 million persons are estimated to have died and experts suggest that this might be a considerable underestimate.

In the United States many city services were strained to the breaking point because so many employees were ill. The telephone company warned people not to make calls. Transportation and other services were hard hit. Bodies accumulated, creating new hazards. Bereaved survivors had to dig graves for their own dead.

We do not yet know how this virulent pandemic came about. Conceivably something like it, or worse, could happen again. Possibly in such an eventuality our improved ability to develop and manufacture effective vaccines would help us forestall catastrophe. At the same time, some molecular biologists suggest that virulent virus forms could emerge which in an age of rapid air transport could spread and kill large populations before vaccines would be developed, let alone be manufactured and utilized on an adequately massive scale.

In 1976 a previously unknown disease was contracted by about 150 persons in Philadelphia. The mortality rate was high, approaching 25 percent. Many months were required to identify the cause of the disease, and the origins and mechanism for spreading are still not understood. Under such circumstances it would clearly not be possible to develop quickly either a vaccine or a cure.

The possibility that a new virulent disease of "natural" origin might suddenly appear is real and will be with us for the foreseeable future. To this we must add the possibility that such diseases could appear as the result of experiments in genetic manipulation.

In recent years a new technique has been developed which makes use of a class of enzyme that operates on deoxyribonucleic acid (DNA) molecules. These spiral molecules are inside the nucleus of every cell and are the basic self-replicating units of life that are able to recombine. The recombined fragments give rise to new forms of DNA molecules that can, under the right circumstances, infect bacteria and reproduce themselves within the cells. These new DNA molecules are called "recombinant" DNA.

These new techniques offer much promise. The ultimate medical and agricultural benefits of such research could be enormous. Furthermore, there are substantial insights to be gained concerning the genetics of living organisms. Yet there are also real dangers.

In principle, genes can be inserted into bacteria that enable them to resist antibiotics or to form dangerous bacterial toxins. It is possible to create a new bacterium that is injurious to humans, yet resistant to our presently useful antibiotics. It is also possible to link segments of DNAs from likely cancer-producing viruses with elements of DNAs that are capable of reproducing themselves in bacterial populations that live in humans and other animals.

Clearly, scientists are not likely to engage knowingly in experiments which would endanger large populations of human beings. But mistakes are always possible. Under the circumstances, new man-made diseases—which can attack animals, plants, or people—must be watched out for as diligently as new "natural" diseases. Both are dangerous. Both involve factors which cannot at present be fully estimated.

The fact is that in our present world new diseases can be spread with unprecedented rapidity. When we couple this fact with the possibility that new diseases, whether of natural origin or man-made, can suddenly appear, we appreciate that our vulnerability to such developments could be not only substantial, but unprecedented.

(13)

We have seen that the greatest vulnerability of the industrial states lies in the probability that they will destroy each other with their military might. At the same time, we cannot ignore the possibility that the poor countries might collectively bring about the destruction of the rich ones. Such a prospect may seem to many farfetched at this particular time. But when we examine the diverse ways in which the world is changing, the rich countries should not feel too sanguine about their relationships with the poor ones. Those relationships are changing rapidly.

Already the frustrations within the poor countries are enormous and there are tendencies to lash out in many directions, often irrationally. We see growing antagonisms in black Africa toward whites, and it would appear to be but a matter of time before the white governments of Rhodesia and South Africa are overthrown. Attitudes in Latin America and Asia toward the United States are hardening. There is little in the way of a positive bond between the People's Republic of China and the Soviet Union.

What will the frustrations in the poor countries be like in another generation, when their populations have doubled once again and they are still poor? How will the changing pattern of climate affect those frustrations? What will their outlook be in a few decades when their population approaches 8 billion persons, most of them poor, hungry, and crowded into vast slum cities? How desperate or radical will their leadership become as the years go by? What would they have to lose were they to lash out in an attempt to bring the rich to their knees, hoping eventually to rebuild the world according to their own image of perfection? They might, of course, lose lives, but by then they would be able to lose collectively about 150 million persons each year through military action without reducing their population.

Obviously, a willingness and an ability to tolerate huge losses, though important, would be inadequate. What about their weapons? Could they really do much harm to the industrial states which possess such vast storehouses of nuclear armaments and other sophisticated weaponry?

The first, and perhaps the most powerful, weapon available to the poor countries would be to cut off all supplies of raw materials—crude oil, minerals, agricultural products. This would have a profound effect upon Europe, Japan, and the United States, which might in turn threaten to take over the oil fields, mines, and plantations by force. But such a move could be forestalled in several ways. The weapons of the poor countries are growing in sophistication with each passing year. Were the Soviet Union to align herself with the poor countries, she could of course threaten to make use of her nuclear arsenal. Were this not the case, terrorist groups from the poor countries could place a number of nuclear bombs (which they will probably soon possess in quantity) at strategic locations in the cities of the rich countries and threaten to explode them. Even if the bombs were nonexistent, the deterrent effect could nevertheless be substantial.

Superimposed upon such actions we might anticipate the launching of any one of a number of possible levels of more conventional nonnuclear warfare. Here it is important that we keep in mind the long and difficult experiences of the United States in Korea and Indochina. As we have seen, peasant-village cultures are extremely resilient.

But far more important than the use of conventional armed forces would be the use of small groups of well-armed terrorists who would be able to destroy key elements of the complex industrial networks of the rich countries. The border between the United States and Mexico is long. That between the Soviet Union and China is even longer. The coastlines of Europe, Japan, North America, and Australia are also very long and penetrable. So a prolonged war of terrorism of unprecedented magnitude would by no means be out of the question. One can imagine such actions combining with internal problems of the rich countries, including dissidence, to accelerate their decline.

Such a fate befell Rome under quite different technological and social circumstances. There is little reason for us to suppose that it can't happen again.

(14)

As we have seen, there have been numerous developments in modern Western society which have greatly complicated our lives and which make it increasingly difficult to arrive at meaningful decisions. The most important of these complications stem from our rapidly changing technologies which have led to the numerous societal vulnerabilities which we have briefly discussed. We must now ask what the collective effects of those vulnerabilities might be upon individual liberty and democratic institutions.

John Stuart Mill's "Essay on Liberty" has helped guide Western democracies for well over a century. Mill argued for complete freedom of thought and discussion, and stressed that there should be strict limits to the authority of society over the individual. Although these ideas are widely held and cherished, they are by no means universally held. J. F. Stephen, who engaged in a classic debate with Mill, argued that the majority of people are incapable of discriminating between different ideas on a rational basis, and that therefore in a completely free society reason cannot triumph. Stephen stressed that the state had a role to play irrespective of the popular will, and therefore social coercion is a necessary part of the evolution of civilization.

For the most part the world's democracies have subscribed more to Mill's views than to Stephen's. Nevertheless, in times of political and economic chaos, people have demonstrated a willingness to surrender a considerable measure of individual liberty if they believe that by doing so political and economic order will be restored. For example, in 1932 the people of the German Republic voted to abolish democracy, believing that by so doing they were trading liberty for stability—and they much preferred the latter. Today we see individual liberties being eroded in most parts of the world, in large measure because of the overwhelming complexities of the problems now being confronted by virtually all societies.

Democracy has now all but disappeared in the poor countries, in substantial measure because the goals which these countries have set for themselves simply cannot be achieved through democratic institutions. Major reforms such as more equitable distribution of income or the destruction of a traditional oligarchical system cannot be brought about by a parliament—it requires an autocratic regime of some sort. Thus we have seen the emergence of a vast spectrum of totalitarian regimes ranging from the Maoist theocracy of China to the former one-woman rule of India, to the assortment of military regimes in Latin America.

Among the rich countries, the totalitarian communist regimes seem likely to be with us for a very long time. They suffer from enormous bureaucratic inefficiencies, witness the substantial difficulties the Soviet Union is having with agricultural production or the comparison of production figures between West and East Germany. Nevertheless, they are able to minimize or circumvent certain of the economic problems which plague capitalist society, such as large oscillations in production, inflation, and unemployment. Further, in a field of competition such as armaments they are able to impose a much heavier burden on the people than any democratic government could possibly get away with. There are, of course, groups of dissidents who offer a certain amount of resistance to the regimes, but the instruments of persuasion and coercion in the hands of the rulers are extremely powerful.

The true democracies of the world now embrace little more than 15 percent of humanity. This proportion is bound to decrease as the result of differential birth rates. Beyond that, will the proportion decrease still further as a result of the sweeping impact of the array of societal vulnerabilities upon individual democracies?

At one end of the spectrum, Great Britain is a nation to watch carefully. She is confronted by a horrendous array of economic problems, including low growth rate, a substantial and growing state control of the economy, low production efficiency, and extremely powerful trade unions. She must export if she is to feed herself, yet she is encountering increasing difficulties competing with other, more efficient exporters. There are many who believe that Great Britain is rapidly approaching a state of economic breakdown and social chaos which will require extremely strong actions on the part of government—and more North Sea oil than is probably available—to forestall. Will she be able to retain her democratic institutions during this period of stress?

At the other end of the spectrum is the United States, which has been the most successful and longest-lived democracy in history. But as the federal bureaucracy has grown in size and complexity, and as the difficulties of making lawful decisions concerning complex problems have multiplied, there has been an erosion of individual liberties and democratic institutions. We went from the inhumane horrors of the McCarthy era of the early 1950s into the age of the "military-industrial complex," into the Vietnam War with all of its duplicity. We experienced illegal wiretapping, internal spying, terrorism, scheming by the CIA and the FBI, the development of "security" dossiers. From Vietnam we moved into the sordidness and dangers of Watergate.

In spite of these problems, or perhaps because of them, there emerged in the nation a dramatic recommitment to democratic values. Public outcries caused the government to make peace in Vietnam. The reaction to Watergate led to a variety of investigations and trials. Even the formerly untouchable CIA and FBI were investigated in depth.

Added to this, people were making their voices heard about a variety of environmental problems ranging from supersonic transports to nuclear power plant siting to strip mining coal. Indeed, democracy seemed to be taking a new form.

Nevertheless, as we examine the tremendous array of problems now confronting the United States, one cannot help but wonder what will happen when chaos is upon us. We might be very close to that time. Thus far neither Congress nor the Executive branch of the government has really come to grips in a meaningful way with even a part of the awesome spectrum of vulnerabilities which face us. At the same time, we have spent a great deal of effort challenging authority and exposing its abuses. These two facts are probably related in the sense that it is now extremely difficult for anybody to govern the United States.

In the aftermath of Vietnam and Watergate, the American people are now very tired. When the time arrives when governmental inactions lead to chaos, what will happen? Will we search for our own strong man and show a willingness to cut ourselves loose from a number of democratic procedures? Will our individual liberties lessen in importance and will our government increasingly take on aspects of a totalitarian state, keeping track of its citizens and coercing them but being impervious to their wishes? Perhaps not. But we should not be overconfident. We must keep in mind that the tools of persuasion and coercion which modern technology has placed in the hands of rulers of nations are unprecedented in their power. The road to totalitarianism appears to be a one-way street.

(15)

Industrial man now lives in a complex and largely synthetic ecological system, new in the human experience and inadequately understood. We have seen that there are many kinds of serious shocks to which that system might be subjected. Those which have been described here are simply illustrative and represent only a fraction of those which deserve attention.

Synthetic ecological systems probably possess the same kinds of complex behavior patterns as do natural ones. One of these, expressed in mathematical terms, is *nonlinearity*, which means that the effect of a strain or shock upon the system is not necessarily proportional to the magnitude of the strain or shock. In certain cases there are *threshold* effects. Some species of fish, for example, may be able to tolerate a 10-degree rise in water temperature without ill effect, but a 12-degree rise would be fatal. At low concentrations carbon monoxide does not appear to have adverse effects upon human beings, yet above a certain concentration it is fatal. There is also the phenomenon of *diminishing returns*, as in agriculture where increases in yield per hectare above a certain point can be achieved only by disproportionate increases in inputs such as fertilizers and pesticides.

Finally, and probably most important in a discussion of vulnerabilities, are the problems associated with *synergisms* in which the effects of two or more inputs to the system exceed the sum of the individual inputs had they been applied separately. For example, carcinogenic substances in particulate matter associated with city air can cause cancer of the lung. In the presence of sulfur dioxide, the effect seems to be magnified, not because sulfur dioxide by itself necessarily causes cancer, but rather because it impairs the self-cleaning mechanism of the lungs, thus increasing the time that the carcinogenic particles spend in the lungs before being discharged.

• The outbreak of a major nuclear war is an obvious example of a nonlinear reaction to inputs. It is analogous to the breaking of a rubber band once it has been stretched to a certain limit.

• Decreases in energy availability can be coped with up to a point, but beyond that something in the system must give way.

• There is sufficient buffering in the plant-animal-human food system that even the Japanese could survive a major decrease in food imports, but again only up to a point.

• Industrial civilization could probably cope adequately with modest increases or decreases in mean atmospheric temperature—but only within certain limits, wherever those might lie.

But how will all of these inputs, together with others we have discussed, interact and perhaps magnify each other? To what extent are they synergistic? We know that energy, food, climate, and environment are related. Terrorism cannot be divorced from armaments, the fragility of technological systems, or from hunger and poverty. Because of such relationships and interactions it is essential that we study vulnerabilities collectively as well as individually.

Finally, the study of resilience is an essential element in the study of vulnerabilities. Resilience can be increased by building redundancies into the system, by endowing the system with more effective means for repairing itself, by establishing buffering mechanisms such as improved storage facilities for food and raw materials. But the issue of the improvement of resilience versus the proliferation of vulnerabilities will be with us for a very long time.

CHAPTER X

The Future

The hill of the Capitol, on which we sit, was formerly the
head of the Roman empire, the citadel of the earth, the
terror of kings. . . . This spectacle of the world, how is it
fallen! how changed! how defaced! the path of victory is
obliterated by vines, and the benches of the senators are
concealed by a dunghill.

—Poggius (b 1380; d 1459),
as quoted by Gibbon in
*The Decline and Fall of
the Roman Empire*

(1)

Let us imagine for the moment that we are near-immortal cosmic creatures
examining the earth from afar, placing the records of all of man's actions and
inactions into a cosmic computer which we have programmed to forecast the
human future in terms of probabilities. Each year we feed new data into the
computer, following which we cluster around the display to see how the
forecasts have changed since the year before. By now, having done this for so
long, we are hardly surprised that in the last century the forecasts have
changed very little. In spite of the fact that we as near-immortal cosmic creatures know better, it almost appears that the human future is predestined.

We remember the situation a million years ago, long before manlike creatures were really firmly established on the earth scene. The forecast for humankind then was not very favorable. But once humans had populated all of
the continents the probability curve for survival turned sharply upward. It
moved up sharply again following the invention and spread of agriculture.
Today, the probability of the survival of humanity as a species is so close to
100 percent that even the invention of a powerful new weapon such as the
hydrogen bomb produced but a minor perturbation on the computer output.

Clearly, only a cataclysm of truly cosmic proportions could drive humankind as a species to extinction. Such a cataclysm, although possible, is highly unlikely in the foreseeable future.

Thus, the computer tells our little group of near-immortal cosmic creatures that humankind is probably destined to be a part of the earth scene for a very long time in the future. We know that this forecast has not changed for countless millennia.

But there are other forecasts to be obtained. What will human society be like in the centuries ahead? Where lies the future of peasant-village culture? Where lies the future of industrial societies?

As we press the buttons our thoughts go back some 3000 years, long before "industrial civilization" was a term our computer could come to grips with. At that time the probability of survival of peasant-village culture was very close to 100 percent. However, the calculated life expectancy of an individual city, dependent as it was upon the peasants and the villages and plagued by disease and war, was seldom more than a few hundred years. The computer told us emphatically that peasant-village culture is extremely stable, that the cities which depend upon the villages are basically unstable.

With the onset of the Industrial Revoluton the probability curves began to change. As industrialization spread throughout Europe and North America, and as colonialism spread throughout Asia, Africa, and Latin America, the probability of survival of peasant-village culture decreased somewhat and a new culture was introduced to the computer's vocabulary. During the eighteenth and most of the nineteenth centuries the computer's estimate of the liklihood of survival of the new form of civilization increased.

But as we cosmic computer-watchers know so well, the developments of the twentieth century have dramatically changed the probabilities. The probability of survival of peasant-village culture is once again very close to 100 percent. The probability of survival of industrial civilization is very close to zero. In effect, the computer is telling us that industrial societies are extremely vulnerable to disruption and that the likelihood of disruption is high. It is telling us further that such societies may well be a short-lived aberration on the earth scene. Like countless living species in the spectrum of evolution, industrial civilization was born, found nourishment, flourished for awhile, only to become extinct as its needs outstripped its supplies and as the complexities of its organization outstripped its capacity to organize.

If there really were a cosmic computer, I suspect that is what it would try to tell us.

Unfortunately, although near-immortal cosmic creatures might be able to program a cosmic computer in such a way that the human future might be forecast with a reasonable degree of accuracy, ordinary mortals cannot do this although they might possess extraordinary mathematical skills. One reason for this is that the forces which impinge upon human beings, both individually and collectively, are so enormously varied and complex. Another reason is that those forces interact with each other, and humans in turn interact with those forces. Thus, in a variety of ways the forces and their effects upon society become modified.

Even were human behavior not a critical factor in determining the human future, the complex interrelationships between the forces which affect human society are difficult to describe in mathematical terms. When we include human behavior as a major variable in the picture, mathematical modeling becomes nearly hopeless. In substantial measure this results from the fact that we are still far from the point where human behavior, either individually or collectively, can be described with any degree of precision in mathematical terms.

We can appreciate some of the difficulties of global modeling when we examine a relatively simple and straightforward question: How many automobiles will there be in the United States in the year 2030? Here we can examine the wealth of history concerning the birth and death of automobiles and the exponential growth of the automobile population. We can attempt to understand the multiplicity of factors which affect those rates, such as the cost of automobiles relative to income levels, economic booms and depressions, wars, convenience, status, safety, and the availability of alternative forms of transportation. Then we can examine various factors which might ultimately limit the population of automobiles, such as traffic congestion, maintenance cost, or the number of automobiles which are actually needed by a family. Following this we can examine technological competitions or innovations which might seriously affect the demand for automobiles.

Clearly, even in this relatively simple case, human decision factors can be of critical importance and yet more often than not such factors cannot be predicted. Were the government to take any of a number of plausible actions to achieve certain transportation and pollution goals, what would otherwise have been a reasonable forecast would be rendered hopelessly inadequate. Taxes on automobiles and fuel might be greatly increased, networks of bicycle paths might be built, new transportation technologies might be developed, migration from large cities to small urban centers might be encouraged. Such decisions are not easy to reduce to mathematical terms that can readily be handled by a computer.

Another relatively simple and straightforward question, yet one of critical importance, is that of population growth. If we know the birth rates and death rates in a given society as a function of age, and if we also know the present numbers of people of each age, the population at any time in the future can be described mathematically with considerable precision. But as we know so well, both birth rates and death rates are subject to numerous outside influences and can change rapidly with time.

Thus far it is not possible to describe in meaningful mathematical terms the effects of the growth of affluence upon individual human decisions to have or not to have children. Furthermore, could a computer have anticipated a decision on the part of the Indian government to penalize families of government employees which produce more than three children? Or could it have anticipated a decision on the part of the government of Singapore to refuse public housing to families larger than a specified size? Obviously not. Yet, global modelers must necessarily assume that at least collections of such decisions can be reduced to mathematical terms and anticipated.

We must face the fact that global mathematical modeling is still a primitive science. This does not mean that attempts to create models, such as those commissioned by the Club of Rome, should not be encouraged. In our attempts to develop models we gain insights concerning interactions between forces which cannot be obtained in any other way. But at this stage of development we should avoid looking upon the output of the computer as necessarily being a description of the real world.

Thus, rather than attempting to model mathematically the changes which are taking place in the world today, it is perhaps more useful to make use of the integrative powers of the human brain (which in its own way is an exceedingly effective computer) and examine past, present, and possible future configurations of human society for conditions of stability and instability. Here, as we have already seen, the level of technological capability and the specific ways in which technology is applied are of the utmost importance.

Earlier we saw that a worldwide food-gathering society is extremely stable for as long as it does not have to compete with the more efficient and technologically more advanced peasant-village agricultural society. Once agriculture was invented, food-gathering society began the long decline toward extinction.

We have also seen that peasant-village agricultural society is even less sensitive to major disruption than is food-gathering society. By contrast, industrial civilization as it is at present constituted is confronted by a number of dangers or vulnerabilities, any one of which or any combination of which could result in total collapse. It is not possible to forecast what the exact combination of forces is likely to be, nor the exact time over which they will operate. But we must face the fact that as matters now stand and unless something dramatically new is injected into the picture, industrial civilization, at least in its present form, will probably perish.

(2)

On a relatively short time scale we can conceive of a number of plausible sequences of events which could lead industrial society down the pathway to disaster. Clearly, at least during the next 25 years, events will be strongly shaped by the following geopolitical considerations.

1. Of all major industrial states the Soviet Union appears to be least susceptible to catastrophic disruption. She is basically independent of the rest of the world for her fuels and minerals. Although she is having agricultural problems, in part because of organizational difficulties and in part because of agricultural sensitivities to weather, she is basically self-sufficient with respect to calories and protein. The rulers appear to believe strongly in what they are doing, and they also appear to have a great deal of self-confidence. Like the democracies in the last century, the Soviets believe that history is on their side. They can afford to wait and see what happens, perhaps using a push here and there just to be on the safe side.

On the negative side, the Soviet apparatus is remarkably ponderous and inefficient. Decision making is highly centralized. The outsider cannot help but suspect that the society has built into it an appreciable degree of vulnerability to natural systems failures. When we add to this the human element, Soviet vulnerability to systems breakdown appears to be substantial.

Dissidence in the Soviet Union is not as yet a real threat to the fabric of the Soviet political structure. At the same time it cannot be ignored by the rulers. For the most part the Soviet citizenry, remembering the deprivations of the past, appears willing, at least on the surface, to trade individual liberty for growing affluence. A few strongly believe otherwise and have become sources of great irritation to the authorities. Were the dissidents to grow substantially in number and were they to develop effective tools of terrorism and disruption, the vulnerability of the Soviet Union would increase substantially. At the same time we should not underestimate the power of the tools of persuasion and coercion in the hands of the Soviet leaders.

Another element which affects the stability of the Soviet Union is the People's Republic of China. The Soviet Union is far more vulnerable than is China to disruption brought about by nuclear attack, with the result that although China in the near future is not likely to have available very many thermonuclear weapons together with the means of delivery, she nevertheless is in a position to cause substantial damage to important Soviet centers. She is also in a position to disrupt Soviet operations through the use of sabotage and terrorist activities, particularly in Soviet Asia. For the foreseeable future, China, like the U.S.S.R., will be basically independent of the rest of the world for her fuels, minerals, and food, but like the Soviet Union her agriculture is very sensitive to changes in weather.

The Eastern European socialist countries have become increasingly dependent upon the U.S.S.R. for their supplies of fuels and other minerals. In particular, the Soviet Union provides most of the crude oil and natural gas used by the European socialist countries. Under the circumstances, the linkages of these countries with the Soviet Union will become increasingly strong during the next few decades—indeed, far stronger than the Soviet Union could maintain using military power alone.

2. Japan lies at the opposite extreme of the vulnerability spectrum from the U.S.S.R., being heavily dependent upon imported foodstuffs, energy, and other raw materials. It is estimated that Japan today is only 70 percent self-sufficient with respect to food, and that by the turn of the century the shortfall will be something like 50 percent. Today her major overseas suppliers are the United States, Canada, and Australia.

The petroleum resources of Japan are negilgible but she does have useable reserves of coal. However, the coal seams are thin and costly to mine, and thus since 1957 domestic coal production has fallen precipitously. Japan's major energy needs are now largely met by imported petroleum and to a much lesser extent by imported coal. Similarly, most of Japan's requirements for nonfuel minerals, such as iron ore and bauxite, must be imported.

Japan has at present strong economic and military links with the United States, her largest customer for manufactured goods, her major source of imported foodstuffs, and her military protector. But in recent years the relationships between the two countries have been disturbed. In 1970 and 1971 the U.S. government criticized Japan for selling manufactured goods so aggressively in the United States and threatened to cut back trade between the two countries. More recently the U.S. has put increasing pressure upon Japan to invest more in her own military establishment. The Japanese are strongly resisting such a move for they full recognize the enormous economic advantage which a low level of military expenditure gives them.

The energy crisis of 1973–1974 hit the Japanese economy particularly hard. In part as a result of that experience, the Japanese are now attempting to achieve greater diversification in their sources of crude oil. Greater emphasis is being placed upon Indonesian oil, and discussions are taking place with the Soviet Union concerning the development of Siberian oil and with China concerning the possibility of increasing imports of crude oil from that country. Although it is virtually impossible to forecast with any degree of accuracy what is likely to happen to Japan's economic ties in the next 25 years, it can be said with some certainty that the geopolitics of crude oil are likely to be a major determinant.

The geopolitics of nonfuel minerals, for example iron ore, further complicate the picture. Nearly half of the ore used by Japan's steel industry comes from Australia with a large part of the balance being provided by India, Brazil, and the Philippines. About 85 percent of the imported steel scrap used by the Japanese comes from the United States. With respect to the customers for Japan's exports of steel products, in recent years there has been a trend toward decreasing proportions of sales to the United States and Western Europe and increasing proportions of sales to developing countries.

Looking to the future of her steel industry, Japan faces some extremely serious problems. Foremost among these is the difficult availability of energy and raw materials, including scrap steel and coking coal. By no means the least of the difficulties is pollution. The steel industry is a heavy polluter of the environment and Japan has already reached the point where she can tolerate little in the way of increased pollution levels.

To Japan's vulnerable situation with respect to food and raw materials we must add her high degree of vulnerability as a complex, interconnected system. The Japanese archipelago has in effect become a single, vast, complex city in which every part is connected directly and indirectly with every other part, not to mention her lifeline connections to sources of raw materials. It is obvious that her vulnerability to aggressive military action aimed against her makes her experience during World War II pale into insignificance. But quite apart from military action, the vulnerability of Japan to internal disruption is high, no matter whether we consider natural systems failures, problems of the environment, or the effects of human intervention such as strikes, sabotage, or terrorism.

Although Japan's incredible development since World War II is often attributed to the ability of the Japanese to work together as a people and to reach a consensus rapidly when that is needed, there is increasing evidence that discontent has become widespread. A recent Japanese survey among young people in Japan and ten other countries showed that dissatisfaction and frustration were more prevalent among youth in Japan than anywhere else—in spite of the fact that the Japanese "standard of living" as measured conventionally is higher than in most of the countries surveyed. Such dissatisfaction has led to political violence, notably in the universities, and to increasing distrust between the diverse sectors of Japanese society.

Of all of the highly industrialized parts of the world, it would appear that Japan occupies the unenviable position of possessing the highest degree of vulnerability. This fact is bound to have a profound effect upon Japan as a nation, as well as upon her relationships with the rest of the world.

3. Western Europe is by no means as dependent upon imports of food, energy, and raw materials as Japan; nevertheless, her level of dependency is high. Rapidly growing affluence has caused her to become a heavy importer of feedgrains, primarily from North America. Although there are substantial coal reserves in the region, following World War II the nations of Western Europe quickly fell into the same energy trap as the United States. Today the region meets the greater part of its energy requirements with imports of crude oil from the Middle East and North Africa. The bill of the region for imported oil is twice that of the United States.

Western Europe was hit very hard by the rise in petroleum prices in 1973–1974 and by the Arab oil embargo. Her vulnerability in this respect will be eased to a certain extent once the field of crude oil in the North Sea is in full production. But as a whole Western Europe will still be heavily dependent upon Middle Eastern oil.

Clearly Western Europe, like the United States, has great need for a unified regional energy policy. Her situation is more difficult in principle because so many sovereign states are involved. In spite of the fact that the nations are linked together in the European Economic Community, unified decisions are not made very easily.

There is now serious discussion in Europe concerning the desirability of utilizing nuclear energy on a very large scale. Such a path presents many dangers, but the alternatives are increasing dependence upon the Middle East, and possibly the Soviet Union as well, for supplies of crude oil and natural gas.

Western Europe, like other major industrial areas, is rapidly becoming a single, vast, interlocked system which is subject to a broad spectrum of vulnerabilities. In recent years the seriousness of these vulnerabilities has been emphasized by a wide range of strikes and terrorist activities. Here the United Kingdom appears to be in a particularly vulnerable situation. Indeed, so deep seated are her difficulties, there is some doubt that even her wealth in the North Sea will recue her. Italy and France also appear to be highly vulnerable.

From a military point of view, Europe is protected by the U.S. nuclear umbrella and by the presence of substantial numbers of U.S. troops in Germany. One of the great unanswered questions is the extent to which the U.S. presence in Western Europe can be decreased without putting Europe in a position vis-à-vis the Soviet Union not unlike the present position of Finland. Of course, were the nations of Western Europe to become substantially dependent upon the Soviet Union for supplies of energy and nonfuel minerals, the ties between Europe and the U.S.S.R. would become even stronger. The ultimate consequences of such a development can only dimly be perceived.

4. For some time in the future the Middle East and North Africa will remain the area which is most likely to trigger major worldwide disruption. There is little question but that the mixture which exists there is explosive, consisting of an unprecedented concentration of wealth and political power, tremendous poverty, numerous ethnic and ideological conflicts, unrestrained emotions, terrorism, sophisticated military technology, and worldwide dependence upon the output of the oil fields. When we add to this the disruption which would be precipitated by a major oil embargo, the dangers rise to levels not previously encountered in history. And over this entire explosive mixture lies the nuclear umbrella which could be triggered by Washington or Moscow.

We have recently watched the slow, painful dismemberment of the once-beautiful and relatively well-off city of Beirut. We watched as this jewel of the Middle East was transformed into a vast garbage heap, virtually destroyed by groups which would rather see the city die than coexist and share power on an equitable basis. In the face of such strong polarization, can there be any hope for a real peace in the Middle East?

Of course, the Arab-Israeli conflict dominates the military picture of the region and it seems unlikely that any truly effective long-term settlement will be reached in the near future. An agreement involves the return of nearly all of the Arab territories captured by Israel in 1967, the satisfaction in some way of the national aspirations of the Palestinians, and the recognition of Israel's political legitimacy; and if it is to be effective it must arise from within the region rather than being imposed from without.

The present uneasy truce is not likely to last much longer. The seemingly endless series of maneuvers which have occupied so much time and effort in the past is bound to come to an end, and the consequences are likely to be more upheavals, another war, and perhaps another oil embargo.

5. As we have seen, the Asian mainland can be divided into two major groups of nations and one lesser one, which differ greatly from each other in their degree of resource self-sufficiency, in their present level of development, and in their economic potential.

The first group, centering around the People's Republic of China, includes Vietnam and the Korean Democratic Republic, and has a population of about 900 million persons. These nations are basically self-sufficient with respect to resources, and if we are to judge from the experience of the People's Republic of China, can move forward with plans for economic and social development even in the absence of substantial outside assistance. Raw materials, together with potential agricultural products and manufactured goods which can be exported, appear adequate to pay for needed imports.

The second group of countries, centering around India, includes Afghanistan, Bangladesh, Laos, Nepal, and Pakistan, and has a population of about 800 million persons. These number among the poorest of the poor countries and there seems little prospect of development taking place very rapidly in the next few decades in the absence of substantial help.

The third, much smaller group, consisting of Hong Kong, Singapore, Taiwan, and the Republic of Korea, is tied directly to the market economies of the industrial world and for the time being their 40 million people are doing well economically. But their continued existence as viable entities is by no means certain. Hong Kong is scheduled to be returned to China. The truce between North and South Korea is an uneasy one and were it broken the United States (almost certainly) and China (probably) would be involved.

Both China and India have invested very heavily in armaments, the former much more than the latter. In 1973 China appears to have invested about $12 billion in her military establishment and maintained nearly 3 million men under arms. At the same time, India has invested some $2.3 billion in her military establishment and maintained somewhat fewer than a million men under arms. In viewing these substantial differences we must keep in mind that China is substantially larger than India. Further, the Chinese armed forces play a much larger sociopolitical role in the nation than do those in India.

Both China and India possess the technological expertise and resources to develop and produce nuclear weapons, together with the means for their delivery. At the moment China's limited (but not negligible) nuclear capabilities appear to be directed primarily at the Soviet Union. The animosity between the two countries is intense and has historic, racial, and ideological origins. The Chinese view much of the Soviet Far East as being rightfully theirs, going back to the golden days of the Middle Kingdom. They resent Soviet Caucasian attempts to absorb the underdeveloped people of Asian ancestry in the region. To this must be added the widely differing official views of Marxist truth held by the two countries. Considering the emotional nature of these deep-seated animosities, it is always possible that hostilities will break out someplace along the 7000-kilometer Chinese-Soviet border.

The embryo nuclear force now possessed by India was developed in part as a matter of prestige, particularly in the developing world. With little question this will be built up in the next few years into a credible striking force which could be used to ensure Indian domination of the subcontinent and as a deterrent against China. Fifteen years have not yet erased the humiliation suffered by the Indians at the hands of the Chinese when they invaded India in 1962.

For the time being at least, the Chinese appear to have come to grips effectively with problems of population growth, food production, income distribution, and public health. When we consider this together with her resource base, it would appear that China is presently heading toward a level of development which will enable most of her people to lead reasonably comfortable lives—by no means affluent, but nevertheless comfortable. It remains to be seen whether the Chinese approach to development can be maintained in the face of considerable internal strife. If not, the effect upon the world as a whole would be profound.

India, by contrast, has thus far not been able to come to grips with most of these problems very effectively. Although she has had a population policy for many years, implementation has been difficult and therefore birth rates are still extremely high. Her largest cities, such as Calcutta and Bombay, have become vast slums. Although agricultural production has improved, the problems of distribution are enormous. Problems of public health, particularly in the cities, are nearly insoluble. When we add to these problems conflicts arising from diverse religions and languages, concerning which emotions run high, we are forced to the conclusion that India's major development problems are not likely to be solved for many decades. In the meantime we must anticipate an almost endless sequence of internal upheavals, such as famine, civil strife, and pestilence, and possibly further armed conflict with Pakistan and perhaps China.

6. Africa south of the Sahara seems destined to be a subcontinent in turmoil for many decades. South Africa and Rhodesia, both dominated by whites, are relatively rich. The white minorities are intensely hated by black Africans both inside and outside the borders of the two countries, and there is little question that there will be continuing strife between the two groups until the whites relinquish their power. This is not likely to happen peacefully.

In the meantime South Africa may well become a nuclear power, not in the strategic sense so much as in the tactical sense. Now that Angola has strong ties with the Soviet Union, the injection of nuclear armaments into the African scene could well transform that area into the first nuclear battleground south of the equator.

Black Africa is the home of an even greater number of ethnic antagonisms than exist on the Indian subcontinent. Coups, revolts, and political murders, many of which are of tribal origin, often seem to be the rule rather than the exception. Some of the new nations, notably Nigeria, Zaire, and Zambia, are very rich in natural resources. But the rest, for the most part, number among the poorest of the world's nations. These latter areas will pass through the development process with the greatest difficulty, and then only with considerable assistance from outside. In the meantime we can look forward to continuing turmoil and even to outright warfare between blacks and blacks as well as between blacks and whites.

7. The nations of Latin America are generally more highly developed economically than those of Africa and Asia. Some of the countries, notably Colombia, Mexico, and Venezuela, are sufficiently well endowed with natural resources, particularly energy, that in principle they can undergo the development process without receiving appreciable help from the outside. Venezuela is a member of OPEC and Mexico could be if she desired. Colombia has sufficient petroleum to satisfy her needs for a long time.

Many Latin American nations are well endowed with mineral and agricultural resources. Vast agricultural and grazing lands have helped Argentina become relatively rich. Copper deposits accelerated Chilean development. Brazil's vast resources both above and below the ground have helped her maintain the most rapid rate of development of all Latin American countries for several years. The per capita gross national product of Latin America is nearly four times greater than that of Asia, including the Middle East but excluding Japan. In spite of these relatively favorable economic conditions, Latin America has long been a tumultuous region.

Major problems in the region include extremely high rates of population growth, rapid urbanization, grossly inequitable distribution of income, high rates of inflation and unemployment, coupled with rates of development which lie far below the potential. To this must be added a plethora of coups, revolutions, counterrevolutions, guerrilla activities including terrorism and rioting, and the virtual disappearance of meaningful democratic institutions. The predominant form of government is now the military government of the right or the left. The strong, and not always benevolent, interests of the United States in the economic and political affairs of the area must also be considered.

U.S. investments in Latin America are substantial and her desire to keep anything out of the region that looks like socialism or communism or Soviet-bloc influence are very strong. On numerous occasions over the decades the United States has interfered directly and indirectly in the internal affairs of Latin American nations. In the last 20 years the Soviet Union has made enormous efforts to move beyond her success in Cuba and develop a strong foothold on the mainland, thus far with only modest success, notably in Peru.

But even her modest successes thus far raise the question of whether Latin America might not eventually turn out to be a major area of Soviet–U.S. confrontation.

The turmoil in Latin America seems destined to increase substantially, and in the process it seems likely that the United States will be seriously affected. A great part of the turmoil will probably result from failure to distribute income more equitably. Today the wealthy families in Latin America number among the righest in the world while the poor people of the region number among the poorest. In many countries economic development only results in the rich becoming richer, with little of the new wealth filtering down to the poor. In large measure because of the extremely high rate of population growth in the greater part of Latin America this situation is likely to get worse before it gets better.

By the year 2000 the population of Brazil is expected to increase from 114 million to more than 200 million, that of Mexico from 60 million to more than 130 million, that of Peru from 16 million to 26 million, that of Venezuela from 12 million to 25 million inhabitants. Most of the additions will enter life as members of very poor families. To improve their lot above the poverty level will be extremely difficult.

As soon as they are old enough, a very large proportion of these additions to the ranks of the poor will head for the cities. Since World War II the growth of Latin American cities has been explosive and there is no indication of a slackening. Mexico City, currently approaching a population of 11 million, is projected to have a population of over 30 million by the year 2000. Other projected populations for the year 2000 include São Paulo and Rio de Janeiro, with 25 million and 18 million, respectively, Buenos Aires with 14 million, and Lima with 10 million.

As urban complexes grow to such prodigious size the pressures of providing jobs and services will be enormous. The combination of unemployment, slums, hunger, and inadequate city services can provide fertile ground for political upheaval and revolution.

Such developments in Mexico will almost certainly have a profound effect upon the relationship between Mexico and the United States. We have seen that some 1 million Mexican nationals now enter the United States illegally each year in search of jobs and higher pay. Many of these are apprehended and returned, but most are not. As the population of Mexico increases, in the absence of more equitable income distribution the situation is likely to worsen considerably. How will the people of the United States react when illegal Mexican immigration becomes the dominant element of population growth in the country, and a major factor in unemployment and crime?

Within Mexico, dissatisfaction with the ruling class is increasing. Whether or not this leads eventually to widespread upheaval, including rioting, guerrilla activity, coups, and perhaps even civil war, is uncertain. Recent events suggest that all of these are possible.

8. The United States, the most powerful nation on the earth, militarily, economically, and technologically, finds herself surrounded by this vast assortment of geopolitical uncertainties and at the same time confronted by her own array of internal vulnerabilities, which have already been discussed. It will be difficult enough for her to cope with her internal vulnerabilities over which, at least in principle, she has some measure of control. But how can she effectively come to grips with her external problems, particularly in view of the fact that a major transformation appears to be taking place in the international political order?

For some time now the old coalitions which evolved during the cold war have been disintegrating. It is too early to say where this will carry us, but one possibility is clearly an anarchic world in which every nation must determine its relationship with every other nation and in which many groups have the power of starting major conflagrations.

There are, of course, alternatives to this drift toward anarchy. The major industrial nations of the West, for example, might form a coalition aimed at establishing joint policies and taking joint action concerning certain critical problems which they share in common, such as energy, food, and mineral resources. But it is extremely doubtful that such a coalition, or others like it, could be formed quickly or that they would be very effective once formed. Strong nationalistic feelings are likely to dominate the world political scene for a long time.

(3)

Thus, given the volatility of the world in which we live, it is not difficult to imagine any one of a number of sequences of events, or combinations of them, which could eventually contribute to the fall of industrial civilization. Let us stretch our imaginations and attempt to visualize a few of them, recognizing that in the sociopolitical realm causal chains cannot be identified with precision nor can we expect events to occur in predictable order. The sampling of "plausible sequences of events" described below are simply illustrative of the great variety of possible sources of disruption to which complex modern societies are vulnerable. Indeed, we must always keep in mind the probability that no single chain of events would take place by itself. One development can trigger another, leading to a cascading effect which can give rise to a wide variety of sequences.

1. Let us make the plausible assumption that a revolutionary group takes over the government of Saudi Arabia and quickly assumes the leadership of the group of Arab states associated with OPEC. By that time the dependence of Western Europe, Japan, and the United States upon imported oil has increased substantially over the needs which existed in 1973. The initial objective of the revolutionary group is to bring the Western industrialized world to its knees, and it attempts to do this by establishing a total embargo on sales of crude oil by Arab states to the Western industrialized nations.

The United States, Western Europe, and Japan agree to threaten, and if need be, to undertake joint military action in the Middle East. The Soviet Union issues a warning to the effect that such an action would have the direst consequences. That the Soviet Union might actually use her nuclear striking power against the Western powers does not seem to be a credible assumption, so the United States spearheads a very large paratroop and naval attack aimed at securing the Middle Eastern fields. This is countered by the destruction of the petroleum production and distribution facilities by the Arab military forces.

The Western powers are weakened seriously by the shortage of crude oil and the effect is intensified when other oil-exporting nations, including Indonesia, Nigeria, Venezuela, and Mexico, join the embargo. The United States takes military action and successfully takes over the Mexican fields, but the production and distribution facilities are seriously damaged in the process.

In the meantime, Western Europe and Japan are on the verge of collapse and the Soviet Union takes advantage of the situation by launching a massive, yet cautious, ground attack against NATO forces using conventional weapons. The attack is countered with tactical nuclear weapons and soon nuclear weapons are used by both sides. The Soviet Union takes over all of Europe. In desperation, the United States launches her strategic nuclear arsenal against the U.S.S.R. and retaliation is prompt.

2. Let us imagine that we are in a time, a few decades from now, when virtually all crude oil in the world has been consumed and the industrial powers have become completely dependent upon other sources of energy for their survival. Coal and nuclear power are now the primary sources of energy in the United States and the U.S.S.R. Western Europe and Japan rely almost entirely upon nuclear power, although its effective utilization was brought about extremely slowly, partly because of the social resistance to nuclear power

which had developed in the 1970s, generated by fears concerning technical and environmental safety problems, the safeguarding of nuclear fuels, and the storage and disposal of nuclear wastes.

Legal efforts to curtail expansion of the nuclear power industry were intensified in most OECD countries following the stoppage of the construction of nuclear power plants in the Netherlands and the injection of the issue of nuclear power development into the 1976 Swedish elections. Further nuclear developments were postponed in the United Kingdom, West Germany, France, and Japan. Incidents of sabotage against nuclear power plants increased sharply. As a result of the intensified antinuclear campaign the construction of new nuclear power plants came to a complete halt in OECD countries. As the pressures were further intensified, operations of older plants were curtailed. As the world energy situation became increasingly critical, nuclear power plants once again were designed and put into operation, but by that time 20 years had passed and the economic damage had been considerable.

Steadily increasing energy costs contributed to the maintenance of a high rate of inflation. In the noncommunist countries this led to tremendous dissatisfaction, strikes, and various sorts of terrorist activities. As time passed the terrorist activities became increasingly effective and soon the terrorist arsenals included nuclear explosives.

In order to combat such developments the central governments became increasingly authoritarian and indeed evolved into versions of military dictatorships. These developments resulted in greatly increased terrorist activity which eventually led to the onset of rapid economic decay not unlike that which had taken place in Argentina several decades earlier, only considerably more severe. Eventually, as the system disintegrated there was widespread starvation and pestilence.

The communist countries were by no means free of these problems. Dissension increased markedly after the disturbances of the 1970s and terrorist groups emerged. Some obtained their weapons locally; others obtained them from China. The dissenters quickly appreciated the vulnerability of the Soviet production and distribution system to disruption, and soon that country also found itself in a precipitous economic decline which led to deprivation, hunger, and disease.

3. Let us imagine that the cooling trend in the Northern Hemisphere continues for a few years until the global heating caused by increased carbon dioxide concentration in the atmosphere reverses the trend. Injection of chlorofluorocarbons and nitrous oxide into the atmosphere accelerates the warming process. As a result of these changes, significant shifts take place in

atmospheric circulation patterns and in rainfall. Weather becomes increasingly variable.

Food production in North America, Europe, and the U.S.S.R. drops precipitously. Food production in the monsoon areas, notably Africa and the Indian subcontinent, falls far short of needs as a result of the changing patterns of rainfall. Drought reduces Chinese wheat production and extensive shortage of rainfall in the United States results in sharply reduced corn and wheat harvests. World reserves of cereals drop to virtually zero.

Widespread famine strikes Africa and the Indian subcontinent, with deaths numbering in the tens of millions. As many as 100 million people try to migrate from the countryside into the already heavily crowded cities in hopes of finding food and water. Terrible violence erupts. The Chinese government succeeds in controlling the movements of her own people and in distributing her remaining reserves of cereals on a reasonably equitable basis so real catastrophe is avoided there, at least temporarily.

In the meantime the affluent diets of the Europeans, Russians, and Japanese are severely curtailed. Rations of meat, milk, and eggs are drastically reduced. Rations are also severely cut in the United States because the country needs foreign exchange and the high price of food makes it an important product to export for foreign currency.

The high price of food fans inflation worldwide and accelerates the growth of discontent. As in the second hypothetical sequence of events outlined above, this leads eventually to the decline of the industrial economies.

4. Let us suppose that a number of radical governments of poor countries, angered by the lack of progress in north-south economic discussions, decide collectively to attempt to coerce the industrial countries into accepting their demands. With widespread covert support from the rest of the developing world, these governments engage in a sustained campaign of disruption of the economic, social, and political life of the American, Japanese, and Western European peoples. They are helped by radical elements in those countries, whose needs for militancy are now given "a cause of universal significance." The campaign combines acts of economic warfare, such as oil and mineral embargoes, boycotts of imports, interference with air traffic and electronic communications, with acts of terrorism, including sabotage of power plants and industries.

The United States and its allies attempt to embargo economic transactions with the developing countries participating in the campaign in an attempt to coerce them into stopping their aggressive acts. Military measures are threatened and some small ones are taken. As the situation slowly but relentlessly goes out of control, the effects upon the social and political lives of the Japanese, Europeans, and Americans are profound, exceeding those during the war in Vietnam.

At this point the Soviet Union decides to enter the arena as an active participant, in the hope of emerging from the crisis as the dominant world power. The results are catastrophic.

5. After the militant period of the late 1960s associated with the Vietnam war, students ceased being politically active in opposition to existing American society but the cultural critique of "the system" became much more widespread as the result of Watergate and other disturbing revelations about discrepancies between prevailing doctrines and practices. The incapacity of governmental institutions to cope quickly and effectively with the accumulating problems facing the United States is highlighted by the persistence of unemployment and inflation despite changes in economic leadership. In time the latent radicalization of large numbers of young people is activated by a succession of traumatic events, but notably by the breakdown of the administrative apparatus in a number of metropolitan centers, including New York, Chicago, and Los Angeles.

The breakdowns are brought about by renewed high inflation, which drives up the cost of public services while preventing the collection of additional local taxes and the sale of municipal bonds. Sharp curtailment of police and fire protection, lack of public transportation, stoppage of waste collection, and a breakdown of public education turn these large urban agglomerations into dangerous concrete jungles from which the population tries to escape to other less-affected places.

Politically militant groups, primarily made up of young people, emerge in many parts of the United States, responsive to old and new political ideologies glorifying violence and emphasizing the need for structural changes of American society. Senseless but sophisticated acts of nihilistic destruction are justified in terms of the slogan "worse is better."

The flight from the major cities degenerates into mass hysteria that quickly spreads to other areas. Work stoppages occur. Social controls cease functioning. Looting and vandalism become commonplace and an atmosphere of fear spreads over the land.

The president establishes martial law. Constitutional guarantees are ignored as military units attempt to reestablish order. They try, with varying success, to force employees back to work, to halt the panic-driven migration, and to stop vandalism, looting, and terrorism. Vigilante forces are hastily formed and clash with extremist groups.

By the time order is restored much damage has been done. Domestically, democratic institutions are weakened and some disappear. The federal government attempts to compensate for its seriously weakened condition by abolishing constitutional guarantees. Revolutionary groups move underground. The civil strife seriously erodes the international position of the United States and the faltering U.S. economy results in a serious weakening of the economies of Western Europe and Japan. In time the United States becomes increasingly vulnerable to acts of hostility and aggression from outside, which reinforce the growing disruptive forces within.

6. The population of Mexico continues to increase at a rate of nearly 3.5 percent per year, which implies a growth from 62 million in mid-1976 to 130 million by the turn of the century. By that time the population of Mexico City reaches 30 million. Ineffective Mexican governments, paralyzed by explosive social tensions and endemic terrorism, fail to achieve rates of economic growth capable of providing employment for the rapidly growing labor force. Income distribution remains grossly inequitable.

Illegal migration into the United States, already accounting for an estimated 9 million illegal aliens in residence in 1976, becomes a flood which even expanded border patrols fail to contain. Mexican immigrants settle in metropolitan areas which offer the protection of anonymity and in areas where Spanish-speaking inhabitants are common. By the early 1980s more than a million illegal Mexicans live in Los Angeles alone. Crime rates increase rapidly.

Attempts by the United States government to halt illegal immigration result in unprecedented infringements of civil liberties, including mandatory identity cards. Such measures amplify the alienation of the younger generation of Americans and provide additional justification for civil disobedience and disregard of law.

As the flow of illegal aliens across the border escalates, a radical-nationalist Mexican government, incapable of solving that country's difficulties, embarks on a militant policy against the United States. Asserting that the millions of illegal Mexican residents of California, Arizona, New Mexico, and Texas "have in fact always lived there," it claims the "right of self-determination" for those territories and covertly sponsors a broad range of terrorist activities.

Mexican irredentism quickly obtains moral-political and even material support from other developing countries in the form of embargos, boycotts, and hostility to American citizens abroad. Eventually, the conflict broadens into a major confrontation between the developing countries, led by the governments of Latin America, and the Western industrial democracies.

(4)

We could, of course, make many additions to the sampling of plausible sequences of events briefly discussed above. Nuclear war triggered by third countries, a nuclear power plant catastrophe, the triggering of a major atmospheric upheaval of a kind which is thus far not suspected as being possible, another prolonged military encounter between north and south, armed conflict between the U.S.S.R. and China, the economic collapse of Europe, attempts by a rearmed Japan to secure adequate and predictable supplies of raw materials and food, the use of tactical nuclear weapons in a full-scale war in Africa—the list could be a very long one indeed. But even a partial listing is sufficient to convince one that industrial societies, and particularly the industrial democracies, are probably headed for some extremely troubled times.

In the absence of our injecting dramatically new attitudes and actions into the world system, industrial civilization seems headed for extinction. Perhaps this will come about in two stages, with the industrial democracies perishing first; then the Soviet Union will become the dominant industrial power for a time, following which she will also perish in the face of powerful external and internal forces. Although we cannot say how long the process will take, nor can we specify the precise sequence of events that will lead to the end result, the odds that this will happen seem high.

This, of course, is a very pessimistic conclusion and stands in sharp contrast to the outlooks of some modern technological optimists, for example Herman Kahn, who states confidently that humankind is headed toward a period of unprecedented affluence and well-being. Kahn and his group predict, for example, that in another two centuries the gross world product (GWP) will be $300,000 billion (constant 1975 prices), corresponding to $20,000 per person (assuming a world population of 15 billion persons). There would still be rich nations and poor nations but the gap between them will have been narrowed to a factor of 4, compared with a factor of about 20 today. By that time the per capita GNP of the rich nations would be about $40,000 and that of the poor nations about $9000, or four times greater than the present average per capita GNP of the rich nations. Indeed, according to Kahn and his co-workers, by that time the average person in poor countries such as India and China will have an income greater than that of the average American today.

One cannot fault Kahn's group on the basis of purely technological considerations. They correctly point out that the energy resources yet to be harnessed are vast, that nonfuel minerals are in the long run no major problem, and that considerably more food can be grown in the world than is being grown today. Near-term environmental issues can be handled in such a way as to ensure "clean air, clear water, and aesthetic landscapes." Kahn does express concern about the long-term environment, but concludes optimistically by saying, "we believe that in time society will be able to cope with any technological problems—and we are confident that there will be sufficient time, though not always enough to avoid all trouble."

But the question of whether or not we have the ability to develop new technologies and to cope with technological problems is not really the significant question confronting mankind today. From a technological point of view we already know how to achieve energy independence, but we are not heading in that direction very rapidly. From a technological point of view we know how to grow enough food to feed the hungry, yet the food situation in the world is being improved at a snail's pace. From a technological point of view we know how to prevent conception, yet the birth rates in the poor countries are falling very slowly. In the meantime, tensions mount and arms proliferate.

The main bottlenecks facing humanity, the primary problems which must be solved, are far less technological in nature than they are social, economic, and political. The technological optimists assume that, willy-nilly, society's momentum will enable us to cut through those problems and thus enter a global technological and economic Nirvana. There are those of us, however, who have serious doubts that this will happen. Indeed, some of us doubt that modern industrial societies, as presently constituted, have the resilience to survive the onslaughts of even the next 30 years.

(5)

Were industrial civilization to disappear it would be the greatest of all human tragedies because of what it has yet to offer the human body, mind, and spirit. Virtually all human societies, no matter how harsh their environments have been, have offered individuals some measure of such human pleasures as loving and being loved, companionship, learning, beauty, and understanding. But the shortness and harshness of life has more often than not limited the opportunities for those pleasures. For all of its faults, modern technology has greatly extended the possibilities both in space and in time. People live longer and can devote greater proportions of their time to activities other than their work. Cultural horizons have been broadened.

Equally important, many of the tools and products of technology are also the tools of science and have enabled us to achieve an ever-greater understanding of our universe and of man's place within it. They have enabled us to probe both the infinitely large and the infinitesimally small, as well as life processes which lie in between. One day it should be possible to understand fully the "how?" of our universe and the life which it nurtures. Sometime it might even be possible to understand something about the "why?" But the achievement of that understanding will depend upon the perpetuation and expansion of advanced technology. Should that disappear, the possibility of our achieving the ultimate understanding would also disappear.

A part of the tragedy is that once industrial civilization disappears it will probably not return to the earth scene for an extremely long time—if ever. Industrial society was able to grow as rapidly as it did in part because of the ready availability of high-grade mineral resources including fuels. As time passed and demands rose, the grades of ores gradually decreased. It is clear that as material desires and needs increase in the future, as industrialization spreads and the population of the earth increases still further, we will be confronted by an accelerating diminution of needed substances. The time must inevitably come when ores as such no longer exist and industrial civilization will feed on the leanest of earth substances—the rocks which make up the surface of our planet, the waters of the seas, the gases of the atmosphere, and sunlight. The technology required to carry out processing will become increasingly complex. Nevertheless, as long as the technology is functioning smoothly, industrial civilization can continue to thrive. But should industrial civilization perish, it is difficult to see how it can get started again.

The ancient Romans were extraordinary engineers and organizers. From a purely technological point of view they came close to achieving the maximum of what could be accomplished technologically in the absence of the steam engine. They brought food and raw materials and manufactured goods over great distances from most parts of the then-known world, and this enabled them to support a population of about 1.2 million persons in the city of Rome itself and some 14 million on the Italian peninsula. Many of their buildings still stand and some of their roads and aqueducts are still in use.

In spite of the technological and organizational achievements of the Romans, the empire disintegrated—because of internal and external political and economic pressure, and because of heavy dependence upon imports of food and raw materials. Importation of food was essential, yet the Roman granaries of Spain and Africa were eventually reduced to exhaustion, apparently by a combination of climatic change and land mismanagement. Inadequate food supplies combined with pestilence and war to accelerate the process of decay. As time passed, the Eternal City was cannibalized for its resources. It is essential for us to realize that this could happen again. We are *not* more exceptional than the Romans were.

After Roman civilization with its high level of technology died, many centuries elapsed before a new civilization emerged to replace it. At that time, as distinct from the present, high-grade resources were plentiful. Conspicuously absent were the necessary organizational skills and technology.

That ancient Egyptian monument, the obelisk, provides in a strange way a bridge between civilizations and illustrates how technologies can be lost when a civilization declines.

These extraordinary columns were simple in design and hewn from solid rock—a combination which enabled them to withstand the ravages of time. The large number of such monuments which have stood for twenty or more centuries attests to the astuteness of the designers and to the capabilities of the craftsmen.

With the decline of Rome, Nero's circus fell into disuse and in time an extremely large obelisk in the center of the track fell over, where it remained prone for eleven centuries. In the sixteenth century Pope Sixtus V developed a plan to erect the giant stone in front of the Basilica of St. Peter in the Vatican. To move so huge a mass using Renaissance technology was so complex an undertaking that all mathematicians of Christendom were asked to submit proposals. One plan was selected out of fifty suggestions and on April 30, 1586, after many difficulties, the obelisk was finally lifted, placed on rollers, and hauled to the center of the square to the sound of all the Eternal City's church bells. In September the stone was pulled upright to the cheers of a huge crowd.

This considerable engineering achievement was hailed in song and story. Paintings and poems glorified the event. But few people at the time appreciated that the Romans over twelve centuries earlier had floated the huge pillar down the Nile from Heliopolis to Alexandria, then transported it by ship to the Tibur, then transported it several kilometers overland to Nero's circus, now the site of the Vatican, where they erected it. Further, this was but one of dozens of such objects which the Romans had brought from Egypt and erected in various parts of the city, largely for decorative purposes. With the decline of Rome, the engineering and organizational skills which enabled the Romans to accomplish such gigantic tasks with such apparent ease were lost.

At present, numerous high-grade resources which would be necessary to start a new civilization are simply no longer available. Extremely complex technologies and organizations are needed to develop an industrial civilization from the earth's lowest common denominators.

Were industrial civilization to perish as the result of a catastrophe, or were it to decay in the manner of Roman civilization, the survivors could undoubtedly provide for their needs for a time by cannibalizing the remnants of the deceased civilization. Dead buildings and automobiles are indeed rich sources of raw materials. But there are limits to which a civilization can continue to exist in this manner, particularly if organizational capabilities are lessened.

(6)

In the light of this gloomy prognosis, it is important that we ask whether it is possible for industrial societies eventually to adapt themselves to the dangers which they face. Can we conceive of an industrial-urban counterpart of peasant-village society? Quite apart from the short-range problem of survival, can we conceive of solutions to long-range problems?

If such problems as nuclear war, resource embargos, terrorism, and the rich-poor dichotomy were eliminated from our culture, we could conceive of an interdependent, global civilization in which many of the vulnerabilities discussed earlier no longer exist. We could even conceive of a world which has a government designed to keep the peace and cope with those common aspects of human activity which are global in scope and affect all people.

Unfortunately, the divisions between cultures are deep and the pursuit of an elusive "national sovereignty" seems destined to occupy the attention of the world's politicians more than world unity for at least the next century. Perhaps we will learn how to live with this situation from a political point of view. But if we do, we must also learn how to live with the situation from the point of view of resources and function.

To take the long view, can we conceive of a "city" which together with its surrounding area is self-sufficient with respect to its material and functional needs? When we examine our technological potential it turns out that such units are indeed possible. We can conceive of cities on land which feed on rock, water, air, and sunlight, and which, like peasant-villages, can reproduce themselves. We can also imagine large cities which float on the sea which feed upon the resources of the ocean and which can also reproduce themselves. Such self-sufficient units could each provide comfort for perhaps 500,000 persons. Worldwide, there might be some 20,000 such units, many of which might be united regionally or culturally with respect to certain common problems.

Dividing human society into a large number of self-sufficient, replicative units would be one way to create a global industrial society which has substantial built-in resilience. Given 20,000 such units, few catastrophes could destroy the entire system. Although the units would be self-sufficient, one hopes that there would be considerable trade among them as well as a great deal of cultural interchange.

A land-based unit would derive needed metals and other minerals from deposits of igneous and sedimentary rocks. Complex carbon compounds could be produced from limestone or from plant materials. Water would be obtained from nearby streams and lakes or from the sea. Heat and power would be obtained from sunlight and from uranium and thorium obtained from rock. Food would be obtained from the cultivation of the surrounding countryside.

A sea-based unit would derive its needed raw materials from seawater, deposits on the ocean floor, and the products of photosynthesis. Heat and power would be obtained by making use of vertical temperature differences in the ocean, from direct solar radiation, or from uranium from seawater. Food would be obtained from the sea.

Units built along seacoasts could combine many features of both sea- and land-based units. Depending upon the location these could be the most versatile units of all, and would harmonize with the fact that already in the United States more than half of the population lives well within 100 kilometers of the coastline.

Such installations could be designed to be efficient in their use of raw materials, including energy. Wastes would be recycled and pollution would be kept to very low levels. By building in three dimensions, as the architect Paolo Soleri advocates and is reducing to practice in his city, Arcosanti in Arizona, comfortable and aesthetic environments could be created which would take up relatively little area and which could be designed in such a way as to harmonize with the surroundings, whether they be land, coast, or sea. Ecological disruption could be kept to very low levels.

We cannot expect such units to emerge fully developed in the near future. Other approaches to providing for human needs are at present less expensive and less demanding from a technological point of view. It is important for us to realize, however, that as the resource base decreases and as the need for higher levels of resilience increases, it is technologically feasible for us to move in this direction. It is not necessary for industrial societies as they are presently constituted to reconcile themselves to the likelihood of their extinction.

Present forces seem to be pushing us in the direction of a world made up of a limited number of industrial societies of increasing vulnerability. Recognition of the dangers inherent in the current situation could lead to a movement toward a limited global government, but at present this seems unlikely.

Rather, the process of fragmentation will probably continue to lead to increasing numbers of political units but probably not to increasing self-sufficiency.

We can hope, however, that rationality will in some measure play a role in determining our destiny. Should this come to pass, we can hope that it would eventually lead us toward two goals simultaneously. The first would be toward increased self-sufficiency and resilience in a physical-biological sense. The second would be toward one world in a political-moral sense. Thus any assessment of the future of industrial civilization must take into account the fact that man still has the power to determine his destiny. From a technological point of view he has the ability to create a resilient civilization in which poverty and hunger no longer exist and in which all persons have the opportunity of leading free lives which are rewarding both materially and intellectually. The computer might judge such a development improbable, but although the probability might be low, the fact of overwhelming importance is that man still possesses to some degree the power to determine the future course of his development.

The current odds certainly favor the extinction of industrial civilization. But the odds against us are by no means zero. Indeed, there is reason to suppose that once we fully comprehend the present human predicament, this in itself might substantially change the odds in our favor.

(7)

It is extremely difficult to build needed resilience into the fabric of industrial society within the framework of democratic institutions. Sound policies covering such complex matters as armaments, energy, food, resources, environment, economic and labor policies, urban decay, and crime are arrived at very slowly—indeed, often too slowly to avoid major crises. Under these circumstances the pressures become very strong to take shortcuts, to bypass democratic processes, to endow individuals or small groups with increased power to make decisions and take actions. As our situation becomes increasingly complex and as the dangers become increasingly apparent, these forces will probably become stronger. It seems likely, therefore, that if industrial civilization survives it will become increasingly totalitarian in nature.

Since World War II we have seen these same kinds of forces operating in the poor nations of the world. Democracy has been abandoned in most of Africa, Asia, the Middle East, and Latin America, and the majority of totalitarian regimes have become oppressive, relying upon coercion to attain their objectives. In some situations, democracy has been abandoned because of internal chaos or divisions of power and influence which made it virtually impossible to develop meaningful development programs. In others, democracy has been abandoned to protect the wealthy and privileged minority. In still others, it has been simply a seizure of power on the part of a few who wanted the power and perhaps the wealth associated with it, and who had the weapons to obtain it.

Of the billion or so persons living in the industrialized nations, only 675 million, or 60 percent, live in effectively functioning democracies. This is little more than 16 percent of the world population. The rest live in Eastern Europe, including the Soviet Union, in Spain and Portugal, which are in a state of flux, or in South Africa, which is rife with conflict between black and white and not likely to last much longer.

Of all of the industrialized totalitarian states, the Soviet Union is the largest and most powerful. Her substantial resource base gives her a degree of self-sufficiency not possessed by other industrial countries. It also gives her economic leverage over other nations, particularly those of Eastern Europe. Although the government of the Soviet Union is ponderous and from many points of view inefficient, it seems likely that reasonable facsimiles of that government are destined to control the nation for a long time in the future. During the last two decades there appears to have been a liberalization of attitude on the part of the central government with respect to individual rights, but it seems highly unlikely that this trend will lead to the emergence of genuine democratic institutions in the U.S.S.R. While it is significant that in recent years groups of dissidents have emerged, this phenomenon has caused outside pressures to be placed on the Soviet government to recognize certain basic principles of individual human rights. Laudable as those efforts are, in the long run they will probably have little effect upon the outcome, for the control over the people by the leaders of the government is virtually complete. Although expressions of outside attitudes concerning human rights will continue to have effect upon the short-term policies of the Soviet government, they are unlikely to have major impact upon long-term policies.

Thus, although the industrial democracies and the industrial totalitarian states share many vulnerabilities in common, it is doubtful that the two groups will be able to work closely together on more than a few problems of vulnerability and resilience. There may be exceptions in the areas of arms control and disarmament, as well as in developing common approaches to global environmental problems. But it seems unlikely that we will be able to work together on the really broad problems of those societal vulnerabilities which stem from both internal and external economic, social, and political instabilities.

Under these circumstances, if democracy is to survive, the present industrial democracies must work closely together in an attempt to chart their own destinies, recognizing that the economic vulnerabilities of the industrial democracies are compounded by their political vulnerabilities. Experience with the efficient management of truly representative political systems is as short as that pertaining to the operation of complex industrial systems. Neither existed 200 years ago. They have succeeded thus far in only a small proportion of human society. Indeed, the record so far suggests that stable constitutional democracies are even more difficult to maintain than steady economic development through market mechanisms. What makes the industrial democracies particularly vulnerable is that sudden perturbations of their political processes and institutions tend to disrupt the rest of the system.

Thus if industrial civilization survives, it will probably do so because the existing industrial totalitarian states have a relatively high capability for survival. It seems unlikely that the industrial democracies will be able to generate the sustained effort necessary to preserve their democratic institutions while at the same time preserving their strong technological-organizational base.

(8)

In spite of the gloomy outlook, the fact remains that man has it within his power to create a world in which hunger and poverty are eliminated, in which all people can live comfortably in environments which are not only clean but beautiful, in which people are free to move about as they please, read and write what they please, and live in cultural environments of their own choosing. Although the creation of such a world lies well within our technological capabilities and well within the resource base which our technology can unlock, the task of achieving it is nevertheless a prodigious one. Two preconditions are essential for success. First, the long time scale must be appreciated—we are talking about one or more centuries. Second, there must be the political will to get the job done in spite of the long time scale. This latter precondition may well turn out to be the real stumbling block.

We who live in the United States are extremely fortunate. Although our founding fathers were very wise and got us started down the right path, they could not have conceived of what the new nation eventually was to become. Certainly what we have become was not planned—in a very real sense it just happened, partly as a result of a sequence of fortuitous circumstances. In the process of our national evolution many mistakes were made; but because of our vast natural wealth, those mistakes could be afforded. We had some close calls, for example the Civil War and World War II; but, fortunately, we had the resilience to recover and move to still higher levels of prosperity.

Those days are gone. Today, the margin for error is much less than it used to be, and it is decreasing. Humanity has passed the point where it can afford to wait and see what happens next—the hazards which lie between us and the next age of man, whatever that might be, are too great. The kind of world we are talking about can only be brought into existence through careful planning and dedicated, sustained effort.

Perhaps it will not be possible for humanity to unite upon a program of world development which would take generations to complete. Most people in the Western world are willing to provide for their children, but only until they are grown. A smaller proportion are concerned about the welfare of their grandchildren. Almost none make provision for their great-grandchildren. Why should we be concerned about the welfare of future generations when so many of us are willing to tolerate violence and suffering in the present?

While most humans are primarily concerned about the welfare of their immediate families, it may be that there are sufficient numbers of people who are concerned about future generations—or who would be concerned if they knew and understood the facts—so that a movement for world development could be generated, perhaps starting in the West, but eventually becoming worldwide. A consensus would have to be obtained among millions concerning the seriousness of the dangers in time perspective, the long-term goals, and the actions which should be taken. Such a movement would be difficult to start, but in the absence of something like it, the prognosis for the future will remain dire.

As a start, groups from Japan, Western Europe, and the United States might establish programs aimed at identifying and then examining in detail all major threats confronting their respective industrial democracies. It seems likely that certain synergistic interactions would appear to be particularly dangerous. The disruptive potential of a major upheaval in one industrial democracy on the others would also require special scrutiny.

Once a measure of agreement has been reached from a multilateral perspective, the results should be exposed to the scrutiny of the scientific community, governments, business and labor, the media, and the public at large. Groups should then be established which would examine in depth the available knowledge with regard to specific vulnerabilities, identify deficiencies in our knowledge, and encourage additional research to fill gaps. There should then be a major integrative effort that would explore various combinations and permutations of threats, which by their synergistic impact, whether by accident or by a causal linkage of events, could create crises of such magnitude as to threaten the survival of one or all industrial democracies.

Following this background effort, a major multilateral effort should be made to develop a series of proposed policies aimed at coping with vulnerabilities and increasing resilience. Here, the most difficult problem will be to find ways to carry out these policy recommendations in the real world, with its multitude of conflicting interests, prejudices, suspicions, and inertias.

Parallel with this major effort aimed at developing specific policies to deal with vulnerabilities, there should be accelerated international efforts aimed at decreasing the likelihood of nuclear and conventional war and decreasing military expenditures worldwide. Finally, plans should be formulated jointly by the rich and poor nations aimed at greatly accelerating the process of economic and social development in the poor countries with the goal of eliminating poverty, hunger, and malnutrition.

Given such a program and the concomitant worldwide sustained effort, it is conceivable that the industrial democracies will survive. But the transition will be stormy and filled with dangers. There will be conflict and violence. Civil and international strife will continue for many decades. But if the industrial democracies remain calm, yet forceful and united in their efforts, it seems quite possible that the transition to a new and higher level of civilization which embraces all humanity can be successfully negotiated.

CHAPTER XI

What We Can Do

(1)

Before discussing what we can do about the precarious situation in which we now find ourselves, it is essential that we ask what we wish of life beyond the primitive, narrow, and unsatisfactory goal of simple survival. Survival for what? What do we want to be? If we had the power and could use it effectively, what would our goals be?

Today we are children. We have pried open a box which contains keys to other boxes. We have managed to fit some of the keys to their corresponding locks and have revelled in the contents of the boxes we have managed to open. We have found wondrous toys which we have played with and fought over. We have found wondrous weapons which enable us to destroy each other in our race to open more boxes. But we have not really addressed ourselves collectively to the question of what might lie beyond our toys, our game playing, and our killing.

Today we are children, but finally after a million or so years our childhood is about to end. With the end of childhood three things can happen: we can exterminate ourselves; we can go back to the ways of life of our ancestors; we can make a quantum jump upward to a new level of civilization, undreamed of by the philosophers of the past.

We often hear major criticisms of technology and of the science which supports it. Many problems which now confront us, such as the dangers of nuclear war, problems of the environment, population growth, and urbanization, crises of energy and food, have been pointed to as direct results of modern technological change. In a sense this is correct, for technology made these dangers possible. But it took human behavior to transform the possible dangers into real ones. Technology, like the axe, is a tool. In the hands of some persons it can be used to kill; in other hands it can be used to produce food. In still others it can be used to help us fly to the stars.

When great energies are expended to curb new technologies, we should ask ourselves whether those energies might not be expended more usefully in curbing certain human institutions which misuse technology. Should we not look upon such human inventions as national boundaries, the concept of national sovereignty, contempt for races and classes other than our own at least equally worthy of being curbed? Is it more important to curb nuclear technology as an isolated issue, or the concept of profit at whatever the cost to society?

Our technology gives us power over nature which is unprecedented in our history. From a purely technological point of view, hunger and poverty in the world are now inexcusable. All people can be fed; all can have adequate amenities. Technology makes this possible. Unfortunately, human behavior patterns keep it from happening.

Recognizing the power that the combination of technology and modern science places in our hands, it is possible for us to imagine a world in which hunger and deprivation have been eliminated, together with capabilities for mass destruction. It is a world in which all people are able to lead free, abundant, and even creative lives. The worldwide civilization is humane and people are in tune with nature, using but not abusing the earth's riches. The creation and preservation of beauty, whether of sight, sound, or touch, is a major human objective. The attainment of new knowledge concerning our universe and our place within it is another.

Our technology makes possible the continuous accumulation of new knowledge, but even more important, it expands our horizons of understanding.

Where did we come from?

Where are we heading?

Where lies our ultimate destinty?

We don't know. But these are questions that can eventually be answered, at least in part, if we retain our technological capabilities. If we lose those capabilities, we will lose the greater part of our ability to learn the answers. And we will lose, probably forever, the power to eliminate human hunger, deprivation, and suffering.

In our thinking about such problems, we must also keep in mind the vastness of our universe. Our galaxy contains billions upon billions of stars and there are billions upon billions of galaxies. Why should we humans think that we are alone? The recent explorations of Mars suggest strongly that life on Earth may well be unique in our own planetary system, that only on Earth among the planets were the physical and chemical conditions able to nurture the complex sequence of chemical events which led to the first complex molecule which could reproduce itself. Perhaps Mars was too dry, Venus too hot,

Mercury and the moon too small, Jupiter too large, and Saturn and the outer planets too cold.

Yet, on the basis of what we now think we know about the ways in which stars were formed, planetary systems are probably extremely abundant. Among these there almost certainly are a great many earthlike planets which perhaps are abodes of life. Given life processes, what is the likelihood that, as on Earth, creatures possessed of power of conceptual thought have emerged? Given such creatures, what are the chances that civilizations have emerged? Given civilizations, what is the likelihood that sufficiently high levels of technology have been achieved to permit a civilization in one planetary system to communicate with civilizations in others?

A number of serious scientists believe that the likelihood is sufficiently great to warrant an intensive search for signals. They point out that within the last three decades we on Earth entered a new communicative state. Our radio technique has now been developed to the point where a signal can be sent from Earth which could easily be detected on the other side of our galaxy. An observer of that signal would see our sun as most unusual among stars and would probably suspect the existence of a high level of technology.

Some enthusiasts suggest that a communications network might already connect advanced civilizations in our galaxy and that human civilization is destined to become a part of it as we pass from childhood to maturity.

Others suggest that civilizations based upon high technology, and associated high rates of energy consumption, are basically unstable. High-energy civilizations will come into existence, live for a few centuries, then inevitably perish through the misuse of their great power.

Whatever the real situation turns out to be, it must be stressed that a search for extraterrestrial intelligence would be worthy of the human spirit, as were the construction of Chartres and Notre Dame, or our voyages to the moon and Mars. Contact with another civilization would tell us instantaneously that it is possible for a civilization to maintain an advanced technological state and not destroy itself.

On the other hand, if we do not detect communicative life elsewhere, perhaps our seeming aloneness will cause us to appreciate how precious our culture really is and will stress the importance of our protecting it vigilantly from the human dangers of our age.

Today, humanity finds itself living from crisis to crisis. So intent are we on the business of getting ourselves out of each crisis as it strikes that our sights have become narrowed and we fail to devote sufficient time and allocate adequate resources for truly great projects which help us look outward and thus enhance life's meaning. The creation of the modern equivalents of Chartres and Notre Dame, whether they be cathedrals, space stations, concert halls, national parks, or arrays of radiotelescopes, should be placed and kept at the top of our lists of priorities. Only in that way can our view of humanity be kept sufficiently broad to enable us to come to grips innovatively and meaningfully with the vast array of mundane problems which threaten to destroy us.

(2)

It is important that we recognize that there is no such thing as an isolated solution, whether instant or otherwise, for any of the human dangers which confront us. Instead, there are fabrics of solutions, all interconnected, which must evolve with time as conditions change.

We must learn to think of our problems on three time scales which can be illustrated by the food situation. First, there is the short time scale of, say, one to five years. Here, we in the United States, for example, are faced by the immediate decision of whether to encourage farmers to plant or not to plant. We can be hit by bad weather. We are confronted by immediate problems of using existing agricultural production and reserves in such a way as to minimize the human suffering in the poor countries and to avoid disaster before the next harvest. We want to maximize the dollar value of our agricultural exports without raising substantially the cost of food at home. Many decisions must be made, which will change from year to year.

Second, there is the long-range problem of securing regional self-sufficiency in agricultural production in the world as a whole. The time scale for achieving this is about a hundred years. For success, a worldwide collaborative effort would be necessary, and the decisions would be quite different from those which would be made on the short time scale.

Finally, there is the intermediate problem of expanding and utilizing effectively the food surpluses of the rich exporting nations so that the needs of both rich and poor importing nations can be reasonably met during the transition period.

Most governments are prepared to take action on a short time scale, but few are prepared to take meaningful action on a long time scale. In the United States the budget cycle is one year, the congressional cycle is two or six years, and the presidential cycle is four years. Few individuals are prepared to take meaningful actions when the results will not be visible for much longer times.

Thus, in some way governmental processes must be changed to take into account the need to make decisions on a long time scale. There are a number of ways in which this might be done. For example, agreed-upon appropriations might be made each year to a new type of national institution which is charged in turn with the obligation of funding long-term projects in collaboration with similar groups elsewhere in the world. But however we go about it, we must realize that this is one of the more critical institutional problems we face today. Unless we learn how to cope adequately with issues on a long time scale, most of the critical problems which confront us will remain unsolved.

When we think only on a short time scale we are reduced to crisis management, which in the long run is self-defeating. Increasingly we find ourselves relying upon brute-force tactics instead of upon strategies for avoiding the crises in the first place. As we have seen, the dangers involved in this approach are manifold.

Here it is essential that we establish early-warning systems which will help us anticipate the consequences of past, and possible future decisions. This means developing the art and science of modeling to a level which will enable techniques of forecasting to be used with a fairly high degree of confidence, taking into account the fact that there are many things, such as oil embargos, which can not be forecast.

The recent creation of the Office of Technology Assessment and of the Budget Office in Congress were important first steps. Beyond that we need to establish someplace in government a mechanism for forecasting, on a continuing basis, demands for and availability of resources using time scales of 10, 20, and 50 years. Such forecasts could be used to anticipate problems and, it is hoped, assure that decisions could be made in time to avoid crises.

There are many areas in which such forecasting will be essential in the years ahead, not only on a national basis but on a global basis as well. Coupled with this it is important that certain vital variables are monitored carefully on a global basis. Such variables should include carbon dioxide, ozone, mean atmospheric temperature, aerosol concentrations, radioactivity, and radiation balance. Satellites can be used to monitor the state of the world's croplands and forests, snow and ice cover, and movements of oil tankers.

But monitoring by itself will not be sufficient. It must be coupled with analytical tools which will enable us to anticipate so that we can plan for the future on each appropriate time scale. Although planning is anathema to some people, not to engage in it fully at this stage of our development would be foolhardy.

(3)

A substantial proportion of the vulnerabilities which confront humanity today have their roots buried deeply in the concept of the nation-state. Each nation considers itself to have sovereign jurisdiction over its own destiny even though growing interdependencies make nonsense of that view. But the fact remains that national boundaries cut up what would otherwise be viable and resilient regions into a series of highly vulnerable subunits, few of which are self-sufficient and most of which can wage war upon each other. National boundaries impede human progress by encouraging war, inhibiting the flow of people, capital, goods, ideas, and information, and by creating entities which give power and wealth to small elites while permitting the masses of people to live in poverty and virtual bondage. The vast majority of people in the world today live under such conditions. Only in the industrial democracies is the situation different, but as we have seen, they are now in a precarious position, magnified in no small measure by the boundaries which they themselves also defend vigorously.

Above the nation-state there is almost nothing which is politically effective. The United Nations has no power and very little influence, although it does have some uses, particularly in situations where the United States and the Soviet Union agree. Some United Nations agencies, for example the World Meteorological Organization and the World Health Organization, do extremely useful work which even manages to breach national boundaries from time to time. But they have little effect upon the governance of the system of nation-states. Thus, apart from a large and very complex series of bilateral gentlemen's agreements and a much smaller series of multilateral ones, anarchy prevails above the national level. Although such agreements are important, we must recognize that a nation will usually honor an agreement only as long as it remains in its interest to do so.

The concept of the sovereign nation-state is so deeply imbedded in human traditions that it will remain a major obstacle to human progress for a very long time in the future. If solutions are found for the formidable array of problems which confront us, it will be in spite of nations rather than because of them. Eventually, perhaps, the world will be united under a government with limited yet real powers over institutions and people with respect to common global problems such as keeping the peace, management of atmospheric pollution, and management of stockpiles of food and other resources. Although we can hope that this will happen, the urgency of our problems is such that we cannot await that day. We must search for other means of effectively penetrating the boundaries of the nation-state for the purpose of getting the job done.

One way of doing this would be to strengthen the United Nations itself so that it can be a more effective organization for keeping the peace. This would involve the adoption of many procedural changes, modification of voting rules, and elimination of the veto. It would also involve the establishment of a permanent, well-funded international peacekeeping force together with an effective intellegence unit which would have control of its own satellite surveillance system for watching military movements as well as movements of ships. The unit would monitor international weapons transfers on a continuing basis.

Once experience is gained, the United Nations or its specialized agencies might be given jurisdiction over other satellite systems used for watching changes in weather, monitoring the environment, and surveying agricultural land and forests.

The International Atomic Energy Agency might be given the responsibility for training and deploying a highly professional international army of nuclear facility inspectors who would be stationed permanently at all nuclear facilities in the world for the purpose of guarding against mishandling or theft of nuclear materials, and ascertaining that proper safety precautions were being taken.

The World Bank, which plays an important role in the development of the poor countries, might be broadened, strengthened, and given greater autonomy. It might be authorized to expand substantially its technical assistance efforts, particularly in agriculture.

New intergovernmental organizations might be created outside of or within the United Nations system to manage global stockpiles of cereals, help develop the international agricultural research network, or help manage the resources of the deep sea.

We must recognize, however, that the concept of national sovereignty renders many intergovernmental organizations impotent. At their best they tend to be ponderous bureaucracies which cannot easily arrive at decisions and which do not always attract effective international civil servants. This is a situation which can and should be changed as quickly as possible, although we should recognize that some of the greatest resistance to change will come from within the system itself, which has its own elite.

A hopeful approach is to work outside the intergovernmental system. Organizations such as the International Rice Research Institute in the Philippines, the International Council of Scientific Unions in Paris, and the International Institute of Applied Systems Analysis near Vienna have demonstrated that much important work can be accomplished at an international collaborative nongovernmental level, with minimal interference on the part of governments. Most such organizations depend at least in part upon governments for their funds, so the government presence is there. Nevertheless, many of these organizations have learned how to cope with this situation reasonably satisfactorily.

The International Council of Scientific Unions has enunciated, for example, the "Principle of Free Circulation of Scientists," which says that no matter where scientists live in the world, they have the right to participate in international scientific activities. If a scientist who lives in country A wants to participate in a conference scheduled to be held in country B, then the government of country B should issue a visa to the scientist from country A even if the two countries are not on friendly terms. The organization, of course, has no power of enforcement, but it does have influence. Were country B to refuse the visa, the chances are that the organization would not accept another invitation from that country unless there were assurances that the incident would not be repeated.

Although such conditions are difficult to bring about from an institutional point of view, they have in fact been accomplished. Because of such efforts, scientists from East Germany and Cuba attended conferences in the United States long before formal relations were established between the governments concerned. Israeli scientists attend conferences in the Soviet Union. Almost no scientific conferences are held in the Arab world because the Arab nations will not admit scientists from Israel.

In recent decades non-governmental international organizations have initiated and carried out programs which simply could not have been accomplished by intergovernmental organizations. Two of them were responsible for the so-called Green Revolution and were instrumental in its spread in Asia. Programs involving intimate collaborative efforts such as the International Geophysical Year, the International Biological Program, and the Global Atmospheric Research Program would not have been successful had they been left to governments alone. Clearly, this approach to world problems should be pursued even more vigorously in the future.

Among the nongovernmental organizations, the multinational corporations stand out as being particularly effective in the conduct of business across national boundaries. Their governances are international. Their organizational structures are almost always sufficiently flexible to permit them to accommodate to rapidly changing international and national political situations. They have acquired considerable abilities to move raw materials, manufactured goods, people, services, ideas, and money in and out of nations efficiently. In the process, they have produced cadres of workers at all levels whose views of the world, and even allegiances, are considerably broader than those which have traditionally emerged within the framework of the nation-state system.

For the most part, multinational corporations have learned how to work with governments, and on occasion even to bypass them. Some corporations have misbehaved by deliberately interfering with the internal political affairs of countries, sometimes flagrantly, and in so doing they have occasionally jeopardized the smooth functioning of the system. Nevertheless, they have demonstrated that they have great value to rich and poor nations alike. Although their rules of behavior need to be more precisely defined, they fill a real need and their potential for the future appears to be enormous.

(4)

When we examine the problems which now confront humanity on a global scale, those of most immediate importance are war and poverty. These problems cannot be divorced from each other for, as we have seen, the growing tensions between rich and poor countries could well trigger, directly or indirectly, a nuclear holocaust. The economic and social development of the poor countries to the level where people are well nourished, death rates and birth rates are low, and literacy rates are high would by no means be the total remedy. Obviously, wars are often waged for reasons which transcend poverty. But the elimination of poverty would be an important element in the total assemblage of constructive steps which need to be taken.

Before discussing approaches to the problem of global poverty it is essential that we in the industrialized part of the world understand three basic realities which unfortunately are reflections both of our economic system and of human nature:

1. We can help ourselves in the process of helping other nations.
2. We can manufacture goods, throw them away, and help ourselves in the process.
3. We can give money to the poor nations to spend as they wish and not necessarily help them.

If help is given in the wrong way at the wrong place at the wrong time, it can do great damage. If it is given in the right way at the right place at the right time, it can benefit all parties concerned.

To appreciate the first point, we need only look back at the Marshall Plan which provided for massive U.S. economic assistance to the war-devastated nations of Europe and Japan. A result of this, which surprised almost everybody, was 25 years of unprecedented economic development, not only for the nations being helped, but for the United States as well. By helping to accelerate the recovery of the war-torn nations, the U.S. opened markets for its own industrial and agricultural products. The U.S. benefited further by being able to import European and Japanese goods at favorable prices. A true symbiosis evolved which lasted for many years.

The rich countries can examine their military expenditures to appreciate the second point. We go through endless cycles which involve the following sequence of events:

1. Development of a new weapons system which renders an older weapons system obsolete;
2. Production and deployment of the new weapons system;
3. Scrapping of the old weapons system, perhaps involving the sale of components to developing countries;
4. Development of a still-newer weapons system which renders obsolete the most recently installed one.

As the process repeats itself, millions of people remain employed and millions of stockholders receive dividends. We purchase something which is indeed important, yet rather elusive and indeterminate; we call this "national security." But the process itself has become a way of life, in no small measure because the livelihoods of so many people depend upon its perpetuation.

The entire process teaches us that in principle we could build factories for the purpose of manufacturing useless objects which could be stored for a few years, then dumped into the ocean. In the meantime we could design new factories to build a "new generation" of useless objects. We would, of course, waste valuable resources, but balancing this would be the substantial levels of employment and profits.

Most of us agree that it would be nonsensical, even immoral, to establish such a system. But the "military-industrial complex" which now exists in the rich countries has demonstrated that something very much like this could be done on a substantial scale. Indeed, in the United States the military system operates at a level of $80 billion annually, which amounts to about 6 percent of the GNP. The system keeps about 2 million persons in their prime working years in the armed services and thus out of productive economic activity. At the same time, millions are supported by the industrial and service activities required to keep the military establishment functioning effectively.

In one sense, from the purely economic point of view, there is little difference between building fertilizer factories to be given away to those poor countries which can use them effectively to help combat hunger, and building weapons systems. We would be building, then disposing in a way that is similar to the military case. In another sense, however, through the process of helping to build up the less-developed economies to the point where they can support themselves, there would emerge increased demands for U.S. manufactured and agricultural exports.

The third reality which must be faced is that nations differ greatly in their abilities to plan, to absorb capital effectively, and to solve the vast number of complex problems connected with their development. Often they lack adequate numbers of trained and experienced people. Diversion of funds for the benefit of the elite is common. Military expenditures consume inordinate sums, on the average exceeding expenditures for public health and education combined. In many countries bribes are accepted, and often demanded, at virtually all levels of the government bureaucracy.

These realities suggest, first of all, that the rich countries could afford to make available substantial resources for a massive effort to end hunger and poverty in the world. At the peak of the Marshall Plan efforts, some 3 percent of the United States GNP was devoted to development assistance. That figure is now down to about 0.25 percent, perhaps only half of which goes for purposes relevant to the elimination of poverty and hunger. Certainly the rich nations could easily afford to spend 1 percent of their GNPs for development assistance to the poor countries. Were military budgets curtailed, far more than that could be afforded.

The real limitation stems not so much from what the rich countries can afford, but rather from what the poor countries can effectively absorb in the way of assistance. For reasons already discussed, the absorptive capacity differs greatly from country to country. Any concerted global effort must take this into account.

Several recent studies suggest strongly that, given the political will, hunger and poverty could be virtually eliminated from the world within a generation. A distinguished group recently reported to the Club of Rome[1] that a "global compact" on poverty between rich and poor nations could attain the following objectives in the poor countries by the end of this century: increase of life expectancy from 48 to 65 years; decrease of infant mortality from 125 to 50 or less per 1000 births; increase of literacy rate from 33 to 75 percent; decrease of birth rate from 40 to 25 or less per 1000 persons. The group estimated that the total investment required would be $15–$20 billion annually (in terms of 1973 dollars) during the first decade, with some $10–$12 billion a year of this

[1] See bibliography.

coming from the industrial countries. As we have seen, this is affordable. The real question is how effectively the assistance can be absorbed.

There are many approaches to the institutional problem of handling development assistance. Experience suggests that most capital assistance should be channeled through international institutions in order to minimize the ever-present temptation to use such assistance for political purposes. Such institutions should have sufficient power and influence to be able to refuse assistance when evidence suggests that it cannot be absorbed effectively, or when the receiving nation appears to be spending too much on its military establishment or doing too little about such problems as maldistribution of income and population growth.

Technical assistance should also be offered by appropriate international institutions, but in many situations such assistance can be more effectively given bilaterally than through international agencies. Experience has shown, however, that bilateral technical assistance programs must be planned very carefully and implementation stages must be completely cooperative. Given the wide range of national and human endowments, investments, government policies, and needs, methods and strategies for technology transfer must be tailored to an individual country's national development goals.

Although outside assistance is of great importance, the basic task of development must be undertaken by the developing countries themselves. It is they who must supply the greater part of the needed resources and establish the policies aimed at growing more food, decreasing the rate of population growth, distributing the food and income equitably. The only way they will be able to pay for the substantial imports they will need will be to export commodities and manufactured goods at fair prices. A continuing reduction in trade barriers to the developing countries' goods is as essential an element of a global cooperative effort as a stabilization of commodity prices.

Because food plays such an important role, both to rich and poor and to exporters and importers, it is important to explore how the production, storage, and transfer of cereals might be used to help achieve the goals of eliminating hunger and malnutrition and of accelerating development. As an illustration, let us imagine that a group of nations, both rich and poor, were to create an international agency for cereal distribution. The member nations would share certain common goals, such as increasing regional self-sufficiency of food production; increasing the efficiency of food utilization and distribution; decreasing the rate of growth in demand for food; and establishing a carefully controlled international food reservoir.

All nations which subscribe to these goals would be eligible for membership. Member states would agree to deal only with the agency in the sale and purchase of cereals. The Cereal Agency would maintain a grain reservoir which would be built up and maintained at an agreed-upon level of perhaps 200 million tons. The agency would make purchases from cereal-exporting nations at locally competitive prices, handled in such a way that the reserve would normally fall no lower than 150 million tons and rise no higher than 250 million tons.

The agency would sell grain to rich importing nations at about the average purchase price, but adjusted to take into account ability to pay (per capita GNP). Grain would be sold to poor countries at substantially reduced prices, but the price would depend upon certain agreed-upon indices of elements which are important in the development process, such as military expenditures, birth rate, and income distribution. No nation would be permitted to purchase in a given year more than a certain limit which might be set at Japan's current per capita import requirements. No nation would be permitted to export cereals which are imported from the agency. All member states would pay dues which would be used, in part, to defray the operating cost of the system and pay for agricultural technical assistance, as well as help defray the costs of selling grain to poor countries at substantially reduced prices. Basically a nation's dues might be related to its GNP, but with built-in incentives aimed at achieving agreed-upon social goals.

In this way, cereal prices could be stabilized, and risks of bad crop years could be minimized. Costs would be moderate, perhaps not exceeding 10 percent, including agricultural technical assistance. Were the cereals sold to the poor countries at one-quarter the selling price to the rich importing countries, the deficit to be made up from dues would probably be no more than about $8 billion.

This imagined Cereal Agency is simply illustrative of the kinds of mutually beneficial arrangements which might be established as part of a global program aimed at eliminating poverty and hunger and at creating development incentives, while at the same time providing insurance against sudden major price fluctuations. One can conceive of similar arrangements with respect to other commodities.

In any event, no matter how the job gets done, it is clear that poverty and hunger can be eliminated. Paying for the program is not the real problem. The difficult question is whether the rich and poor nations, working together, can mobilize the necessary political will. Here the rich countries, and in particular the industrial democracies, are in a special position. If they jointly assume their responsibilities, the chances for success are substantial.

Among the rich countries, the attitudes, actions, and inactions of the United States will be particularly important. The United States has the opportunity to take leadership in the creation of a truly effective global development program. If the U.S. fails to do so, it seems doubtful that an adequate effort will be mobilized.

(5)

Although wars have always been horrible and senseless in their inhumanity, until recently they have been tolerable from the point of view of survival. Even during the 30-year period 1915–1945, when deaths from battles numbered about 30 million, industrial society managed to survive and following World War II entered the most rapid period of economic growth and social change in its history. But thermonuclear weapons together with their means for delivery have changed the picture completely. As we have seen, the United States and the Soviet Union have deployed sufficient numbers of missiles armed with thermonuclear warheads to destroy each other utterly. The weapons are all part of a system which we call deterrence, which depends for its success upon the high degree of probability that neither side will strike first because retaliation will be certain and virtually instant.

Thus far, the system of deterrence has worked, and for as long as the U.S. and the U.S.S.R. behave rationally it will probably continue to work, provided other unpredictable forces do not interfere. We have seen, however, that these other forces—ranging in character from accidents to misjudgements to irrational behavior to a strike by a third party to the escalation of a tactical nuclear war—present very real dangers indeed, for the entire deterrent system could be triggered without either nation wanting it to happen. The very existence of this system, possessing such an extremely high level of destructiveness, is the single greatest threat today to industrial civilization.

Ideally, the U.S. and the U.S.S.R. would agree to dispense with the system entirely. Unfortunately, it is too late to do this. How would one side verify that the other had no secret missile base or missile-launching submarines remaining? What about other nations such as England, France, India, and China which possess nuclear capabilities?

The Strategic Arms Limitations Talks (SALT) between the U.S. and the U.S.S.R. will, if successful, stabilize the strategic striking forces of the two nations. But that level will almost certainly be considerably higher than that of today. We know that a nuclear exchange involving the equivalent of some 30,000 million tons of TNT is now possible. The levels made possible by the SALT agreement as now visualized might be some ten times higher.

Thus any foreseeable agreement on arms control would not relieve us from the great danger of a major nuclear war. It would, however, help get us out of the accelerating upward spiral of the strategic arms race with its attendant uncertainties and great costs. The advantages of such an accomplishment would by no means be negligible.

Much more than this needs to be done, however. Admitting that for the time being we cannot totally eliminate strategic nuclear weapons from the earth scene, we could nevertheless greatly reduce their numbers and still provide adequate deterrence on both sides. The question then becomes: How small a nuclear striking force would still represent a significant deterrent to a premeditated offensive strike?

It is by no means certain, but it is possible that the United States could survive the loss of five major cities. In spite of this, would we be likely to launch a strategic attack against the U.S.S.R. if we knew that in the process five unspecified large urban centers would be totally destroyed? Although the numbers game can certainly lead to vigorous debates, it seems likely that the threat that five cities and 20 million people might suddenly be eradicated would constitute a significant deterrent. There is little reason to suppose that Russians care less about their people and their cities than we do, in spite of the rhetoric of the warriors on both sides.

The precise number of cities which must be threatened to constitute an effective minimum deterrent is not so important. Whether it be 1, 5, 10, or 50, the important point is that the number of nuclear-armed missiles necessary to carry out the threat would be very much less than those now in place. Were the system triggered under these circumstances, the resultant catastrophe might reduce the two opposing powers to helplessness, but other parts of the industrial world would probably survive, the ozone layer would not be endangered, and agriculture would continue uninterrupted in most parts of the world.

It would seem, then, that for as long as some kind of deterrent system is necessary, it could function effectively were each side to possess a limited, agreed-upon number of nuclear-powered submarines, each possessing an agreed-upon number of missiles armed with nuclear warheads of agreed-upon size. All would be subject to inspection while in port. Once out of port they would disappear, each under secret orders as to where its journey might take it and what its targets might be.

Under these circumstances all land-based long-range missile sites would be abolished and international inspection teams using satellite surveillance as well as ground inspection could ascertain compliance. The nuclear materials from the discarded warheads could be placed in depots under the stewardship of trained international inspectors, to be utilized over time, with safeguards, in nuclear power plants.

It will not be easy to secure agreement on some such minimum deterrent.

Once agreed upon, a great deal of time would be required to dismantle existing sites and make the new system operational. Past experience suggests that at least 25 years would be required to pass through the entire process. In the meantime, of course, we will continue to live in deadly danger, made all the worse by the likelihood that increasing numbers of nations will come into possession of nuclear weapons.

The problem of nuclear proliferation, then, is next in importance to that presented by the existence of our vast systems of deterrence. The greater the number of nations which possess nuclear weapons, the greater will be the likelihood that the weapons will be used in anger and the greater the likelihood that a full-scale nuclear war will be triggered.

Little can be done about the six nations which now possess nuclear weapons capabilities. However, the strongest possible steps, short of war, should be taken to dissuade other nations from either manufacturing their own nuclear weapons or acquiring them in other ways. Using the argument that the world simply cannot afford to permit an already dangerous situation to become still more dangerous, all nations should again be urged to ratify the nonproliferation treaty. Those which refuse should be subject to such sanctions as withholding shipments of conventional arms. At the first sign that a nation is producing or otherwise obtaining nuclear weapons, much stronger economic sanctions should be used.

Unfortunately, it is unlikely that very many nations can successfully pass through the world energy predicament without making use of nuclear power. In order to lessen the likelihood that nuclear materials will be diverted to military purposes, it is essential that nations which manufacture nuclear power plants use restraint in the kinds of equipment they sell. Above all, we should quickly attempt to achieve agreement on the creation of international cadres of inspectors who would be stationed permanently at nuclear installations to guard against the diversion of nuclear materials.

Last, the present major suppliers of conventional weapons to the rest of the world should exercise greater restraint concerning the types and quantities of weapons they sell or give away. As we have seen, the entire process amplifies an already dangerous situation and greatly impedes the rates of development of the poor countries.

(6)

The industrial nations must increase their resilience to interruptions in the flow of food and raw materials. This can be done by achieving greater measures of self-sufficiency, developing alternative sources of supply, stockpiling, conserving, and recycling.

Heavy importers of food, such as Japan, should make every effort to increase their production of basic foodstuffs to the point where in an emergency people would have enough to eat. During the emergency they might have to eat considerably less in the way of animal products and consume more cereal directly, but they could still have a nutritious diet. Agricultural and land-use policies should be directed toward this goal, with perhaps a two-month supply of cereals held in reserve. Unfortunately, one never knows in what part of the seasonal agricultural cycle an emergency might strike.

Great efforts should be made to guard against further loss of good agricultural land, whether through mismanagement, housing developments, or the encroachment of industries, highways, and airports. To minimize the need for and use of chemical fertilizers, all excrement, both human and animal, should be processed and returned to the soil. Pricing and taxing policies should be altered to make this possible.

With respect to minerals, provision should be made for a certain amount of stockpiling, the extent depending upon domestic production and the potential volatility of the sources of supply. Stress should be placed upon the efficient recycling of metallic scrap, if necessary by providing price and tax incentives. Incentives should be provided to design automobiles and appliances in such a way that life expectancy is higher than at present and so they can be recycled with greater ease and efficiency. In addition, in certain cases, for example aluminum in the United States, incentives should be provided to permit extraction of a significant proportion of our aluminum requirements from domestic aluminum-bearing clays.

As we have seen, disruption in the flow of certain minerals could cause major difficulties. But of all raw materials crude oil is by far the most critical and most likely to give rise to extremely serious problems unless substantial corrective actions are taken very soon.

The industrial democracies, which are particularly vulnerable to disruptions in the flow of their supplies of crude oil, must diversify their sources of energy as quickly as possible. This will not be easy because no matter what route they take, costs will go up. In particular, capital costs will become very large.

Unfortunately, this is a problem which cannot be solved through the free movement of market forces, which would simply lead to continued rapid increases of imports and increased vulnerability. The situation is one in which the government must intervene, providing needed incentives and disincentives plus guarantees. In addition, certain international understandings concerning energy pricing are highly desirable, particularly among the major crude oil importers.

How much should we be willing to pay for our supplies of energy? Are the economics of energy functioning for long-term human benefit when such economics make it so attractive for us to consume most of the existing petroleum and natural gas in the world before we learn how to use coal and oil shale effectively? Are the economics working for our benefit when they dissuade us from investing adequate quantities of capital in the technologies of utilizing coal and oil shale? Are they working for our benefit when they encourage us to burn useful, complicated hydrocarbon molecules to heat water and buildings and to generate power, when such molecules could be used more effectively for the manufacture of a vast array of complex and extremely useful petrochemicals?

Obviously an economic dislocation, such as that which accompanied the sudden fourfold rise in energy costs in 1973–1974, is uncomfortable. The only way that the major importing nations can protect themselves against similar dislocations in the future is to develop options that are truly viable. This would mean using, on a substantial scale, energy sources other than crude oil, natural gas, or other import-dependent technologies.

If such options are to be developed and put into operation on a meaningful scale, the entire price structure of our various energy resources must be reexamined and drastically altered. Here the term *price* is used to include all costs to the consumer, including taxes, less government subsidies.

Ideally, the revised price structure and associated guarantees would make oil shale and coal competitive with crude oil and natural gas (both domestic and imported) for the production of liquid fuels and petrochemicals. Nuclear power (fission) would be made competitive with coal for the generation of electricity. Solar energy would be made competitive with fossil fuels for space heating and cooling. In this way, all of our major near-term energy possibilities would be developed and utilized.

Of course, our energy costs would be greater than they are today, but not dramatically so. Estimated costs of producing synthetic fuels from coal and oil shale are about $20 per barrel, and even making due allowances for underestimation, the cost is not so very far from the current price of imported crude oil. The real problem is to establish the price guarantees that will enable the producers of synthetic crude to invest the very large amounts of capital necessary to protect their investment should the price of crude oil drop drastically. Once this is done and facilities are established on a large scale, further major increases in the prices of crude oil charged by the exporters would simply not be possible.

Here we must keep in mind the fact that even if energy costs (in constant dollars) were to go considerably beyond the present price of imported crude oil, the results need not be catastrophic. In 1971 fuel costs represented something like 2.5 percent of the U.S. gross national product, which is not very large when we consider the amount of wealth that is generated by the energy.

The importing industrial nations must arrive at a common agreement on energy pricing and on taking artificially higher energy costs into account in the pricing of their manufactured products, particularly those for export. To take an extreme case, if Japan were to continue with OPEC oil as its primary source of energy and if Germany were to shift primarily to coal and nuclear energy, for the time being Japan would have a marked economic advantage. Obviously, some compensatory understanding would be necessary to keep the system from falling apart.

It is difficult to see how reasonable levels of energy self-sufficiency can be achieved in the near term unless nuclear energy is used on a substantial scale, particularly for the generation of electricity. The rarity of uranium ore suggests that breeder reactors must sooner or later replace the standard enriched reactor. Unfortunately, the mystique which has arisen in most industrial nations concerning the dangers of nuclear power, and particularly of the breeder reactor, has taken on the appearance of a religious war in which logic and experience have been lost sight of and actions are governed largely by emotions. Reasonableness will not be brought back into the nuclear power picture unless rules are adopted for nuclear power plant siting and generating procedures which make it obvious that: (1) accidents which can endanger human life will be rare; (2) large-scale human catastrophes will be virtually impossible; (3) radioactive wastes can be stored safely; and (4) diversion of explosives-grade nuclear materials will be so difficult that it will not be a matter of serious concern.

From both the technological and organizational points of view it seems possible that these conditions can be met, and a serious effort should be made to establish the rules. As a start, we might agree that breeder reactors should not be scattered broadside over an entire nation but confined instead to a relatively small number of carefully selected sites. One such site might be an isolated atoll, far removed from normal human activity. The power would be used to produce nitrogen fertilizers or methane gas which would be shipped to industrial and agricultural centers. Another such site might be a large artificial island anchored in the open ocean. There are also a number of potential sites on the U.S. mainland which could be used for the large-scale generation of electricity for general distribution.

One advantage of confining power generation to a few sites, embracing no more than about 15,000 square kilometers altogether, would be that continuous policing by resident inspectors would be relatively easy. The inspectors would be professionals who are assigned by an international body and not responsible to the authorities which operate the plant.

Theorizing about the feasibility, safety, and security of breeder reactors is important. But it is equally important for us to gain the necessary practical experience.

Although diversification of energy sources deserves the highest priority, a great deal of time will be required before the results affect the energy situation in a meaningful way. In the meantime, substantial efforts should be devoted to stockpiling crude oil. The Japanese are now constructing a number of large floating steel storage tanks which will be placed offshore to hold a two- or three-month supply of oil. The United States is talking about storing a several-month supply of crude oil in abandoned salt mines.

Conservation of energy can be a critical element in decreasing our vulnerabilities. Here, substantially increased costs of gasoline, fuel oil, natural gas, and electricity will help lower consumption. But a great deal more will be needed, ranging from the redesign of our cities to changes in our ways of life. Why can't we walk to our work and do our shopping without benefit of the station wagon? Why can't we use bicycles to travel intermediate distances without seriously endangering our lives? Why can't mass transportation for greater distances be more effective than it is? The solution of these problems may well require major changes in our entire tax structure and in our zoning regulations.

Finally, it is important to emphasize the development of sources of solar power such as wind, ocean thermal-energy conversion, direct conversion using solar panels, conversion via the biomass, and generation of power by concentrating the sun's rays to make steam. Each of these approaches has advantages as well as disadvantages, but in the long term solar energy gives promise of being one of our major sources of electricity. Geothermal energy, too, shows considerable promise and should be developed fully wherever it is practicable.

(7)

Some of the more difficult problems confronting industrial nations are internal ones which threaten the continued smooth functioning of the vast interlocking system of mines, factories, farms, communication and transportation systems, and power networks. We have seen that this system is vulnerable to accidental disruption as well as to disruption deliberately brought about by sabotage or work stoppages. Further, intimately associated with the smooth functioning of the system are certain random variables such as rainfall and temperature. The system gets strained by droughts and by floods. Unusually cold weather brings about gas shortages; unusually hot weather contributes to blackouts. Superimposed upon all of this are a variety of socioeconomic factors such as unemployment, inflation, income distribution, urban finances, and crime.

One of our major problems in attempting to cope with the vulnerabilities of such a system is that we simply don't understand it in all of its complexity. We are constantly being surprised. It was believed with some confidence that the Great Blackout of 1965 could not be repeated, but it happened again in 1977. It is now clear that the economic forecasts made during the 1970s have been among the least accurate ever made. Such misjudgements stem far less from human foolishness than from lack of understanding of the complex system in which we live.

Obviously, we must do what we can to achieve a better understanding of our system, but we cannot afford to wait before we take certain important remedial actions. For example, we know enough about systems to appreciate that redundancies are essential. If a highway becomes clogged, it is useful to have alternate highways available. If an electrical generator breaks down, it is useful to have standby generating capacity. All of this suggests that we systematically examine our own system and attempt to identify the critical elements and the weak points. We should imagine the kinds of things that might happen, estimate the seriousness of potential breakdowns, and design redundancies which could ease situations which appear to be particularly dangerous.

Parts of our system are now very old and lack of adequate maintenance and replacement have made breakdowns more likely. Some critical elements of the U.S. network, such as cities, are likely to break down because of inadequate care. The decades of neglect clearly call for massive investments of capital for replacement of wornout components and for modernization.

Redundancies and modernization will help protect the system against natural failures, and to a certain degree they can lessen the dangers of breakdowns resulting from terrorism and sabotage. But the latter dangers cannot adequately be coped with by purely technological means. Some critical points of the system can be effectively fenced or otherwise guarded, but this will not always be possible. Stricter controls can be placed on the possession of weapons and explosives. Penalties for trespassing and willfully damaging property can be greatly increased. Suspicious individuals and groups can be kept under surveillance. But although such measures would lower risks, it would be virtually impossible to provide complete protection.

In a sense, work stoppages are potentially far more damaging than terrorism or sabotage. How would we cope with a strike in the energy sector which included all workers in pipeline transport, petroleum refining, coal mining, and oil and gas extraction, totaling only 0.7 percent of the labor force? How would we cope with a strike of workers in the public service area which included all firemen, policemen, and water, steam, and sanitary employees, totaling only 1.0 percent of the labor force? A few years ago we would have thought such situations could never happen, but now we are not so sure. Continuing inflation, rising expectations, and the worsening financial condition of cities have fanned the flames of discontent.

One approach to such problems would be to insist upon compulsory arbitration for all labor disputes in sectors where strikes would have a sudden, serious impact upon the public safety. Indeed, something like this will probably turn out to be necessary. But how far down this pathway can we travel without infringing seriously upon rights and freedoms which we deeply cherish?

Patching up our present system in order to make it less vulnerable to disruption will be a long and costly process. Developing the necessary understanding of the complex socioeconomic elements of our system so that they can be handled effectively for the common good will also be difficult. This is yet another example of our having to think, plan, and act on a long time scale—in this case perhaps a century.

Given the necessary effort, over time we can gradually increase our resilience. But for as long as the United States remains a single complex system, in spite of the redundancies we will never reduce our vulnerabilities to zero. At the very least we will remain vulnerable to such very large shocks as a full-scale nuclear attack. This will also be true of the other industrial nations.

(8)

In light of this vast array of complex problems which now confronts humankind, and considering the time that will be required to take remedial actions, it is essential that we come to grips with the problem of what we really want in life. How do we want to live? Do we simply want more of the same? Or are we in some ways discontented with our lot, whether in spite of or because of our vast material wealth?

To what extent is it a part of human nature to want to own things? In the United States the sheer weight of personal possessions increases every year. The department stores of Japan and Europe seem always to be filled with people who are either buying or looking covetously at the offerings. The lines of people in Moscow looking at goods which they cannot now afford, but one day will, are always long. The Chinese peasant proudly shows off her transistor radio and her new sewing machine. Everywhere people are in love with the automobile.

Is all of this simply a reflection of the fact that we are still children? When we reach adulthood, will all of this stop? Will we suddenly find ourselves becoming highly selective about what we personally own? Will we perhaps live more austerely and less artificially, sharing more things in common? Will we recapture the gentle arts of love, contemplation, introspection, and conversation? Will we once again become doers rather than viewers? Will we return to our roots within the world of nature and wonder at its splendors? Will we make peace with ourselves and with each other?

In the 1960s large numbers of young people in several industrial countries demonstrated against their societies and attempted to establish themselves in simpler, less-technological environments. They shunned conventional jobs, lived on farms and in communes, and tried to be self-sufficient. This movement, for the most part, did not succeed. But the fact that it started at all and that enclaves of such people still exist is significant. Many of those who tried the simple life in the 1960s moved back into the system, where they now work in offices and factories.

It is important, then, for us to realize that in 1977 one-third of all American workers are dissatisfied with their jobs—a higher proportion than at any time in the past 25 years.[2] Only 17 percent of clerical and hourly workers felt that employees are dealt with fairly. And this in spite of the fact that the majority of the workers felt that their pay was satisfactory. This suggests that large numbers of people are now thinking less about personal possessions and more about the meaning and purpose of their lives. Perhaps they find themselves unfulfilled by the routine and often anonymous roles they are called upon to play in gargantuan factories, offices, and stores.

Much has been written about the impersonality of the large institution, which came into existence for straightforward economic reasons. Generally speaking (and up to a point), the larger a manufacturing plant is, the lower will be the cost per unit of output. Added to this, modern technology gives little room for exercise of human judgment in carrying out tasks. Thus, over

[2] Poll conducted by the Opinion Research Corp. of Princeton, N.J., reported in the *Los Angeles Times*, August 10, 1977.

time, institutions have become larger while the human role has become smaller and less meaningful. As long as we continue to make our major business decisions solely on the basis of cost-effectiveness and efficiency this situation will prevail.

This trend carries with it the seeds of social upheaval and even of destruction. As discontent increases, the voices crying out in protest will swell in number and the target is likely to be technology. Indeed, we see about us today numerous signs of the emergence of a new kind of Ludditism, which, were it to take hold, could be disastrous.

Added to such considerations, we are faced by the fact that there are indeed limits to growth. We might argue among ourselves as to exactly where those limits lie. But we must recognize that neither population nor affluence can continue to grow forever. Unless we willfully stop their growth ourselves, nature will stop this growth for us. And she has many ways of doing it. Again, our limited knowledge does not permit our forecasting just what combination of factors will do the stopping.

Human stress and societal tension might be the limiting factors. Or it might be rapid climatic change brought about by increased carbon dioxide in the atmosphere. Ecological disruption, new diseases, environmental pollution, or shortages of food, energy, and minerals could all play roles. Or the major limiting factor could be our declining ability to manage the system as it becomes larger and more complex.

Under these circumstances it behooves us to consider seriously the possibility of intentionally stopping growth ourselves and of adjusting our ways of life to accommodate to this new situation. Here it should be stressed that stopping growth would not necessarily mean stopping change. Society should continue to evolve, century after century, but within the framework of a stabilized population and constant per capita consumption of energy and other raw materials.

We should not—nor could we—stop growth suddenly. Once there is general understanding of the need, the transition should be made gradually. Much damage could be done were the change too abrupt.

In considering the problem of where growth ought to stop, we should experiment with new approaches to the related problems of where and how people work and where and how they live. There are those who suggest that we should develop technologies and industries which are designed more to the human scale. Ingenious proposals have been made for the design of small cities in which people can be nearly self-sufficient and live efficiently and comfortably. We should study such possibilities carefully and experiment with them on a substantial scale.

Were there to be a regrouping of society into smaller settlements and smaller industries, and were each to achieve some real measure of self-sufficiency, the resilience of society as a whole would increase enormously, perhaps eventually approaching that of peasant-village culture. As this process goes on, the responsibilities, pervasiveness, and complexities of central governments would be correspondingly lessened, eventually to be concentrated primarily upon the broadest of national problems and upon global ones.

(9)

As we attempt to peer into the future it is easy to reach the conclusion that industrial civilization doesn't stand much of a chance. We have seen that in the absence of clear decisions and constructive programs the poorer nations are headed squarely toward famine, pestilence, revolution, and bloodshed on a massive scale. There will be discontinuities in the flow of energy, minerals, and food. There will be systems failures, terrorism, and wars. Under the circumstances, how long will the great deterrent systems remain asleep? A few thousand years from now, human beings may well look back upon our age of technological achievements as a short-lived phenomenon which exploded over the earth, then fizzled out.

Yet, we have seen that the fizzling need not take place, that we have the power to create an entirely new level of civilization. Will we make use of that power? Or will we continue to conduct our business as usual?

When we look back into the sweep of history we see that occasionally during periods of great danger societies have risen to the challenge and responded so forcefully that the danger was overcome. It is hoped that the rich and poor nations will collectively rise to the heights that will be necessary to respond effectively to the present challenge. If they fail to do so, it will be history's saddest day.

Bibliography and Suggestions for Further Reading

As was the case with my earlier work, *The Challenge of Man's Future*, anything approaching a complete bibliography of the subjects discussed would be so unwieldly that it would not be very useful. However, an attempt has been made to list a few general reference works together with other works which will provide the reader with keys to the available literature and sources of statistics and other information.

Chapter I of the author's *The Challenge of Man's Future* (New York: The Viking Press, 1954) gives a brief overview of the events which led to the emergence of the human species and to the various stages of cultural evolution including industrialization. To the bibliographic suggestions given there should be added the excellent small volume dealing with historical demography *Population and History*, by E. A. Wrigley (New York: McGraw-Hill Book Co., 1969), and the lengthier work *Populations and Societies*, by Judah Matras (Englewood Cliffs, N.J.: Prentice-Hall, Inc., 1973).

The evolution of the human species is discussed from many points of view in *Evolution of Man*, edited by Louise B. Young (New York: Oxford University Press, 1970). The history of science and technology is admirably and compactly discussed by R. J. Forbes and E. J. Dijksterhuis in *A History of Science and Technology*, available in two paperback volumes (Baltimore: Penguin Books Ltd., 1963). *The Industrial Revolution, 1760–1830*, by T. S. Ashton (New York: Oxford University Press, 1964), is an excellent review of that dramatic development.

Chapter I of this book has been drawn in part from several papers by the author including "Population Growth and Affluence: The Fissioning of Human Society" (*Quarterly Journal of Economics* 89, 1975: 236–46), "Human Materials Production as a Process in the Biosphere" (*Scientific American*, September 1970), and "Some Quasi-Copernican Revolutions in Man's Utilization of Energy," in *The Heritage of Copernicus*, edited by Jerzy Neyman (Cambridge, Mass.: The MIT Press, 1974).

Chapters II and III, dealing with the economic growth of the United States, Western and Eastern Europe, and Japan, make liberal use of the facts available in the *Statistical Abstracts of the United States*, now available annually as a paperback titled *The U.S. Fact Book, the American Almanac* (New York: Grosset and Dunlap). Other useful statistical information can be found in the *Statistical Yearbook of the United Nations*, published annually.

For important insights into modern U.S. industrial society, see John Kenneth Galbraith's *The Affluent Society* (Boston: Houghton Mifflin Co., 1958) and *The New Industrial State* (Boston: Houghton Mifflin Co., 1967). Additional insights are given by Kenneth E. F. Watt in his concise discussion of modern U.S. crises, *The Titanic*

Effect (Stamford, Conn.: Sinauer Associates, Inc., 1974). Useful background information can be found in *America in Our Time*, by Godfrey Hodgson (New York: Doubleday and Co., 1976); *A History of the Modern World*, by R. R. Palmer and Joel Colton (New York: Alfred A. Knopf, 1966); *Contemporary Europe: A History*, by H. Stuart Hughes (2nd ed.; Englewood Cliffs, N.J.: Prentice-Hall, Inc., 1966); and *Economic Growth in the West*, by Angus Maddison (New York: The Twentieth Century Fund, 1964). *The Unbound Prometheus*, by David S. Landes (Cambridge: Cambridge University Press, 1969), is an excellent study of industrial development in Western Europe from 1750 to the present time.

The industrialization of Japan is discussed by G. C. Allen in *A Short Economic History of Modern Japan, 1867–1937* (rev. ed.; London: George Allen and Unwin, Ltd., 1972). Frank Gibney provides a useful discussion of modern Japan in his *Japan: The Fragile Superpower* (New York: W. W. Norton & Co. Inc., 1975).

Excellent discussions of the development of the Soviet economy are given by Harry Schwartz in his *Russia's Soviet Economy* (New York: Prentice-Hall, Inc., 1954) and *The Soviet Economy Since Stalin* (Philadelphia: J. B. Lippincott Co., 1965).

Chapters IV and V, which deal with developing countries, make liberal use of the publications of the Overseas Development Council in Washington, particularly its annual volume, *The U.S. and World Development, Agenda for Action* (New York: Praeger Publishers, 1975, 1976, 1977). Useful statistics are given in the *World Population Data Sheet* (Washington D.C.: The Population Reference Bureau, Inc.), published annually.

Other interesting works concerning poor nations and their relationships with rich ones include: *World Without Borders*, by Lester Brown (New York: Random House, 1972); *The Great Ascent: The Struggle for Economic Development in Our Time*, by Robert Heilbroner (New York: Harper and Row, 1963); *The Challenge of World Poverty*, by Gunnar Myrdal (New York: Pantheon, 1970); *The Wretched of the Earth*, by Frantz Fanon (New York: Random House, 1968); and *Beyond Dependency*, edited by G. F. Erb and V. Kallab (Washington: The Overseas Development Council, 1975).

Two addresses by Robert S. McNamara are noteworthy: one on the population problem given at the Massachusetts Institute of Technology in 1977 and the other given to the Board of Governors of the World Bank in Manila in 1976. Both are available from the International Bank for Reconstruction and Development in Washington, D.C.

For background concerning the chapter dealing with food, the reader is referred to the *World Food and Nutrition Study* (Washington, D.C.: National Academy of Sciences, 1977), which gives an assessment of the current situation together with a useful bibliography. *By Bread Alone*, by Lester Brown and Erik Eckholm (New York: Praeger, 1974), gives a highly readable overview of the world food situation.

I am indebted to Professor J. Gvishiani for the source of the quotation from Mendeleyev as well as the translation. The original (in Russian) is in *Dimitri Ivanovich Mendeleyev, his Life and Activities* by O. Pisarzhevsky (Moscow, 1953), p. 45.

Much of the chapter dealing with energy is based upon an article by the author entitled "Energy in Our Future," published in the *Annual Review of Energy, Volume 1* (Palo Alto, Calif.: Annual Reviews, Inc., 1976). The reader will find much of interest in that volume concerning energy resources and problems. Other useful discussions of the energy situation, both in the U.S. and the world, can be found in *A Time to*

Choose, a report by the Energy Policy Project of the Ford Foundation (Cambridge, Mass.: Ballinger Publishing Co., 1974), and *Energy, Global Prospects 1985–2000*, a report of the Workshop on Alternative Energy Strategies (New York: McGraw-Hill Book Co., 1977).

With respect to nonfuel minerals, the reader is referred to *Resources in America's Future*, by Hans H. Landsberg et al. (Baltimore: The Johns Hopkins Press, 1963); *Resources and Man*, edited by Preston Cloud (San Francisco: Freeman, 1969); *Material Needs and the Environment, Today and Tomorrow*, a report of the National Commission on Materials Policy (Washington, D.C.: U.S. Government Printing Office, 1973); and *National Materials Policy* (Washington, D.C.: National Academy of Sciences, 1975).

Useful volumes dealing with global environmental problems are *Only One Earth*, by B. Ward and R. Dubos (New York: W. W. Norton & Co. Inc., 1972); *Human Ecology*, by P. R. Ehrlich et al. (San Francisco: W. H. Freeman & Co., 1973); *The Genesis Strategy, Climate and Global Survival*, by S. H. Schneider (New York: Plenum Press, 1976); and *The Unfinished Agenda*, a report of a task force sponsored by the Rockefeller Brothers Fund, edited by G. O. Barney (New York: Thomas Y. Crowell Co., 1977). The most recent and authoritative study of the effects of rising carbon dioxide concentrations in the atmosphere was made by the Panel on Energy and Climate of the National Academy of Sciences, 1977.

There are numerous publications dealing with the arms race and the international trade in arms. One of the more useful recent books is *The Last Chance*, by William Epstein (New York: The Free Press, 1976). The Summer 1975 issue of *Daedalus* (the Journal of the American Academy of Arts and Sciences in Boston) is devoted to some excellent expert discussions of arms, defense policy, and arms control. The Stockholm International Peace Research Institute (SIPRI) publishes a yearbook entitled *World Armaments and Disarmament* (New York: Humanities Press) which is useful. One of the best, and certainly the most compact sources of statistics in this area is *World Military and Social Expenditures*, by R. L. Sivard (WMSE Publications, Box 1003, Leesburg, VA 22075), which is published annually. The most useful monthly source of information concerning armaments is *Arms Control Today*, published by the Arms Control Association, 11 Dupont Circle, N.W., Washington, D.C. 20036. Articles included deal with nuclear proliferation, arms control agreements, arms sales, and changing military technologies. *The Bulletin of the Atomic Scientists*, published monthly in Chicago, also presents numerous useful discussions of these and related problems. The complex domestic political-economic aspects of the arms race are discussed in highly readable form by Sidney Lens in *The Military-Industrial Complex* (St. Louis: Pilgrim Press, 1970). The global effects of large-scale use of nuclear weapons are discussed in a report by the National Academy of Sciences, *Long-Term Worldwide Effects of Multiple Nuclear-Weapons Detonations* (Washington, D.C.: National Academy of Sciences, 1975).

Two other aspects of vulnerabilities are discussed in *International Terrorism, A New Mode of Conflict*, by Brian Jenkins (Los Angeles: Crescent Publications, 1975); and *The Night the Lights Went Out*, edited by A. M. Rosenthal and A. Gleb (New York: New American Library, 1965).

An important paper dealing with environmental vulnerabilities is *Multiple Vulnera-*

bilities: *The Context of Environmental Repair and Protection*, by Harold and Margaret Sprout (Center of International Studies, Princeton University, 1974).

In recent years there has been an exponential growth of books dealing with the human future. A useful sampling is given below:

The Next Hundred Years, by Harrison Brown, James Bonner, and John Weir (New York: The Viking Press, 1957)

The Year 2000, by Herman Kahn and Anthony Wiener (New York: The MacMillan Co., 1967)

Mankind 2000, edited by Robert Jungk and Johan Galtung (London: Allen and Unwin, 1969)

The Limits to Growth, by D. Meadows et al. (New York: Universe Books, 1972)

The Coming of Post-Industrial Society, by Daniel Bell (New York: Basic Books, 1973)

Mankind at the Turning Point, by M. Mesarovic and E. Pestel (New York: Dutton/Readers Digest Press, 1974)

An Inquiry Into the Human Prospect, by Robert Heilbroner (New York: W. W. Norton & Co., Inc., 1974)

The Next 200 Years, by Herman Kahn et al. (New York: William Morrow and Co., 1976)

Problems involved with computer forecasting are discussed in:

Thinking About the Future: A Critique of the Limits to Growth, edited by H. S. D. Cole et al. (London: Chatto and Windus, 1973).

The Art of Anticipation, edited by S. Encel et al. (London: Martin Robertson, 1975).

A thoughtful, concise discussion of the problems of forecasting the future is given by Willis W. Harman in *An Incomplete Guide to the Future* (San Francisco: San Francisco Book Co., 1976).

Some interesting books which attempt to come to grips with the problem of what we can do include:

Small is Beautiful, by E. F. Schumacher (New York: Harper and Row, 1973)

The Human Quality, by Aurelio Peccei (Oxford: Pergamon Press Ltd., 1977)

The Futures of Europe, edited by Wayland Kennet (Cambridge: Cambridge University Press, 1976)

Goals for Mankind, by Ervin Laszlo et al. (New York: E. P. Dutton, 1977)

Finally, two important books express concern about the future of democratic institutions:

The New Liberty, Survival and Justice in a Changing World, by Ralf Dahrendorf (Stanford, Calif.: Stanford University Press, 1975)

The Collapse of Democracy, by Robert Moss (London: Temple Smith, 1975)

Index

accidental disruptions, vulnerability to, 196–97
aerosol sprays, destruction of ozone layer and, 171–74
affluence, prospects for increasing, 64–65
Afghanistan, 228
Africa, 69, 81
  relationship between Physical Quality of Life Index and per capita GNP in, 83
  vulnerabilities to disruption of, 229–30
  see also North Africa
age distribution of population, 42–43
agricultural exports:
  of developing countries, 113
    capital accumulation, 97
  of rich countries, 113
  of United States, 113, 124–25, 127–31
    to developing countries, 127, 128, 192–93
    embargo on soybean exports (1973), 128, 131
    increasing demand for, 129–30
    to Japan and Western Europe, 130, 131
    Public Law 480, 127, 128, 192–93
    vulnerability to disruption, 191–94
  see also food prices
agricultural imports:
  dependence on, 125–26
  of developing countries, 127, 128, 192–93
  see also food imports
agriculture (agricultural production), 20–21
  climatic changes and, 164–66, 191, 192, 195, 235
  in developing countries, 100
    fertilizers, 87–89, 96, 125
    "Green Revolution," 125, 133
    increasing productivity, 88–89, 132–36, 193
  in India, 87, 88, 125, 133–34, 229
  in Japan, 76, 130–31
  in Mexico, 132–33
  in the Soviet Union, 73, 191–93
  in the United States, 35–38, 48, 126–30
    climatic changes, 165–66
    crop yields, 124, 126–27, 129
  vulnerability to disruption of, 190–94
  see also arable land; cereals; fertilizers; food production; irrigation
air currents, 161
airplanes:
  hijacking of, 199–200
  supersonic, and ozone depletion, 173
air pollution, 55–57, 63, 65
Alaskan oil resources, 141, 143, 146
alcohol from sugar cane, 155
aluminum, 189, 190
American Indians, 43
Angola, 84
animal products, 122

animals:
  cereals fed to, 122
  domestication of, 20
  as power source, 22–23, 27–28
Antarctica, 114
Antipater of Thessalonica, 23
aquaculture, 136
Arab countries, 83
  Israel and, 108, 227
  see also Middle Eastern countries
arable land
  in developing countries, 136
  loss of, in industrialized countries, 129, 131
Arctic Ocean, removal of ice covering, 175–76
Argentina, 230
armed forces, 69–70
arms:
  nuclear, see nuclear weapons
  privately owned, 203, 269
  see also military aid; military expenditures
arms control, 262–63
arms race, 59–61
arms sales to developing countries, 108–9
Asia, 69, 81
  relationship between Physical Quality of Life Index and per capita GNP in, 83
  vulnerability to disruption, 227–29
atmosphere, 159–60, 194, 196
Australia, 125, 181–82, 189
authoritarian governments, 234
  in developing countries, 103–4
  see also totalitarian states
automobiles:
  air pollution and, 56, 57
  in the United States, 45–58

balance of payments (trade deficits):
  of developing countries, 98–99
  of United States, 128–29, 194
Bangladesh, 87, 91, 228
banks, loans to developing countries by, 98–99
basic research, 39
Belgium, 67
birth control, see family planning programs; oral contraceptives
birth rates:
  in developing (poor) countries, 79, 81, 89–95
  in Europe (19th century), 69
  see also fertility rates
blackouts, 196–97
blacks in the United States, 43–45, 47, 48, 63, 208
Bolivia, 84
"brain drain," 118
Brazil, 91, 131, 151, 155, 184, 230, 231